Gender and Media

Why do some TV genres have the label feminine or masculine? Why do we worry about boys playing video games too much while girls play just as often? Is the TV show *Sex and the City* empowering or not? Why are recent television shows like *Desperate Housewives* post-feminist television?

Gender and Media explores these and other complex questions by offering a critical overview of the contemporary debates and discussions surrounding gender and mediated communication, and by providing students with an overview of the current academic research on these topics.

The book is divided into three parts: representing, producing and consuming, with each section made up of three chapters. The first chapter of each section attempts to answer the most basic questions: 'Who is represented?', 'Who produces what?' and 'Who consumes what?'. The second chapter of each section draws attention to the complexity of the relationship between gender and media, concentrating on the 'why'. The third and final chapter of each section addresses the latest debates in the fields of media and gender, adding a vital layer of understanding of the topic at hand.

This process is aided by text boxes, which provide additional information on the most important concepts and topics and exercises, helping to bridge the gap between theory and everyday life media practices.

This is an ideal textbook for students studying gender and media, and for general courses on gender studies, sociology, cultural studies and women's studies.

Tonny Krijnen is an Assistant Professor in the Department of Media & Communication at the Erasmus University Rotterdam. Her research activities lie in the fields of popular culture, gender, morality and qualitative research methods, on which she has published widely.

Sofie Van Bauwel is an Associate Professor in the Department of Communication Studies at the Ghent University and a member of the research group Centre for Cinema and Media Studies (CIMS). Her research activities involve gender, sexuality and media on which she has published.

Communication and Society
Series Editor: James Curran

This series encompasses the broad field of media and cultural studies. Its main concerns are the media and the public sphere: on whether the media empower or fail to empower popular forces in society; media organisations and public policy; the political and social consequences of media campaigns; and the role of media entertainment, ranging from potboilers and the human-interest story to rock music and TV sport.

Glasnost, Perestroika and the Soviet Media
Brian McNair

Pluralism, Politics and the Marketplace
The Regulation of German Broadcasting
Vincent Porter and Suzanne Hasselbach

Potboilers
Methods, Concepts and Case Studies in Popular Fiction
Jerry Palmer

Communication and Citizenship
Journalism and the Public Sphere
Edited by Peter Dahlgren and Colin Sparks

Seeing and Believing
The Influence of Television
Greg Philo

Critical Communication Studies
Communication, History and Theory in America
Hanno Hardt

Media Moguls
Jeremy Tunstall and Michael Palmer

Fields in Vision
Television Sport and Cultural Transformation
Garry Whannel

Getting the Message
News, Truth and Power
The Glasgow Media Group

Advertising, the Uneasy Persuasion
Its Dubious Impact on American Society
Michael Schudson

Gender and Media

Representing, Producing, Consuming

Tonny Krijnen and Sofie Van Bauwel

LONDON AND NEW YORK

First published 2015
by Routledge
2 Park Square, Milton Park, Abingdon, Oxon OX14 4RN

and by Routledge
711 Third Avenue, New York, NY 10017

Routledge is an imprint of the Taylor & Francis Group, an informa business

British Library Cataloguing-in-Publication Data
A catalogue record for this book is available from the British Library

Library of Congress Cataloging in Publication Data
Krijnen, Tonny.
Gender and media : representing, producing, consuming / Tonny Krijnen and
Sofie Van Bauwel.
pages cm
Includes bibliographical references and index.
1. Sex role in mass media. 2. Women in mass media. 3. Men in mass media.
I. Van Bauwel, Sofie. II. Title.
P96.S5K75 2015
302.23081 – dc23
2014047664

ISBN: 978-0-415-69540-4 (hbk)
ISBN: 978-0-415-69541-1 (pbk)
ISBN: 978-1-315-69459-7 (ebk)

Typeset in Sabon
by Taylor & Francis Books

Contents

List of Figures

Acknowledgements

This book could not have been written without the support of the people around us. Specifically we would like to thank Nena and Remco Schrijver and Gianni Marzo for their patience and coping with the times of our absence necessary for us to write this book. Marc Verboord and Liesbet Van Zoonen we thank for their advice and suggestions that improved our work tremendously. Last, but not least, we would like to thank James Curran, Natalie Foster and Sheni Kruger for cheering us on and replying to our endless list of queries.

Introduction

In July 2009, a Norwegian journalist interviewed Lady Gaga, one of the world's most prominent female pop stars. The journalist asked Gaga if she was a feminist; she responded: 'I'm not a feminist. I, I, I hail men, I love men. I celebrate American male culture: beer, bars, and muscle cars' (Lady Gaga, 30 July, 2009). Critics, including feminists, were quick to respond. At best they called Gaga an anti-feminist, at worst they abused her physical appearance, with the term "horse faced" among the tamest words used. News media fell over each other to have their best critics write analyses on the Gaga-phenomenon. The main question these analyses addressed was whether or not Lady Gaga is a feminist. Most point out that Gaga's appearance, behaviour and statements are highly contradictory; she seems to criticise the expectations of female behaviour and appearance with her own appearance and behaviour – something most authors deem feminist – while simultaneously denying she is a feminist – something that disappoints feminists (Britannica Editors, 2010; Cochrane, 2010; Williams, 2010). As Noelle Williams (2010) concludes: 'I can't help but fantasize about just what Lady Gaga could do by identifying as "feminist". Her immense popularity and youthful, outspoken image could be the perfect set-up for a revolution of the word.'

What is interesting is that most of these critical pieces, blogs and responses gloss over the second part of her answer. After mentioning muscle cars, Gaga tells the reporter that he asked her a different question before which implied that her sexuality may be distracting from her music. Her response to this statement sounds quite different:

> 'You see, if I was a guy, and I was sitting here with a cigarette in my hand, grabbing my crotch and talking about how I make music 'cause I love fast cars and fucking girls,' Gaga retorted, 'you'd call me a rock star. But when I do it in my music and in my videos, because I'm a female, because I make pop music, you're judgmental, and you say that it is distracting. I'm just a rock star.'
>
> (Lady Gaga, 30 July, 2009)

This explanation of gender assumptions is more telling than Gaga declaring she loves men and beer and whether or not she is a self-declared feminist. The concept of gender is important in forming our perceptions and appreciation of pop stars and the music they produce. Blog posts on the subject support this notion when pointing out that male rock stars are very rarely called a "coked-out whore".

There are many things to be considered regarding Lady Gaga's feminist or anti-feminist identity. The same can be said about questions regarding other media producers and their products. For example, 'Is the TV show *Sex and the City* (HBO) empowering or not?', 'Why are recent television shows like *Desperate Housewives* (ABC) called post-feminist television?', 'Why do some TV genres have the label feminine (e.g. soap opera, talk shows) or masculine (e.g. current affairs, action movies) while we know that their audiences are mixed?', 'Why do we worry about boys playing video games too much while girls play just as often?'. These questions are complex and difficult to answer; they refer to many things that do not have manifest, unambiguous meanings. Gender, TV and videogames are all concepts that have many meanings and definitions, and can be looked at from a plethora of perspectives. These meanings, definitions and perspectives are also not mutually exclusive. For example, when we think about boys and videogames, we think about a special group of boys (between 12 and 20 years of age, let's say) who play a certain kind of videogame: realistic and violent games such as *Grand Theft Auto* (Rockstar Games) or *Assassin's Creed* (Ubisoft) – not *The Sims* (Electronic Arts). We know that not all boys are similar. Not only is there a difference between two randomly chosen 15-year-old boys in terms of character, physical appearance, likes and dislikes, and many other features, but there are also differences with regard to culture, history and geographical location.

In this book we address these and other questions and their complexity. We do not try to answer each of them, but aim to create an overview of what exactly we are talking about and what the complicating aspects are. Current debates and discussions will be laid out, together with an overview of current academic research on these topics. Our ultimate goal is to create an environment in which our readers can confidently make up their own minds about the different interactions and relations between media and gender.

Three different fields are discussed: the representation, the production and the reception of (mass) media in relation to gender. All three are important in terms of how we think about media messages, their producers and their audiences. Each of these fields has distinct relationships with gender. The negotiation of meanings of gender takes place on the level of production, representation and reception and is marked by complicating factors. Furthermore, the three fields should be viewed as interrelated. As Liesbet van Zoonen (1994: 41) argued in *Feminist Media Studies*: 'Separately, the elements of production, texts and reception of media make no sense; they are intricately linked in the process of meaning production.' With developments in media technology, boundaries between the fields are increasingly blurred. Audience members are more often also media producers, and media content is less and less tied to one medium. Content is also more interactive in character than ever before. Before exploring the multiple and various relations between media and gender, it is essential to formulate an understanding of both concepts.

Gender

What is gender? In academia, the concept of gender has many different interpretations and approaches. The term is often used with various meanings and intentions and closely related to the sex/gender dichotomies "femininity and masculinity" and "men and women". Mostly, gender is viewed as the socially constructed meanings of one's physical sex. Femininity and masculinity are then viewed as socially constructed conventions and norms with regard to the behaviour and appearance of women and men (Oakley, 1972). Socially constructed means that context and community play a central role in meaning making (Vygotsky, 1978). The meanings of one's sex are thus not a natural given, but constructed through interactions between people in a given society. As societies change, so do communities and contexts, which means that these meanings of gender are dynamic and prone to changes.

The term "sex" is thus usually used when referring to a biological fact. Most of the time, people are expected to perform a gender that fits their sex. As Lady Gaga pointed out during the interview, because she is of the female sex, she is expected to perform according to the norms of feminine behaviour. If she were of the opposite sex, she claims, the interviewer would approach her differently; the interviewer would determine her behaviour to be in line with her sex. In short, individuals of the male sex are expected to behave in a masculine way – in this case 'grabbing my crotch and talking about how I make music 'cause I love fast cars and fucking girls' (Lady Gaga, 30 July, 2009) – while individuals of the female sex are supposed the behave in a feminine way. This view on biological differences determining one's gendered behaviour is known as biological determinism, a gender approach strongly embedded in Western societies.

These understandings of sex and gender dichotomies bring us to our first complexity: both sex and gender are not dichotomies per se and both can be viewed as continuums. Physical sex is viewed as consisting of chromosomal, anatomical and hormonal features of which any kind of mix is possible. For example, there are many women who have some facial hair and there are many men with high-pitched voices (Fausto-Sterling, 2000). In short, one's sex is found on a continuum between female and male.

Similarly, gender can also be viewed as a continuum between femininity and masculinity. Understanding gender as a social and cultural construct already indicates that gender norms regarding behaviour and appearance are dynamic and subjected to change. Though there are lists of masculine and feminine traits, especially among psychologists, most people intuitively think of exceptions when reviewing such lists. For example, when we review the list of gender characteristics as constructed by the Bem Sex Role Inventory (BSRI) scale we read that active, analytical, ambitious and independence are masculine characteristics. As a reader you might recognise yourself in these characteristics regardless of your sex. Psychologist Sandra Bem created the BSRI scale in 1974 as a measure of how feminine or masculine people believe they are, regardless of their sex. Bem's research found that people identify characteristics as clearly feminine or clearly masculine (Bem, 1974). Almost 20 years later, internationally comparative research shows that attributes are contributed to either masculinity or femininity on a global level. In a study among people in 25 different nations (Williams and Best, 1990) show how adventurous, active and aggressive traits are associated with masculinity, while affectionate, attractive and curious traits are associated with femininity. In contemporary society, more than two decades later, ambitious, active and independent are not always defined as masculine traits, showing the dynamic character of such traits. This does not, however, mean that the evaluation of these traits is similar for both genders.

Though interpretations and perspectives on the concept of gender are still debated, the concept of gender has been widely used since the 1970s. The discussion about the differences between women and men and whether or not this difference is biologically determined is much older. Simone de Beauvoir described this discussion in the 1940s:

> One is not born, but rather becomes a woman. No biological, psychological, or economic fate determines the figure that the human female presents in society; it is civilization as a whole that produces this creature, intermediate between male and eunuch, which is described as feminine.
>
> (Simone de Beauvoir, 1949: 8)

The basic assumption that women are "made" rather than being born was central to the development of the concept of gender.

This interest in the concept of gender manifested itself in academia during the 1970s against the backdrop of the women's movement. More and more studies engaged the concept of gender rather than sex (Rakow, 1986). Ann Oakley (1972) was one of the first to distinguish between sex and gender. She indicated that the difference between sex and gender is very clear: '"Sex" is a word that refers to the biological differences between male and female, the visible difference in genitalia, the related difference in procreative function. "Gender", however, is a matter of culture: it refers to the social classification into "masculine" and "feminine"' (Oakley, 1972: 16). This classification had significant influence on later generations of academics.

Over the decades, the concept of gender has been related to other concepts of interest to us as well. In her now classic article *The Traffic in Women: Notes on the 'political economy' of sex*, Gayle Rubin (1975: 165) stressed the link between gender and sexuality and reproduction. In her article she states that every society system 'has a sex/gender system – a set of arrangements by which the biological raw material of human sex and procreation is shaped by human, social interventions'. These "arrangements" are culturally variable and organise human action through certain structures such as marriage. Gender is defined as an imposed social distinction between the two sexes, in which it is conceptualised as a product of social sexual relationships.

An important complication with the construction of the gender dichotomy (and sex dichotomy) is that it is an essentialist approach. Gender is formulated as inherent to sex, and both genders are considered to be essentially different. An essentialist approach therefore formulates gender and assumed differences as natural and unchangeable. As we will see in the coming chapters, such a perspective on gender has major implications on how we view the production, content, and reception of media. If we think aggression comes natural to men, society has to comply with aggressive behaviour; there is nothing we can do about it. If we follow a non-essentialist view, we can study aggressive behaviour and analyse how gender relates to it. The results of such a study would depict a different picture and perhaps change our perceptions of aggression in relation to men and masculinities.

History has repeatedly proven that the essentialist approach is erroneous. For example, in Western society, there is a firm belief that girls like the colour pink and boys like the colour blue. This colour coding of gender is quite recent. According to Jo Paoletti (2012), in the US pink, as a softer shade of red, was seen as a masculine colour while blue, with connotations to the Virgin Mary of Christianity, was associated with femininity; thus, colour coding gender has a history, changes over time and differs globally, and therefore should not be interpreted as innate.

A non-essentialist approach to gender offers us opportunities to think about the meanings of gender. Ann Oakley (1972), Gayle Rubin (1975), Judith Butler (1990), and many other scholars have made tremendous contributions to the advancement of the understanding of gender. The anti-essentialist critique can be defined as the conceptualisation of gender as a social construct and not reducible to the biological. This dynamic nature of gender is emphasised in feminist philosophy. The most famous example is Judith Butler. Butler argued that gender is not so much a noun as it is a verb. By formulating gender as a verb, Butler (1990) emphasises that gender is something we do, not something we have or get. The concept of "doing gender" was first coined by Candace West and Don Zimmerman (1987). In their article they argue that the sex/gender system is confusing as it proposes sex as a "given" (which it not always is), while gender is proposed as an achievement. This dynamic, they argue, strips away the social structures that organise gender and sex. Rather, they say, we 'conceive of gender as an emergent feature of social situations: both as an outcome of and a rationale for various social arrangements and as a means of legitimating one of the most fundamental divisions of society' (West and Zimmerman, 1987: 126). Gender should therefore be viewed as a fluid and dynamic concept that is continuously reconstructed. In her later work *Bodies That Matter* Butler

(1993) argues that one performs gender. Performativity does not mean that gender is something you put on in the morning and take off when you go to sleep. Rather, gender is assigned to the body through performativity. Our ways of doing gender produce something real, they construct meanings of gender inscribed to the body. To articulate it more crudely, according to Butler (1993), the sexed body does not exist without gender. This also leaves room for the individual to reinvent their gender.

This view on gender performativity has raised a lot of debate and critiques. For some scholars, the emphasis lies too much on subjectivity and individual action (Dunphy, 2000) and the difficulty of using Butler's theory in empirical work (Edwards, 1998). The approach of doing gender and performativity is an important critique on the sex/gender dichotomy described earlier and is still current in studies on gender and sexuality, which we will explore in coming chapters.

A related but slightly different critique on essentialism has been formulated in terms of intersectionality. The concept of intersectionality was originally coined by Kimberlé Crenshaw (1989), formulating a black feminist critique of the tendency to treat gender and race as two separate categories of experience. Basically, intersectionality claims that the concept gender should be understood in relation to other concepts such as class, age, sexuality and ethnicity (Phoenix and Pattynama, 2006). Like gender, these concepts are also viewed as social constructs whose meanings change over time. Intersectionality places gender into context, but it also increases the complexity of meanings.

In this book we understand gender as a fluid concept with a meaning that is continuously negotiated and intersects with many other features. We will focus primarily on gender and only speak of the related concepts such as class, age, ethnicity and sexuality when needed to explain the relation of gender within the media. As we will see, there are many instances when we have to consider the relation of gender and the media as intersecting with class, age, ethnicity and sexuality. Yet, it is not the aim of this book, nor feasible, to write a comprehensive overview of all the meanings of gender and all of its intersections. As Donna Haraway (1988) argues, the list of important characteristics is an endless one. Therefore, it is more important to realise that different characteristics have different consequences in different times and places. We will emphasise intersectional relations throughout the book when they are relevant.

Media

The second major concept we need to comprehend before we delve into the exploration of the relationships between gender and media is media themselves. In this book we are concerned with what are commonly called "mass media". By mass media we refer to media that aim to reach a relatively large audience of usually anonymous receivers with much the same information. Examples include newspapers, magazines, television, (popular) music, videogames and film (Croteau and Hoynes, 2014; McQuail, 2005).[1] Mass media, however, is a rather old-fashioned term. Over the last few decades the media have changed due to both societal and technological developments. While the major societal development is increasing globalisation, the major technological development is the blurring boundaries between the production, content and reception of media.

Globalisation is of course not a concept only applicable to media, but to the world in general. It includes, for example, economic factors such as the increase of multinational corporations, and human factors such as the increase of migration and travelling. According to Diana Crane (2002: 1), globalisation is 'a complex and diverse phenomenon consisting of global cultures, originating from many different nations and regions'. In the early days of media studies, (Western) academics usually referred to the media in general, while their research usually focused on Western media mostly located in the Anglophone countries; hence they claimed that their theories and perspectives of the media in the US or the UK were valid on a global level. Over the decades this view on the media has been critiqued immensely. Instead of generalising local research results to the rest of the globe, authors have started to concentrate more on the dispersion of (mainly North American) popular media to other countries (Curran and Park, 2000). This view is summarised as cultural imperialism. Cultural imperialism refers to the domination of powerful nations over weaker nations, imposing their norms and values. Ultimately, this imperialism leads to homogenisation of culture globally (Crane, 2002). The short interview fragment with Lady Gaga demonstrates a few examples of the different perspectives described above. When she refers to rock musicians, she refers to the Western idea of rock music. Similarly, when she refers to "men" she even explicitly refers to American men and male culture. As a musician she locates herself in American culture. Her concert tours take her all over the world and she is globally popular. Should we interpret this as an example of media imperialism, with Lady Gaga promoting American values to other peripheral countries? When ambiguities in her promotion of gender, feminist and other values are indicated by critics and fans of Lady Gaga alike, it becomes hard to believe that she promotes American values.

Many have critiqued media imperialism. James Curran and Myung Jin Park (2000) formulate three lines of argumentation that counter this view of globalisation. The first line shows how the dispersion of media should not be understood as a one-way flow (from the centre, i.e. US, to the periphery). Other centres of media production are of importance, such as the film industries in India and Nigeria (Bollywood and Nollywood), the TV industry in Brazil exporting telenovelas to European countries, and the increasing popularity in Asia of popular culture products from South Korea (the so-called "Korean Wave").

The second line of argumentation against media imperialism focuses on the resistance of US domination, both by nations themselves as well as by audiences. Nations have different ways of protecting their own local cultures (this is called protectionism). Simultaneously, audiences should not be understood as sponges absorbing whatever media content they consume. Depending on their local context and history, they can attach different meanings to a media product (Curran and Park, 2000).

The third and final line of argumentation attacks the fussiness of the concept of cultural imperialism: 'American, Western, and capitalist – can be used almost interchangeably in the media imperialism argument' (Curran and Park, 2000: 6). A more nuanced use of these concepts is necessary to de-trivialise the concept of cultural imperialism.

The last development within perspectives on media and globalisation is a more positive view. Globalisation is viewed as something that takes place on a global scale (and not as a Western phenomenon) enabling the creation of new communities and identities and cultural exchange (Curran and Park, 2000). Authors in this field have found wonderful insights on cultural hybridity, localisation of cultural products and the like.

Often these latter perspectives are viewed as oppositional to media imperialism, also called the homogenisation vs. heterogenisation debate. However, this debate itself has recently been challenged. As Timothy Dowd and Susanne Janssen (2011: 519) argue: 'Although scholarship on both cultural imperialism and hybridization has generated substantial insights, it also has its limitations, because neither approach captures fully the global situation of creative works.' Instead, according to Giselinde Kuipers (2011: 543), we should view the media industry as one of the transnational fields that are 'best understood as polycentric systems with multiple competing centres'. In Chapter 4 we will explore the globalisation of the media industry more in-depth.

The concept of media globalisation is contested as much as the concept of gender. In this book, we aim to understand the meanings of gender and media within their contexts and intersections. Throughout this book the most general media theories and perspectives will be discussed in relation to gender, but we will also discuss their scope on a global level. Media production, content and reception are contingent on the place of origin while simultaneously being part of diverse global media systems. This place of origin might sometimes refer to nations with their history, ideologies and traditions, but also to regions. For example, media production is dependent on the media system adopted in a country (Hallin and Mancini, 2004), but it does matter as well where the production company originates. Habits of media use can also differ tremendously by country or region.[2] Hence, we will draw attention to this context of media as much as to the fluidity of gender.

The second major development in media is technology. Like globalisation, media technology has been a field of scholarship for a long time. The impact of media technology on the dimensions of time and space has been a primary focus of attention. For example, media enable us to view events happening on the other side of the world at a time we ourselves find convenient. For example, we can watch Lady Gaga's concerts through live streaming on our PCs or download parts of it on YouTube.

This alteration of time and space by media technology is sometimes believed to have a major impact on society. One of the most popular views on this impact is Marshall McLuhan's (1962) idea of the global village. Through media technology, the era of print would end and be replaced by an oral culture. This development would change the individualistic and fragmented society into something like a village, with a more collective identity and a sense of inter-connectivity. Many people view the web as proof for McLuhan's predictions of this global village.

Similar to globalisation, McLuhan's view (and those of others) have been criticised throughout the years. The most important criticism is technological determinism. In this view, technology is considered to be the cause of social change. Raymond Williams (2003: 5) describes technological determinism as the belief that:

> New technologies are discovered, by an essentially internal process of research and development, which then sets the conditions for social change and progress. [...] the steam engine, the automobile, television, the atomic bomb, have *made* modern man and the modern condition. [italics in original]

McLuhan's arguments state that it is the invention of technology that will change society at large. Raymond Williams (2003) counters this perspective with three arguments. First, he argues, not all technological inventions are intentional. Second, we should look at the social history of media technology. As society changes, people's needs and desires change, which then has an impact on research and the development of technology. Third, the social use of media technology should be taken into account. When television was introduced as a mass medium, the frame of usage for this medium was similar to the one for radio.

The debate on technological determinism is still ongoing. Again similar to the debate on globalisation, academics have voiced a need for a more productive account on media technology. As Leah Lievrouw and Sonia Livingstone (2006: 4) argue: 'People always have choices about how technologies are created, understood and used. However, when certain technologies become very extensive, embedded and taken for granted [...] they can also constrain or limit the range of available choices.'

In the chapters that follow, we will use this view on media technology as a context for understanding the relation between media and gender. Media technology has major consequences on media production, content, reception and the relations to gender. One of these consequences is the convergence of media technologies. Using a smartphone we can access the newspaper, watch television and update our profiles on social network sites (SNS). It is more and more common to use one device (in this case a smartphone), and we also post videos on SNS or share newspaper clippings with each other through SNS. This development changes the concept of media itself.

Another consequence is the organisation of social relationships and media industries, termed the network society (Castells, 1996) or "network sociality" (Wittel, 2001). Societies are organised in networks with various centres, which has important repercussions for processes of production, experience, power and culture. This development is not only of importance for the organisation of the media industries, but also for our everyday life experiences.

Connected to this idea of network sociality is the concept of mediatisation. Mediatisation is simultaneously an old and a new concept in the study of media. Old because the concept has been used in work as early as the 1930s; new because it has recently become a specific field in media and communication research (Couldry and Hepp, 2013). Mediatisation can be understood as a concept used 'to capture somehow the broad consequences for everyday life and practical organisation (social, political, cultural, economic) of media, and more particularly of the pervasive spread of media contents and platforms through all types of context and practice' (Couldry and Hepp, 2013: 191). Mediatisation promotes a more holistic approach to studying media. Underlying this development (Couldry and Hepp, 2013) identify three trends in media studies. First, media are increasingly ubiquitous in our everyday lives. Much of our communication is mediated in some way. Second, research into how media shape our everyday experiences and how these experiences in turn shape media became more persistent. Third, an approach to power that not only locates power with large social institutions but in everyday life micro-politics became more present in media studies. Together, these three trends have enabled the rise of this new field of mediatisation.

Last but not least, the rapid development of media technology seems to have an impact on the concepts used in studying the media. As the boundaries between production, content, and reception of media are increasingly blurred, the jargon common in academia to study these phenomena is challenged (cf. Lievrouw and Livingstone, 2006). For example, traditional media companies sometimes produce media content but it is more and more common for media users to create their own content and publish it, enabled by new media technologies. The number of uploaded videos on YouTube produced by what we would traditionally call consumers is enormous. However, consumer in this case is not an appropriate word, neither is audience nor user.

This blurring of boundaries complicates our investigation in yet another way; it adds another layer of understanding the concept of media production, content and reception. It also indicates a more active approach to media production, content and reception, all of which could be considered as verbs instead of nouns. In the following chapters we will draw on the concepts discussed here, paying attention how they impact our thoughts and current debates on the relationship between gender and the media. Before we embark on this journey, we will briefly outline the history of academic work on media and gender.

Gender and Media Studies

Work on gender in relation to the media has a long and rich history that coincides with feminist movements. Though academic work on media came into existence as early as the rise of media, most of this work showed great disinterest in women as a topic of investigation. Indeed, this was an important point of critique delivered by feminist scholars in the early 1970s (Van Zoonen, 1994). Themes and theories in academic studies often suffered from male bias (for example, by presenting male experiences as universal), and women were under-represented in universities, both as students and professors.

The second wave feminist movement, starting in the early 1960s in the US, is thought to have contributed to some gender awareness in academia. However, as Liesbet Van Zoonen (1994) argues, this was only possible because the topics raised by feminists were already part of the traditional communication research agendas of that time. Three research themes of feminist academic enquiry emanated there from: work on stereotypes and social roles, ideology, and pornography (Van Zoonen, 1994). Each of them has a specific tie to feminist activism. The first theme, social roles and stereotypes, is inspired by the thought that by the under-representation and stereotypical representation of women in the media, female audience members lack positive role models to model their behaviour on (Tuchman, 1978; Van Zoonen, 1994). Over the years, there have been an enormous amount of studies devoted to this theme and two strands have developed. One strand focuses on the representation of women in the news media industry and news media themselves. The second strand focuses on the representation of women in advertising and popular culture. Both strands will be explored by us in Part I – Representing. This paradigm is still popular in academia. Some journals, like *Sex Roles*, are devoted to it. Recently, more and more studies are devoted to questions of intersections in stereotypical representations, masculinity and diversity in femininities.

The second theme, ideology, is tied to feminist activism in a slightly different way. Ideology as a theme was and is part of the domain of critical inquiries of the academic domain cultural studies. Critical scholars from the Centre for Contemporary Cultural Studies (CCCS) in Birmingham were studying subcultures (that are often tied in with the media) from what was called a Marxist perspective. Further inspiration was derived from Louis Althusser's postulation of media as "ideological state apparatuses" (media are agents of the ruling class) and his concept of "interpellation" (ideologies hail us, draw us in) (Hermes and Reesink, 2003; Van Zoonen, 1994). Last but not least Antonio Gramsci's ideas on "hegemony" were built upon. Hegemony can be understood as an elaboration of Marx's ideas on ideology. The ruling class, Gramsci argues, does not dominate by sheer force but consent of the subordinates. This consent is gained by translating ideology in common sense assumptions, naturalising power relations. For example, women are considered as naturally more caring than men. If we take caring as a natural character trait of women it is also natural that women take care of the children. Hence, a societal structure that confines women to the private sphere of the home and men to the public sphere of work is thus naturalised. Taking these concepts as a starting point, their research was directed to sub-cultures that were exclusively male. In 1978 the Women's Studies Group of the CCCS (consisting, among others, of Angela McRobbie, Charlotte Brundson, Dorothy Hobson, Janice Winship and Rachel Harrison) formulated a strong critique on this bias in their paper *Women Take Issue*. The working group was related to the Women's Liberation Movement (though they state the ambiguity of this relation) and their political viewpoints became apparent when they stated: 'It is through the questions that feminism poses, and the absences it locates, that feminist research and women's studies are constituted as one aspect of the struggle for the transformation of society which would make "women's studies" unnecessary' (Women's Studies Group, 2007 [1978]: 7). Their paper opened up the discourse at the centre and it became more inclusive towards "the Other".

The academic work on gender and media from a cultural studies perspective has flourished ever since, in both the investigation of media texts and their audiences. There are quite a few journals devoted to cultural studies in general, while there are some that specifically focus on gender (for example, *Feminist Media Studies*). In Part I – Representing and Part III – Consuming we will investigate work on ideology in-depth. Many of the authors that were part of the Women's Studies Group have contributed extensively to insights in the relation between gender, ideology and the media during the decades that followed.

The last, but not least, important theme in academic work on gender and media concerns pornography. In early work on pornography, feminist debates clearly contributed to the research agendas (Van Zoonen, 1994). In general, pornography is considered to objectify women. Women are usually treated as objects of male sexual desire, and usually are not present in pornography as active sexual agents. In its most radical form, pornography is objected to as a cultural expression of men's hatred against women, expressed in the slogan 'Pornography is the theory and rape the practice', coined by Robin Morgan in 1977. Pornography, from this perspective, should be considered a violent act against women. In 1988 Andrea Dworkin and Catherine MacKinnon formulated pornography not as a violent, and hence criminal, act, but as an act against women's equal civil rights. In the appendix they draft a model ordinance in which they argue: 'Pornography is central in creating and maintaining the civil inequality of the sexes. Pornography is a systematic practice of exploitation and subordination based on sex which differentially harms women' (Dworkin and MacKinnon, 1988: np). Underlying these arguments are important assumptions about media texts and their effects: enjoying pornographic material is thought to have a direct effect on human – or in this case male – behaviour. This is an oversimplification of media consumption in general which we discuss in Part III. Recent research shows that the pornographic images are understood in a variety of ways and often evoke contradictory reactions (Attwood, 2005), complicating the relation between text and audiences. Additionally, Susanne Paasonen (2009) stresses the importance of situating debates on pornography in their social-historical contexts. Ideas, thoughts and normative viewpoints are culturally specific, resulting in different arguments and viewpoints with regard to pornography in society in different regions of the world.

Academic work on pornography and gender is still not very popular, even though very recently an academic journal *Porn Studies* was founded. The aesthetics of porn imbuing our society has gained more attention and is caught in the term "pornofication". Pornofication refers to the notion of mainstream cultural products being imbued with aesthetics of porn. For example, there are many clothing items carrying the *Playboy* bunny or T-shirts with the slogan "ex-porn star", and there is much use of nudity in music videos and advertising. This trend is intimately tied to debates on sexualisation, which we will discuss in Chapter 9. Pornofication is also a crucial point of debate in contemporary feminist activism and scholarly work with a feminist political agenda. In *The Aftermath of Feminism* McRobbie (2009) takes issue with pornofication and sexualisation. The commercialisation of sex and sexuality is, on the one hand, hailed as "girl power". Women, and especially young girls, are positioned as having the freedom of choice to celebrate sex and sexuality. However, McRobbie (2009) argues, this appropriation of girl power and feminist vocabulary by commerce (including media) is a very normative affair. Young women are "forced" to participate in sexualisation and pornofication in order to obtain femininity. In her book, McRobbie sets up a nuanced debate on femininity, media and sexuality in contemporary society. However, we feel that underneath these nuanced accounts the assumption of the media text having a direct effect on human – in this case female – behaviour is still emphatically present. We will take further issue with this debate in Chapter 9.

As you might have noticed, with the title of her book McRobbie refers to "post-feminism". As a concept, post-feminism in general refers to a development in society in which women are thought to enjoy the benefits of feminist activists' hard-won freedoms, but are not willing to carry the burdens of positioning themselves as feminists (Press, 1991). Indeed, sometimes it feels like feminist is a dirty word. Though this is attributed to post-feminism, it is not really that new. In her seminal work *Feminist Media Studies* Van Zoonen shows how 'Reinharz's description of the past still holds: "At first, the very act of discovering sexism in scholarship was revolutionary [...] it was radical simply to study women"' (Van Zoonen, 1994: 15). At the time of writing, we cannot fully subscribe to Reinharz's statement any more. There are lots of women present in media and communication departments. In some departments, the majority of students are female. Nevertheless, the ratio of male and female professors is still less than desirable. For example, in 2012 in the Netherlands 33.2% of the assistant professors are female, 21.5% of the associate professors are female, and only 14.8% of the full professors are female

(Gerritsen, Verdonk and Visser, 2013). Most international academic organisations on media and communication (like the International Communication Association, European Communication Research and Education Association, and the International Association for Media and Communication Research) each have a gender division. Nevertheless, calling yourself a feminist sometimes still means that you are positioned as an angry, man-disliking woman, who is never satisfied with all she has. Many people strongly believe that gender equality in Western societies is a fact. There are many things wrong with this observation. The first one is that gender equality in many domains is not a fact. Salary gaps, for example, do exist in all countries on this globe. Additionally, it also articulates gender as a dichotomy and as monolithic. Gender, we argue, is not the only element of our identities that determines our position in life, and gender is not experienced similarly among all women. Gender intersects with class, ethnicity, sexuality, age, (dis)ability and many more things. As students from the feminist authors discussed in this chapter, we feel privileged. For us, our entry to a university education was never a point of debate, our position is foremost as a scholar (be it female ones, as we are commonly called Mrs. Prof. contrary to our male colleagues who are called Prof.), and our writing of this book was frowned upon by some colleagues not because it was about gender, but because it was a lot of work that is not esteemed highly these days in an academic career path. Nonetheless, we do feel frustration when Lady Gaga positions feminists as not liking men, and not liking beer and cars. Frustration, as it shows little respect for the energetic, engaging work of the women and men before us. With this book we therefore hope to contribute to a more balanced view by giving the reader the tools to form their own, well-informed opinions about current debates on gender and the media.

Structure of the Book

To address our main question – how to understand the relation between gender and media with all its complications – this book is divided into three distinguishable parts: representing, producing and consuming. Each part is divided into three chapters. The first chapter attempts to answer the most basic questions: 'Who is represented?', 'Who produces what?' and 'Who consumes what?'. In these chapters we will provide an overview on each topic. Partly, these overviews are numerical, showing, for example, how many women and men are present in the media industries. These chapters also address the key concepts within the research fields under scrutiny. The second chapter of each section draws attention to the complexity of the relationship between gender and the media, concentrating on the "why". For example, after the chapter 'Who consumes what?', it is useful to look into the various explanations of why the relationships are what they are. What is the relationship between watching action movies and gendered identities, for example? The third and final chapter of each section addresses the latest debates in the fields of media and gender, adding a last, vital layer of understanding of the topic at hand. With regard to media representations, for example, we will engage with intertextual representations.

This set-up serves various purposes. It serves to ease the reader into the different topics and to create an overview of the field before tackling debates and complicating factors. We believe it is useful to first fully understand the most important concepts of a given field before addressing more theoretical questions. This process is aided by text boxes, which provide some additional information on the most important concepts and topics. Each chapter also contains exercises, bridging the gap between theory and everyday life media practices. Additionally, the division into three parts enables the reader to focus on the topics most relevant at that moment in time.

The clear focus of the book also has some limitations. Some debates and concepts are not discussed as elaborately as they deserve. To compensate, we have added notes with suggestions for further reading at the end of each chapter.

Notes

1 This also means that media used for interpersonal communication, such as the (mobile) phone, email and letters are left out of the discussion.
2 Till now, we have discussed globalisation in terms of countries and regions. The importance of the nation state and what the impact of globalisation on the existence of the nation state may be is a relevant and important debate, but beyond the scope of this book.

Part I

Representing

Chapter 1

Who is Represented?

Switching on the TV we notice that Lady Gaga is not the only controversial character in terms of gender in popular media. The sexually ambiguous character Frank Underwood in *House of Cards* (Netflix), *Grey's Anatomy*'s (ABC) Miranda Bailey, who is definitely female but displays a style of management that might be deemed masculine, the emphasised femininity of Penny featuring in *The Big Bang Theory* (CBS), the kind but romantically incompetent (mostly) male farmers in *Farmer Wants a Wife* (Channel 5) and many, many more, are all examples of media representations of gender that challenge gender norms in one way or another. While these examples suggest an enormous diversity in the representation of gender, there certainly are clear patterns to be distinguished that contradict this diversity. While none of the above characters' gender (or sexuality) is the point of big debates in society, we see how Miranda Bailey is called "the Nazi" by her interns and how Penny is pictured as unintelligent and is countered by the very intelligent, but highly unattractive character Amy in the same series. These female characters are then either ridiculed (Penny's misunderstanding of the male protagonists' work is a continuous source for jokes and puns), or even punished (calling someone Nazi is a very negative statement after all). While simultaneously Frank Underwood and the male farmers' masculinity are no reason for concern or question at all. In this part, we will examine these and other patterns of representing gender in the media. In Chapter 1 we present an overview of what representations actually are and what patterns we can distinguish in gender representations in different types of media. In Chapter 2 we will address questions of what these patterns actually mean. In the last chapter of this part, Chapter 3, we will turn to complicating factors in contemporary gender representations.

Box 1.1 Exercise: The Bechdel test

A fun example, and a quick test, of how to review gender representation in popular media is the so-called Bechdel test. Designed by cartoonist Alison Bechdel, one of the characters in the comic *Dykes to Watch Out For* says she only watches movies if they meet three requirements. Since then, these requirements have been known as the Bechdel test and form three easy steps to assess whether a medium provides us with a proper representation of women. Now think about your favourite movie or TV serial and answer the following questions:

1. Does it have at least two women in it?
2. Do they talk to each other?
3. Do they talk about something besides a man?

Of course, this test gives a simplified view on gender representations and it provides us with a normative view of what a *good* representation is. We return to the question of what is a 'good representation' in Chapter 2.

The representation of men and women, of masculinity and femininity in the media has been an important topic of feminist inquiries and academic research into the media for over five decades. Realising that gender and its attached meanings are social constructs, feminist academics turned to analysing representation of gender in the mass media, as media were considered to be one of the sources in which meanings of gender were constructed. Even in contemporary academia, examining representations is a core business. In both cultural studies as well as more psychological approaches, a large body of work exists on gender representations in the media. The notion of representation has a double meaning. On the one hand, representation refers to the re-presentation of men and women in the media, referring to questions that stress the disparity in the number of men and women present in media and the roles they fulfil. On the other hand, representation refers to the portrayal and imagining of gender, questioning how women and men are portrayed in media and the meanings attached to these portrayals. This dual meaning is routinely present in work on gender representations.

Both of these meanings of representation relate to the premise that media representations have important consequences for social, cultural, and political meanings of gender. A crucial question in debates regarding gender representation is how representations relate to reality. Stuart Hall (2013) distinguishes three categories of theories that attempt to answer this question: the reflective, the intentional, and the constructionist approach. Academics adhering to the reflective view on representation postulate that the numbers of women and men present in the media should mirror those in a given society. The intentional theorists promote a perspective that scrutinises what the producer of the representation wanted to say. Lastly, scholars that endorse a constructionist approach see representations as negotiations of meaning. From this point of view the meaning of representation is not fixed in the representation itself but is co-created by its audience. Meanings are therefore dynamic. The reflective and constructionist views on representations are well researched, (as we will show), while the intentional view is less common. The reason for the unpopularity of the intentional approach is that is poses a very thorny viewpoint; by scrutinising the content the researcher concludes something about the producer(s) of that content, without ever asking the producer her or himself. In our view, research from the intentional approach leaves us with rather hollow results when only a content analysis is conducted. The reflective and constructionist views on representation each have their impact on the kind of research conducted.

What are Representations? – Different Views, Different Research

Representation has a dual meaning. While the first, representation, refers to a numerical analysis of women and men's presences in the media, the second is more complex to understand and involves study of the ideologies of gender. The media are thus viewed as an arena for the struggle of cultural meanings. We might wonder how this works. How do representations of men and women relate to the cultural meanings of men and women in society? Hall, one of the most important cultural studies scholars on representations, formulates the relationship between representation and culture as follows:

> To put it simply, culture is about "shared meanings". Now, language is the privileged medium in which we "make sense" of things, in which meaning is produced and exchanged. Meanings can only be shared through our common access to language. So language is central to meaning and culture and has always been regarded as the key repository of cultural values and meanings.
>
> (Hall, Evans and Nixon, 2013: xvii)

It is important to note that Hall *et al.* speak of *shared meanings*. As discussed in the introduction, the media do not create meanings by themselves; the media industry and audiences are both part of this construction.

Due to the dual understandings of the concept of representation, research on gender representations in media is manifold. We can distinguish different disciplines where psycho-analysis, semiotics, social psychology and discourse analysis are the main approaches. The first field, psycho-analysis, has its roots in film analysis. Using insights from authors such as Jacques Lacan, Laura Mulvey (1975) formulated the most important theoretical insights on gender and media: gaze theory. In her essay *Visual Pleasure and Narrative Cinema,* Mulvey discusses how a movie evokes the pleasure of looking at another person as an erotic object – called *scopophilia.* Movies then construct characters as objects for this pleasure, enabling a particular way of "looking at" people, exercising *the gaze*. The gaze has the psychological effect that the subject of this gaze loses some sense of autonomy upon realising that he or she is a visible object (Mulvey, 1975). Male characters in movies are more often bearers of the gaze, while female characters are more often subjected to it. Often this is formulated as "looking-at" and "to-be-looked-at-ness" (Mulvey, 1975). Contemporary examples of the gaze are found aplenty, for example in print advertising. Look for example at these two stills from TV commercials for perfume:

Figure 1.1 Still from J'Adore Dior TV commercial

Figure 1.2 Still from Acqua di Gio TV commercial

The male model (featuring in a commercial for Acqua di Gio) looks straight at us, hence defying our attempt to make him the object of our pleasure. The female model (featuring in a commercial for Dior's J'Adore), however, looks away, offering us the chance to let our eyes wander over her face. By exercising the gaze, one becomes an active subject; while being submitted to it, one becomes the passive object.

Though Mulvey's insights are still considered of crucial importance for the study of gender representations, and sometimes even described as the "Mulvey effect" (Pisters, 2011), her essay also received a lot of critique. Main points of criticism were directed at the strict gender binary Mulvey implies, the position of the female audience, and the heteronormative viewpoints. By positioning the male as active and the female as passive, Mulvey (1975) reconstructs and reifies the gender dichotomy, leaving no space for active women or passive men. This dichotomy also has repercussions for the audiences. From Mulvey's point of view, female audience members cannot enjoy movies as their position is rather masochistic: they would be watching themselves being objectified. Last but not least, Mulvey's (1975) ideas are exclusively heteronormative viewpoints. Sexual lust and desire only exists between men and women. In 1981 Mulvey (2009) replied with afterthoughts claiming that female viewers might oscillate between female and male coded viewing positions. This oscillation between viewing positions opens up space to negotiate spectatorship by gay, lesbian and bisexual viewers. More of these negotiations will be explored in Part III.

The second field, semiotics, refers to a structuralist approach that concerns how signs work. Largely derived from the work by Ferdinand de Saussure, semiotic analysis starts with an understanding of the sign as "dyadic" or a two-part model of the sign. De Saussure (1983 [1972]) defined a sign as being composed of: a "signifier" – the *form* that the sign takes – and the "signified" – the *concept* it represents. The *sign* is the whole that results from the association of the signifier with the signified. For example, the three-letter word CAT (the signifier) refers to a furry animal found in many homes (the signified). What is important is that the relationship between signifier and signified is unstable and arbitrary (we do not know, for example, what kind of cat you pictured in your mind, or how you feel about cats). The meaning of a sign is therefore never entirely fixed and the relationship between signifier and signified is a constructed one.

Roland Barthes (1994) further explains this multi-layered signification when he distinguishes between first- and second-order signification. The first order of signification is called denotation, the more literal meaning of a message. For example, in the commercial for Acqua di Gio discussed previously, we see a handsome male face looking at us, and the picture is in black and white. Though this is indeed literally what we see, the second order of signification, connotation, is equally important in coming to a full interpretation of the ad's message. The male face is handsome and his gaze is brooding, so it's not just any male, but a male who has a deep inner life that we cannot entirely fathom.

The black and white setting of the commercial enhances his brooding gaze, but also connotes a certain style or class. Together, the connotation and denotation create a message telling us that the perfume Acqua di Gio is for men who are self-confident with a rich inner life, who can afford a certain lifestyle. According to Barthes (1994), denotation and connotation enhance each other; connotation is not a hidden meaning, underlying the denotation. We have to perceive them as a doubled meaning, one strengthening the other and vice versa.

Michel Foucault formulates one of the major critiques on the semiotic perspective. Foucault argues that the semiotic approach leaves no room for the subject(s). Objects, or in this case representations, do not enclose meanings, Foucault argues, but meanings are produced continuously by subjects. Representations can therefore be seen as *signifying practices*.

> Representation functions less like the model of a one-way transmitter and more like the model of a dialogue – it is, as they say, *dialogic*. What sustains this dialogue is the presence of shared cultural codes, which cannot guarantee that meanings will remain stable forever – though attempting to fix meaning is exactly why *power* intervenes in *discourse*.
>
> (Hall *et al.*, 2013: xxvi)

These questions of power segue into the third field of scholarly work on representations: discourse analysis. Discourse analysis specifically looks into how meanings are produced, by whom and how power intersects. Representation is therefore considered a process where a constant interchange and interaction takes place between the material world and the mental maps (conceptual ideas, associations and impressions) in our heads. Most media and gender scholars stress in one way or another that the construction of the mental maps can possibly result in certain behaviour or signifying practices. Many scholars worry that stereotypical representations therefore result in stereotypical behaviour, and, as such, limit an individual's freedom to behave in whichever way they desire (Brouns, 1995; Smelik, 1999; De Clercq, 2003). In Chapter 2 we will further explore these ideas.

The fourth and last field in the study of gender representations is the social psychology approach. In general, social psychology can be defined as focusing on 'the effects of social and cognitive processes on the way individuals perceive, influence and relate to others' (Smith and Mackie, 2007: 5). With regard to gender, the social role theory formulated in 1987 by Alice Eagly is best known. Social role theory endorses the viewpoint that gender behaviour is regulated by social norms that are applicable to the social roles people occupy. One is socialised into this behaviour, for which several institutes are deemed relevant: family, peers, education and the media. Media images show us what the appropriate gender behaviour is, taking into account our role and status in society. Social psychologists today aim their studies at discovering what kind of gender norms and behaviours are promoted in contemporary media, and specifically in advertising.

The four fields (briefly) discussed each generate specific insights on gender representations in the media. While psycho-analytical and discourse approaches relate representations to questions of power in society, semiotics is more interested in the structures of meaning, and last but not least social psychology tries to investigate the gendered norms on appearance and behaviour. Each of these approaches is also marked by a focus on a specific type of media.

Represented Where?

Research on gender representations focuses on all media but can be characterised by type of medium. Early work on representations focused primarily on advertising, while later studies focused on popular culture. A third type of media heavily scrutinised for its representation of gender is news and current affairs. As we will see, with regard to the numeric representations of women and men in the media we can only draw one conclusion: women are grossly outnumbered by men. Reviewing research from different regions, the similarities in results are stunning. Nevertheless, there are some telling differences between advertising, popular culture and news media.

Advertising

Gender representations in advertising have generated a large body of work from the 1970s onwards. It was around this time that television became a mass medium and (Western) societies became more media saturated than ever before. Bombarded by representations of womanhood and gender relations in the mass media (TV, radio, newspapers, magazines), media became the centre of attention for feminist research and critique (Gill, 2007a). The feminist movement, second wave, considered advertising as a disturbing and (gender) biasing culture (Van Zoonen, 1994). In the welter of research on gender and advertising, studies can typically be categorised into either "Goffmanian analysis" or "Sex Role analysis". The first refers to a method of analysis developed by sociologist Erving Goffman, results of which nowadays are usually connected to questions of power and hence related to discourse analysis and/or psycho-analysis. The second method was based on Social Role Theory (Eagly, 1987) and is therefore connected to social psychology. We will discuss both types of analysis and the status quo of gender representation in advertising at the time of writing this book.

Almost 35 years after the publication of Goffman's *Gender Advertisements* (1979), his analysis is still considered seminal, and his method of analysis is still a foundation for work on gender analysis. Goffman's analysis of the representation of gender in advertisements started with the idea that expressions of gender, what Goffman calls "gender displays", are socially learned and socially patterned, and that they function as a ritualistic affirmation of the social hierarchy. As Goffman (1979: 6) emphasises, '[t]hese expressions considerably constitute the hierarchy; they are the shadow *and* the substance'. Goffman's view is not so different from the idea of signifying practices. The main difference is that, as a sociologist, Goffman is interested in how gender is organised in society, discovering patterns, while discourse analysts are more interested in the question of power, focusing more on the ideological meaning of patterns.

Furthermore, Goffman takes advertisements as the starting point of his analysis, as ads, with their "commercial realism", give us insight into something richer than "real" glimpses of gender displays. Goffman argues that this is the case for three reasons (1979: 23):

> First, ads [...] are intentionally choreographed to be unambiguous about matters [...]. Second, [...] they can be shot from any angle that the cameraman chooses, the subjects splayed out to allow an unobstructed view [...]. And finally, [...] a real person is very considerably restricted as to the sorts of live scenes he will be allowed to glimpse from whatever angle.

In this sense, Goffman emphasises, it is useful to look into commercial photography if we want to know what kind of gender displays a culture has generated.

We would like to add another reason for the importance of looking at commercial photography. Commercial photography has a clear and obvious persuasive function. It is meant to persuade us to buy something or believe something. One of the main functions of ads is to grab our attention and communicate a certain message in a very short amount of time. In that fleeting moment we need to interpret several cues and judge them as suitable or not suitable for us (interpellation is at work here). Hence, cues have to be very clear for the reader, and commercial photography therefore uses unmistakable gender displays (among others) and stereotypes.

Goffman (1979) developed tools for the analysis of gender displays and their relation to power structures (i.e. Relative Size, Feminine Touch, Function Ranking, The Family, The Ritualization of Subordination and Licensed Withdrawal). These gender displays emerge in advertising over and over again (they are repetitive frameworks). In many advertisements we see women depicted while touching something delicately, for example a perfume bottle, a small child or dog, a glass of wine, or her own face. This display is what Goffman would call the Feminine Touch: the tracing of the objects or oneself mimics the '"just barely touching" of the kind that might be significant between two electrically charged bodies' (Goffman, 1979: 29). Hence, the feminine touch eroticises objects. These tools of analysis, the displays, are still used today to analyse gender in advertising and other media (Kang, 1997; Bell and Milic, 2002; Diaz Soloaga and Muñiz, 2013).

Most studies on gender displays in the media are confirmative of Goffman's early analysis of gender advertisements (cf. Kang, 1997; Lindner, 2004). Katharina Lindner (2004) for example, shows how women in magazine ads are often represented in stereotypical roles, though magazines aimed at a female audience (i.e. *Vogue*) do this more often than magazines aiming for a general audience (i.e. *Time*). Additionally, as her study encompasses almost 50 years' worth of ads, she shows that stereotypical gender display has only slightly decreased.

However, Goffman (1979) emphasises the importance of historically and geographically situating the analysis he developed and the tools that result from it. In other words, the meaning of the gender displays that Goffman describes are referring to the social mores of 35 years ago in an American society. Undoubtedly, the same gender displays are still amply available in contemporary media. However, the meanings have changed in interesting ways. Women have reclaimed some of the traditional stereotypes that indicated a submissive position to express the exact opposite.

Another change in this regard is the role reversal that takes place with regard to gender displays. For example, Goffman described "Function Ranking" as follows: 'In our society when a man and a woman collaborate face-to-face in an undertaking, the man – it would seem – is likely to perform the executive role [...]'. This function ranking shows particularly well in ads, with Goffman giving examples of male doctors and female nurses, men instructing women, et cetera. In contemporary advertising, these images are quite hard to find, and often contradict the stereotypical ranking Goffman described. So, while function ranking remains an interesting tool for analysis, its meanings for the relationship between men and women have changed over time.

The second large body of work on gender representation in advertising follows a different approach, based on social role theory (Eagly, 1987). This perspective endorses the viewpoint that gender behaviour is regulated by social norms that are applicable to the social roles people occupy. One is socialised into this behaviour, for which several institutes are deemed relevant: family, peers and education, but also media are thought of as important with regard to the socialisation of gendered behaviour. Media images show us what the appropriate gender behaviour is, taking into account our role and status in society.

Box 1.2 The Bem Sex Role Inventory

A lot of research on sex roles in the media uses the Bem Sex Role Inventory (BSRI). Developed by Sandra Bem in 1971, the BSRI is a measurement tool that 'provides independent assessments of masculinity and femininity in terms of the respondent's self-reported possession of socially desirable, stereotypically masculine and feminine personality characteristics' (Bem, 2013). The tool is made up of 60 personality characteristics that are considered either very feminine, very masculine or gender neutral (20 of each). The

characteristics in the BSRI are used to assess the behaviour of media
characters on gender stereotypicality.
Curious? You can find (unofficial) versions of the BSRI on the web!

Activists such as Jean Kilbourne started research in the late 1960s on the
portrayal of women in advertising. She travels around the globe with her
lecture titled *Killing Us Softly* (at the time of writing with the fourth edition of
this lecture), where she examines the way women are represented in ads
and its relation to health issues such as eating disorders (Kilbourne, 2013).
From this approach sprang a new academic discipline: media literacy. Academics in this field promote the view that (especially young) people need to be
educated to read the media in a critical and evaluative manner to prevent
harmful effects. The field is often criticised for its normative views on both the
audience and media content. We will discuss this debate regarding what audiences, including young people, do with media representations more in-depth in
Part III.

The sex role perspective is not so different from Goffman's, though scholars
in both traditions rarely use each other's method or jargon. While "Goffmanians"
usually analyse advertising along the lines of the displays developed by Goffman,
"Sex Role Students" usually direct their attention to three elements: gender of the
main character, setting and product category. The main difference is the relation to
questions of power, which is more common with the first approach than in the
latter. In general, findings show that men outnumber women in advertising, that
women are more often placed in the private sphere while men are situated in
the public sphere, and that women are more often related to product categories
such as cosmetics and household detergents (so-called domestic products), while
men are more often related to product categories such as cars and mechanical
tools (non-domestic products).

These results are common for all types of media advertising. For example,
the first major study of television advertising by the National Organization of
Women (Hennesse and Nicholson, 1972) analysed more than 1,200 commercials
shown on US television. The analysis shows that more than one third of ads
show women as "domestic agents", and in half of the ads women were portrayed
as "household functionaries". Though this study did raise some severe critiques
on the mode of conduct of the study (e.g. the use of untrained coders), later
studies confirmed these findings (Gill, 2007a).

Interestingly, results from both traditions are overwhelmingly similar.
Though studies continue to prove that stereotypical representations of gender
are still easy to find in contemporary advertising, more and more studies also
show contradictory results. In a meta-analysis, Wollin (2003) shows how some
studies found a decrease of stereotyping, some an increase, and yet other studies
found few stereotypical representations of gender in advertising. From the
1990s onwards especially, women are being represented in a larger scope of

occupational roles (MacDonald, 1995). For example, more women are depicted in the public sphere or as professionals in high status jobs. While some feminist authors celebrate this development as proof of changing representations and underlying societal structures, others, like Van Zoonen (1994), warn against it. The image of the working woman can also be interpreted as an attempt by the advertising industry to target a new niche market of the "new woman". This new image is then a new stereotype of the working woman that is related to her economic independence and her ability to consume. In other words, this image can be used by the industry to target a specific audience (the working woman) as they form an interesting audience group for advertisers (Lotz, 2006). Instead of being liberated of stereotypical representations, women are made into a commodity for the media industry to earn money from.

Recently, the "new woman" has transformed into "super woman", simultaneously being a good wife, mother, friend, lover, boss or employee, and overall being an available and self-assured sexual being (Gill, 2007b). The self-assured sexual being aspect is debated, as some authors would argue that this image is repetitive of the everlasting depiction of women as objects of desire instead of subjects; the self-assuredness is a thin layer disguising objectification. Once more we would like to point out that this point of view also promotes a normative view of audiences (as audiences do not copy-paste these images). Nevertheless, we should interpret changing gender representations with a critical awareness about social structures that impact the production and content of the media.

Parallel to the similarities of results in both traditions, results of studies in gender representations in advertising are remarkably similar all over the globe (Bresnahan, Inoue, Liu and Nishida, 2001). For example, Adrian Furnham, Twiggy Mak and Liza Tanidjojo (2000), Russell Luyt (2011), Carolyn Michelle (2012), and Atif Nassif and Barrie Gunter (2008) all show how men outnumber women in advertising in New Zealand, the Arab region, Asia and South Africa, respectively. On a larger scale, Adrian Furnham and Stephanie Paltzer (2010) show how these figures are globally similar in a discussion of 30 studies on sex roles in TV ads. This resemblance in results is partly due to the fashion industry that is generated primarily in Europe and the United States (Diaz Soloaga and Muñiz, 2008). In a sense, the fashion industry creates "global fashion". Brands like Nike, Calvin Klein and Hugo Boss are not just popular in the Western part of the globe. On the contrary, they are desired by many people in many regions (Global Brands Magazine, 2013). Hence, advertising is relatively similar across the globe as well.

Most interesting about these studies though, are the results regarding the intersectionality of gender and ethnicity. While it might be true that men outnumber women in advertising representation on a global level, these studies show with scaring precision how multifaceted the notion of gender and representation actually is. For example, Luyt (2012) shows how men in South African ads are represented differently depending on their race. While white males are dominant and represented along the lines of hegemonic masculinity, black males are marginalised and represented along the lines of alternative masculinities. Black males are represented as less successful in achieving masculinity compared to white males. This shows how the concept of masculinity is multi-layered and should be understood within the context of a certain country/region or, rather, in the light of the social structures present there. As Luyt (2012: 49) argues, '[t]hese representations arguably mirror the inequitable distribution of economic, political and social power within SA [South Africa]'. In Chapter 2 we will investigate these complexities more thoroughly.

Of course, the intersection of ethnicity and gender is not the only valid intersection. We might expect that features such as class, age and sexuality are of equal importance. For pragmatic reasons it is impossible to take all features into account, as the list of features might be endless (Haraway, 1988). The essential thought here is that we must try to situate our results and interpretations within a broader context than "just gender". In other words, we should be careful to not simplify gender analysis into categories such as men and women in general and limit it to biological sex.

Popular Culture

Popular culture recently turned into a topic of investigation when cultural studies scholars directed their attention to "lowbrow culture". The early studies by cultural studies scholars focused on the culture "of the people" – often meaning their own elite, highbrow culture – and not on popular or mass (lowbrow culture) mostly consumed by workers. When attention was turned to popular culture, popular culture was stipulated, like high culture, as a cultural artefact that was worthy of studying. Till that time, popular culture as an important part of the identity, leisure time and media consumption among a large share of the audiences was rarely studied. In contemporary academia, research engaging with popular culture is mostly taken seriously (we say mostly, as some parts of the academic community still view popular culture as undeserving of serious attention).

Interestingly enough, though many academics discuss, criticise and study the representation of gender in popular culture, there is little to be found in terms of numeric investigations of males and females present in popular culture. This is peculiar, as we know about the figures in advertising and news media, but not popular culture, one of the largest chunks of media consumption. In general it is assumed (and sometimes shown in research) that, like in advertising, women are under-represented in popular media. As Malia Schilling (2013) states: 'Girls [TV series] may have won a Golden Globe this year, but media representation of women is nowhere close to achieving gender equality.'

Similar to advertising, scholarly work on gender in popular culture can be categorised into different fields, with cultural studies and "sex-role approaches" as the two most prominent. However, these approaches traditionally focus more on how males and females are presented than on presence itself. In Chapter 2 we discuss the how of representations. The few studies that provide us with numerical insight into the presentations of females and males in popular culture sketch an interesting picture that is similar for various media; in general women are outnumbered by men.

With regard to television, an analysis of 67 hours of TV drama and comedies in the 1996–97 season broadcasted on the three major networks in the US shows how men clearly outnumber women in several regards (presence, main characters and speaking time) (Glascock, 2001). In a more comparative analysis during the same period, Nancy Signorielli (1997) shows that in all popular media women are under-represented. TV has the highest proportion of women, with 55% men and 45% women. Movies have almost two men (63%) for every woman (37%). Music videos have almost four men (78%) for every woman (22%), although much of this difference may reflect the composition of popular music groups. The only medium that has more women than men present were magazines directed at teen girls. Magazine articles have 70% women to 30% men, and magazine advertisements have 82% women to 18% men (Signorielli, 1997). Almost one decade later, an analysis of prime-time TV in the Netherlands from 2003 to 2004 shows a similar picture. In an analysis of "moral subjects" (who gets to speak on moral matters on prime-time TV) men outnumber women 56% to 44% (Krijnen, 2007).

Recent analyses on a newer medium, video games, show a slightly different picture. While in the genre of "video games" (think of elaborated games such as *World of Warcraft* (Blizzard Entertainment) et cetera) men outnumber women in overwhelming fashion. In casual games (think of games such as *Candy Crush* (King), *Tetris* (Nintendo), and *Farmville* (Facebook)), however, women outnumber men as primary characters (Wohn, 2011). Checking for appearance, Donghee Wohn (2011) notes there is little difference in how males and females are represented. Arguably, there is a genre difference within the medium. In Chapter 2 we will explore whether this kind of difference among genres within a medium type occurs more often.

News

As with studies regarding gender and media production, research on who is represented in the news is ample. Gaye Tuchman's (1978) foundational work *The Symbolic Annihilation of Women by the Mass Media* set off a welter of studies in both popular media and news media. The initial idea, symbolic annihilation, refers to the under-representation of women in mass media in general, referring to a notion presented by George Gerbner and Larry Gross (1976: 182) who wrote about representation: 'Representation in the fictional world signifies social existence; absence means symbolic annihilation.'

Box 1.3 Female Politicians in the News

Studies in the representation of politicians in the news media forms a specific strand of research in the broader field of 'gender in the news'. In general, these studies point to the marginalisation and trivialisation of high-ranking female politicians. More recently, qualitative analysis shows how gender is reinscribed with concern to female politicians (Luenenborg, Roeser, Maier and Mueller, 2011).

The absence of an equal representation of females and males (or ethnic groups, social classes, disabled and abled people, et cetera) means that audiences form a view of the world in which women are symbolically absent in certain spaces. The emphasis lies in symbolic, as "real life" women are present in these spaces. A good example is the winner of Wimbledon in 2013, Andy Murray. News media all over the world announced Murray as the first British winner since 1936. This is indeed true for male participants of the tournament, but not for female participants such as Viriginia Wade, who was the British Wimbledon champion in 1977. Announcing Murray as the first British winner in 77 years symbolically annihilates Wade's victory in 1977.

Although the relationship between (the absence of) representation and its effects on the audience has been criticised severely (for it is difficult to draw conclusions on the impact of what audiences do not experience), this relationship still stands in research on gender and representation. In various academic disciplines the concept of symbolic annihilation is a core element of the work on representation and identity. For example, Stuart Hall (1986: 9) stresses the idea that some people or identities are central in media representations and others 'are always "represented" only by their eloquent absence, their silences'.

Altogether there are (at the time of writing) almost four decades worth of insights on the way in which men and women are represented in news stories. In 1979, Mieke Ceulemans and Guido Fauconnier conducted a first inventory study. In their report on the image, role and condition of women in media, they show how women are under-represented in all media, including advertising, radio, TV and print. Additionally, they show how women are presented in comparison to men (see Chapter 2 for further discussion). Ceulemans and Fauconnier's study was the first of its kind.

The most current and longitudinal project in this regard is the Global Media Monitoring Project (GMMP), which started with a relatively simple question that arose at the Women Empowering Communication conference held in Bangkok in 1994: 'What does a snapshot of gender in one "ordinary" news day look like?' (GMMP, 2010). The initiators wanted to map the representation and portrayal of women in the world's news media and create media awareness. They strongly emphasised the portrayal of women in news stories, but the data collection and data analysis also included information on the representation of men in news stories on television, radio, newspaper and, in the last version, monitoring online news websites. This monitoring is conducted every five years (so far 1995, 2000, 2005, 2010 and 2015) and analyses one-day of news stories globally, and more specifically the representation and portrayal of women. The snapshots reveal astonishingly similar results of gender representation in news media on a global level; men in news media grossly outnumber women.

The latest (as of writing) monitoring conducted in 2010 includes 108 countries, 1,281 newspapers, radio and television stations, 76 news websites, and eight international news websites. The global results of the GMMP study are also reflected in other national studies on the portrayal of men and women in the news (Eie, 1998; Van Zoonen, 1988; Lont, 1995; Spears and Seydegart, 2000; De Clercq, 2003; Ross and Carter, 2011).

In this last GMMP monitor, only 24% of the people heard or read about in print, radio and television news are female. In contrast, 76% of people in the news are male. This is a significant improvement from the analysis of 1995 when only 17% of the people in the news were women (GMMP, 2010: viii). The under-representation of women in traditional news media seems to be carried over into the virtual news world; women are only present in 23% of the stories in news websites.

Additionally, women and men are present in different categories of news stories. For example, while women remain lodged in the "ordinary" people category, men are far more represented in the expert category; women are identified by their family status four times more often than men; women's age is twice as likely mentioned as men's age; 18% of women in news stories are portrayed as victims in comparison to 8% of men. The GMMP monitor concludes that men outnumber women in almost all occupations. When women do make the news it is primarily as "stars" or "ordinary people", not as figures of authority (GMMP, 2010: viii). These results have slightly changed over the past two decades, but are confirmatory of other studies regarding this issue. For example, Margaret Gallagher (2001) discusses the under-representation of females in the news in terms of the priority towards traditional news subjects like politics and governance. Van Zoonen (1988) stresses that females in the news are more likely to be present in relation to topics like culture, education, nursing, wellbeing or consumption, while males are more likely to be present in subjects on finance, economics, politics and foreign news.

Representations and Reality?

One pressing question we have not addressed yet, is the relation of gender representations with "the real world" or "reality". It is a pressing concern, as it underlies a lot of the research discussed in this chapter. Results are constantly compared to "real world statistics" or to power relations in the "real world". Reality, though, is a rather slippery term and has been a point of debate for thousands of years. Starting with Plato's cave, philosophers have continuously debated the ontological and epistemological character of reality. In other words, we do not exactly know what reality is.

Representations, being photographs, movies, pop song lyrics or newspaper clippings, are not reality, even when we as audiences are tempted to judge them as such (Croteau and Hoynes, 2014). Representations are the end result of a production process in which many decisions and selections are made. Another question David Croteau and William Hoynes (2014) raised in this regard is connected to the intentional view of representations. They argue that 'the media usually do not try to reflect the "real" world' (2014: 189). However, representations do relate to our social world in fundamental ways. As Goffman (1979: 8) puts it: 'Gender displays, like other rituals, can iconically reflect fundamental features of the social structure; but just as easily, these expressions can counterbalance substantive arrangements and compensate for them.' By analysing the gender representation, we argue, we at least get a view of contemporary social structures in specific locations.

The importance of location and time as the context of interpretation of representations is emphasised by authors such as Stuart Hall, Jessica Evans and Sean Nixon (2013) and Goffman (1979). The interpretation of representations is dependent on the geographical location and the time of their production. For example, the picture of Marilyn Monroe, which is a still from the movie *The Seven Year Itch* (20th Century Fox), caused a lot of consternation in 1955, the time in which the original movie was produced.

The movie was an adaptation of a play with a similar name, and is a romantic comedy. However, producing the movie met some difficulties, due to

Figure 1.3 Still from *The Seven Year Itch* (1955)

the moral codes of that time. From 1922 until 1966, a self-regulatory institution existed in Hollywood, called the Hayes Office. This office initiated a Production Code in 1930, stating in the first two articles of the "Sex" section:

1. 'The sanctity of the institution of marriage and the home be upheld. Pictures shall not infer that low forms of sex relationships are the accepted or common thing.'
2. 'Adultery, sometimes necessary plot material, must not be explicitly treated, or justified, or presented attractively.'

(ArtsReformation.com, 2006)

These kinds of moral conventions, and the status of Marilyn Monroe as a sex symbol of her time, made the picture controversial as the connotations of the upwardly billowing dress refer to adultery. However, if we interpret the billowing dress with today's contemporary mores, we see a rather demure and innocent woman who alludes to naughty fun. This picture is also iconic; meanings and different interpretations are restricted. We all recognise Marilyn Monroe, the picture is black and white (dating it to old times), and it is recognisable as a still from a Hollywood (and hence US) movie. These and other features all cause the interpretations of the scene in this picture to be situated in time and place.

Several questions arise when we take this clear attachment of the meaning of representations to time and place into account. Firstly, the concept of place has become more complicated in the light of globalisation. With converging media industries, it is not only harder to pinpoint the location of the production of representations, but representations also travel around the globe in different ways than they have previously. This has at least two consequences. First, as discussed earlier, images produced in the US travel around the globe, meaning that a certain type of aesthetics is becoming the standard form in representations. Second, gendered images have to be suitable for audiences around the globe and are stripped of features that might be offensive to a certain group of people.

Similarly, time is also a tricky concept. While in the 1950s debates focused on representations and their relation to adultery, contemporary debates focus on porn, the headscarf and underwear (Duits and Van Zoonen, 2006, 2007, 2011; Gill, 2007b), each concept provoking equally fierce debates and as heated arguments as the debates of the 1950s. In spite of the change in topics, the debates on gender and media representations still revolve around the female body (Duits and Van Zoonen, 2006). While in the 1950s the image of Marilyn Monroe was considered threatening to the sexual mores of the time, nowadays the visibility of sexuality that was previously bound to the realms of pornography is seen as threatening. There is one significant difference though; contrary to the 1950s debates, modern debates do not only take place between the media industry and regulatory bodies, but also within academia with a noticeable feminist voice (Duits and Van Zoonen, 2006, 2007, 2011; Gill,

2007b). When interpreting media representations today, it is not only the social mores of the contemporary times we take into account, but also the contextualising debates and the voices within these debates (Moss, 2011).

Conclusion

In this chapter we have looked into the first meaning of the concept of representation. Women are outnumbered by men overall on a global scale. The meaning of these numbers are manifold, ranging from symbolic annihilation of women to patriarchal power structures in societies across the globe. We might ask ourselves if and how 'fair and equal representation' is beneficiary. Is it really true that once women and men are present in equal numbers, social structures with regard to gender will change? The short answer to this question is simply, no. The long answer to this question is much more complicated. It is not only who is represented, but also how one is represented. For example, it is not only important to find out that women in TV ads are usually presented in the domestic sphere promoting a household product, it is equally important to think about what this kind of representation means for everyday life. As Tuchman (1978) argued, these media messages lead to the fact that girls in particular believe that their social horizons are more limited than boys do. The signifying practices as discussed earlier in this chapter are pivotal to understanding gender representations in full. In the next chapter we will delve deeper into the "how" aspect of representation.

Further Reading

To find out more about the theories discussed in this chapter we recommend the following volumes:

- Goffman, E. (1979). *Gender Advertisements*. New York: Harper and Row Publishers, Inc.

Goffman's analysis of gender displays in advertising is a real eye opener, because of the clear and recognisable patterns analysed. However, the book is also rather old and the gender displays should, at the very least, be reflected upon in a historical sense.

- Hall, S., Evans, J. and Nixon, S. (Eds.) (2013). *Representation* (2nd edition). London/Thousand Oaks/New Delhi: Sage Publications.

This edited volume offers an eloquent introduction to representations in visual media from a discursive perspective.

- Mulvey, L. (1975). Visual Pleasure and Narrative Cinema. *Screen*, 16(3), 6–18.

This article by Laura Mulvey introduces the important concepts of psychoanalysis to look at visual representations, such as the gaze, scopophilia and voyeurism.

Last but not least we would like to draw attention to:

- Van Zoonen, L. (2005). *Entertaining the Citizen: When Politics and Popular Culture Converge.* Lanham: Rowman & Littlefield Publishers.

Research into the representation of politicians in the news was only briefly addressed in this chapter. However, it is an interesting and very important field of inquiry. In her book, Van Zoonen gives a broader account of the convergence of politics and popular culture than representation, addressing political issues in popular culture and the use of popular culture by politicians.

Chapter 2

Subject Positions

In 2002 Benny Benassi (2002) produced a song *Satisfaction* in which the lyrics, inviting the listener to provide satisfaction, are accompanied by a music video featuring women operating heavy machinery, while lip-syncing (the voice is synthesised, alternating a male and female sound). This combination creates a disturbing spectacle; the women are very attractive and wear skimpy outfits, yet they operate masonry drills, belt sanders and angle grinders. Intensifying the confusion even further are the ad-like texts that appear on screen highlighting the mechanical details of each power tool. The music video and the accompanying lyrics invite a critical reading that would judge the text sexist; the women in the video are objects to be gazed upon, indicated by batting their eyelashes, the fragmentation of their bodies, and the erotic movements they make. The power tools are handled in a sexual manner. The lyrics reify this reading even further. Last but not least, the genre of the song – electro house – is not known for its emancipatory merit which creates a context to deem this video as sexist.

However, this reading does not explain the contradictory and confusing atmosphere that this music video creates. They might be women in skimpy outfits, but they are not mere objects to be looked at. First of all, they are active and in control, as they are handling power tools. Second, by alternating the female and male voice to sing the lyrics, it is unclear whose satisfaction is demanded, creating confusion about who is the object and who is the subject. Third, the in-screen texts on the tools' details might be seen as a tongue-in-cheek addition to the video critiquing the objectification of women in ads. The music video as a whole is so over the top that it might also be read as an ironic critique on sexism.

The various uses of this music video also indicate that it enables more than one reading. The song was used to promote beer, but also a hamburger chain, and it appeared in a movie and several video games. In this brief, and rather crude, analysis of the video, we see how many elements are of importance when interpreting the meaning of the song. The meaning of the song is not dependent on the women appearing, but on *how* they appear and in which context. In the previous chapter we examined the numerical representation of

Figure 2.1 Still from *Satisfaction* (Benny Benassi)

men and women in the media. We concluded that, in general, men outnumber women in almost all media types and genres. The social psychological approaches on sex roles in the media formed the first indication that, next to quantitative measures of representation, qualitative measures are of importance. Even though the duality of male/female may be a socially and culturally constructed division, it does have real consequences for the subjectivities for women and men (Gray, 1992). In this chapter we delve deeper into the question of how representations (re)produce or challenge power in relation to gender and how media products relate to the subject and subjectivity.

The Subject and Identity

In the previous chapter we saw that the main difference between psycho-analysis and discourse analysis with semiotic and social psychological analysis of media content is its relation to power and, as we will see, to gendered subjectivity and identity. While subject, subjectivity and identity are very closely related, their meanings are distinct. Subjectivity refers to 'the condition of being a person and the processes by which we become a person; that is, how we are constituted as cultural subjects and how we experience ourselves' (Barker, 2012: 220). While identity refers to 'how we describe ourselves to each other' (Barker, 2012: 11). Identity hence includes a social and a self-identity. While the social identity denotes what others expect of us (social role theory is very much related to this), self-identity concerns the conceptions we have of ourselves and how we feel about that. Both subjectivity and identity are thought to be informed by the media (though media are certainly not considered as the only informers). To fully understand this relation we need to turn to the origin of subjectivity and identity in both psycho-analysis and discourse analysis.

Subject, Subjectivity and the Media

From a psycho-analytical view, subjectivity – what it means to be a person – is located in language. A student of Sigmund Freud, Jacques Lacan, postulated that we become persons when we acquire language. We are born in a world in which language is the main way of communication. We need this language to express ourselves and experience ourselves. For example, we learn words to express our emotions: happy, sad, angry. At the same time, we also start to feel happy, sad and angry. However, we can only use the tools in the language available. This language uses words such as "I" and "we", but also "man" and "woman" and attaches meanings to these words. We start to think about ourselves in terms of male or female, man or woman with its attached meanings. Language therefore also directs and structures our experience of what it means to be a woman or a man (Van Zoonen, 1994; Flitterman-Lewis, 1992).

One of the major problems with this psycho-analytic viewpoint of gender subjectivity is its reproduction of the sex/gender dichotomy. Sticking to this dichotomy does not allow for more fluid conception of one's subjectivity and reproduces it as well. As Teresa De Lauretis (1987: 1, 2) argues:

> To continue to pose the question of gender in either of these terms, once the critique of patriarchy has been fully outlined, keeps feminist thinking bound to terms of Western patriarchy itself, contained within the frame of a conceptional opposition that is "always already" within the frame of a conceptional opposition, [...]

Instead, De Lauretis (1987: 2) proposes to view gender as not so tied up with this difference in physical sex, but as produced by discourse:

> [T]o propose that gender, too, both as representation and as self-representation, is the product of various social technologies, such as cinema, and of institutionalized discourses, epistemologies, and critical practices, as well as practices of daily life.

De Lauretis (1987) was inspired by Michel Foucault's "technologies of the self" and postulated the media as "technologies of gender": discursive practices of gender. Foucault's (1982) notion of technologies of the self refers to specific techniques humans have to understand themselves within the context of discourse. We will now outline Foucault's ideas on discourse and technologies of the self as they form a turning point in the study of (gender) representations.

Let's start with the notion of discourse. Though in general terms discourse refers to conversation or writing, Foucault developed a different understanding of discourse (Hall, 2013). Interested in how meanings and knowledge were produced, Hall summarizes Foucault's thoughts on discourse as follows:

[A] group of statements which provide a language for talking about – a way of representing the knowledge about – a particular topic at a particular historical moment.[...] Discourse is about the production of knowledge through language. But [...] since all social practices entail *meaning,* and meanings shape and influence what we do – our conduct – all practices have a discursive aspect. [italics in original]

(Hall, 1992: 291, in Hall, 2013: 29)

Discourse refers to the circulating of meanings in society and includes, next to language, social practices. So, it is not only language that produces the meaning of gender (as it is from psycho-analytical point of view); also "what we do" contributes to the production of meaning (Hall, 2013). We do not only think of ourselves as male or female, but most people also behave as male or female, for example, by wearing the gender appropriate clothes. When a woman wears a dress, she also simultaneously articulates a certain type of femininity. The media are important contributors to meanings circulating in society. In the media, meanings of gender are constantly negotiated, constructed, deconstructed and so on, and hence contributing to the discourse on gender. This constructionist view on media represents an important development, as gender representations thusly became an important point on the research agenda in the social sciences and humanities (Hall, 2013). To understand media's contributions to gender discourse, we have to look into relations between power, subject, knowledge and discourse.

First, discourse is seen as producing knowledge. Meanings are not created by an identifiable author or an individual that consciously creates meanings. Of course material texts are created by one or more individual subjects. However, the subject can only do this within the regime of truth of a particular period and culture. A regime of truth can be understood as types of discourses that are accepted in a certain time period and function as the truth. It is a regime, as this distinction between true and false is related to power and regulated by societal institutions such as jurisdiction and science (Foucault, 1989). For example, the idea of a biological sexual difference (male or female) is not only a part of our language, it is also maintained by social institutions such as governments, educational systems, and so on. When we apply for identity papers, for example, we have to check the box: male/female.[1] This happens so often in our lives that most of us do not think about this essentialist notion of our sex, it is a naturalised meaning in most societies. In Foucault's opinion meanings are *made* true, and many people police the boundaries of regimes of truth. For example, transgender people – people whose gender expression does not match their biological sex – encounter a lot of problems, including violence imposed upon them by others who want to maintain the sex/gender dichotomy.

So, discourses produce knowledge and are related to power. Gender representations in the media can be understood as discursive formations of ideas on gender during a particular time and place. With regard to the subject, media texts present us with 'figures who personify the particular forms of knowledge which the discourse produces. These subjects have the attributes we would expect as these are defined by the discourse […]' (Hall, 2013: 40). In other words, media present us with representations that show us what femininity and masculinity are according to the prevalent discourse at a certain time and place.

We can now understand the confusion caused by Benassi's music video a bit better, seeing as the display of women in skimpy clothing is part of contemporary Western discourse on gender, it is (for some) a normal view. What is, however, not "normal", what is not within the regime of truth created by the discourse, is the women operating power tools (as it is not part of normal activities for women). The meaning of gender is at least negotiated here. The discourse on femininity is problematised. This problematisation is thought to be of importance for the audiences: their sense of the self, their subjectivity, is impacted by gender discourses.

However, there is yet another way in which mediated gender discourses relate to subjectivity. Media texts, Hall (2013) argues, also produce a place for the subject, a place for the reader from which 'its particular knowledge and meaning most makes sense' (Hall, 2013: 40). The reader is subjected to the discourse and its regime of truth and the media text only makes sense if the reader identifies with the position constructed by the discourse. Think about the commercials discussed in the previous chapter, for example. These images tell us what a man or woman is supposed to look like and how she or he is to behave, however the commercials are only meaningful if and when we feel addressed by them. To "get" the J'Adore commercial we have to subject ourselves to the discourse on women as objects of desire. Generally, this place of the subject is indicated as "subject positions" created by the text.

It is important to understand that the text could be understood as creating multiple subject positions (Weedon, 1987). Not all texts do this, and some do it more than others. Benassi's music video creates more than one subject position. We identified two subject positions already, one that deems the video sexist, one that deems the video a critique on sexism. However, maybe we could identify even more positions. For example, the women in the music video seem to have tremendous fun and enjoy flaunting their sexuality. Hence, these women can also be interpreted as sexually liberated, and therefore as a strong symbol for female empowerment (cf. McRobbie, 1984). In Part III, "Consuming", we address questions on how audiences and individual members take on subject positions and how their decisions are structured. For now it is important to grasp the notion of multiple subject positions. Yet, we should not forget that these positions are always created by discourse and are therefore not endless in their variety. Some texts open up more possibilities than others and have greater polysemic potential (cf. Fiske, 1987).

Identity and the Media

The reason these complex issues of subjectivity and subject positions are important is that they relate to our identities. Identity is a very opaque term, in the sense that is hard to define. Hall understands identity as follows:

> The point of suture, between on the one hand the discourses and practices which attempt to "interpellate", speak to us or hail us onto place as the social subjects of particular discourses, and on the other hand, the processes which produce subjectivities, which construct us as subjects which can be "spoken". Identities are thus the points of temporary attachment to the subject positions, which discursive practices construct for us.
>
> (Hall, 1996: 5–6)

Our identities are dependent on our subjectivity and how we relate to these subject positions. Our self-identity and social identity are informed by our subjectivity. However, as the word "temporary" indicates, our identities are not fixed but are dynamic constructs.

Our identity, Antony Giddens (1991) argues, should be considered a discursive project. It is not a set of traits, but a reflexive narrative about the self that one tries to sustain. This reflexive narrative is discursively constructed from, among other elements, media representations. Considering identity as a discursive project has two consequences for our understanding. First, it positions identity as central to issues of agency and politics. Identities are not only constructed in terms of who we are, but also in terms of who we are not. With regard to representations, this means that the images we see do not only have an impact on how we view ourselves, but also on how we view others. It is only through our relations to the Other, to constitutive outside, that an identity is discursively constructed. For example, when we experience our social identity as masculine, this also means "not-feminine". Discourses on femininity and masculinity inform our sense of gender. Second, it features identity as a non-essentialist notion. The unity and internal consistency of identity are not natural – they are produced in discourse. A person's identity is not a set of identifiable, fixed character traits. Gender then, an important part of our identity, is not a predetermined essential part of us, but a construct. De Lauretis (1984) stresses this fluid notion on identity and subjectivity: identities are not fixed but perpetually produced.

Box 2.1 Exercise: Gender Biography

Write a short biography starting with the sentence: 'I realised that I am female/male/queer/feminine/masculine/other* when … ' Use a maximum of two pages. Reflect on what this experience has meant to you and how you experience yourself. Were there other experiences that reinforced or contradicted this first experience?

*pick whatever suits you best

Media as technologies of gender inform the narratives of our identities and our subjectivity. This insight underlies studies on gender representations done by discourse or psycho-analysts. Questions that some of these academics raise about the rightness and realism of representations (not only in numbers but also in non-essentialist manner) become understandable. However, the "rightness" of representation is a complex, ambiguous and normative affair. Examples of questions raised in academic studies are 'Do these representations affirm existing stereotypes?' and 'Are these representations realistic?' (cf. Dhaenens, 2013). Scholars who concentrate on this matter often find themselves focusing on stereotypes as they are usually considered as significant markers of regimes of truth and embodiments of the boundaries between what is deviant and what is not. We will now look into stereotypes and how they function as a technology of gender.

Stereotypes

The word stereotype is derived from two Ancient Greek words, stereos (firm) and typos (impression). Walter Lippmann coined its current use in 1922 in his book *Public Opinion*. Lippmann discusses stereotyping as a psychological mechanism; people make categorisations to understand the world around them. The negative connotations the word has are developed later. For our purposes, we use Hall's conceptualisation of the word stereotype: 'Stereotyping reduces people to a few, simple, essential characteristics, which are represented as fixed by Nature' (Hall *et al.*, 2013: 247). Stereotyping is a signifying practice and therefore productive; they produce knowledge of the Other and of the Self. Stereotypes are important for our subjectivity and identity. Usually stereotypes' contribution is not considered benevolent. With their reductive potential, stereotypes are an articulation of essentialist notions of gender, and deny the dynamic nature of gender (Van Zoonen, 1994).

Box 2.2 Ain't I a Woman?

Critiques on racial stereotypes often use the phrase 'Ain't I a Woman?' This phrase is the title of one of the most famous speeches in feminist history. In 1851, at the Women's Convention in Akron, Ohio, Sojourner Truth (an emancipated ex-slave) addressed an almost entirely white audience pointing out their ethnocentric points of view. You can read the entire speech at: www.feminist.com/resources/artspeech/genwom/sojour.htm.

As products of discourse, stereotypes are fluid concepts; they change over time and are geographically situated. Think, for example, of the Western stereotype of blonde women as less intelligent than everyone else, which does not work in many other parts of the world. Additionally, most gender stereotypes intersect with other characteristics such as ethnicity, age, sexuality and class. At the end of the 1980s, criticism of academic work on gender representations functioned as turning point for feminist scholarship. According to many feminist scholars, gender representations were highly complex and it was time for a 'critical interrogation of characters' gender, race and class'. Important authors such as bell hooks (1992), Ruth Frankenberg (1993), Philomena Essed (1982) and Jacqueline Bobo (1995) criticised the mainstream media for their negative portrayals of African-American women. They were portrayed as being close to nature, exotic and sexually assertive. Common stereotypes used were the mammy, the jezebel and the welfare mother. Asian-American women on the other hand are more often portrayed as mysterious and exotic, while being sexually submissive. Common stereotypes are the dragon lady and the China doll. As Michelle Lazar (2005) argues, this pan-Asian femininity is reproduced in advertisements all over the world, as is the case for women of African descent. As stereotypes articulate essentialist notions, these stereotypes do not only articulate Asian-American and Afro-American women as in terms of a certain gender, but also as inherently different to white women.

These stereotypes are prolific in contemporary media. For example, the character of Christina Yang played by Sandra Oh in ABC's *Grey's Anatomy* is often considered an example of the model minority stereotype commonly used for Asian-Americans. She works hard, is ambitious, a real go-getter and slightly unsympathetic. The character of Christina hence contributes to the construction and naturalising of an essentialist notion of people of Asian descent. Nevertheless, stereotypes are also challenged in contemporary media. Over the seasons, Christina Yang becomes more sympathetic and the issue of race is discussed overtly in the show. In this way the stereotype is undermined, instead of the model minority, Christina becomes "just Christina".

Resisting stereotypes is more common in the media. Some media genres are famous for the space they provide to resist stereotyping. Hip-hop music, for example, is known to represent black women as objects of desire; her body is a commodity. However, the genre also forms an important site for self-definition.

Box 2.3 Reversing Gender

A fun way to discover stereotypes is to practice "role reversal". Role reversal refers to changing features of media characters in one's mind to see if they still would work in the given media product. What would the character of Christina Yang be if we turn her into a white man for example? Would the character still be deemed ambitious go-getter and slightly unsympathetic, or would our judgment on the behavior change? Lots of examples are found on YouTube where music videos are changed, most often to critique the original or to draw attention to certain issues. An example of the latter is found in a music video featuring Benassi's song (*Satisfaction* – the granny remake for Equal Payday), raising awareness for equal pay in Belgium. In the video, older women have taken the place of younger ones while wearing similar clothing and making similar movements. You can find the link at: www.youtube.com/watch? v=ZB4QoCIXdg4.

As Murali Balaji (2010: 8) convincingly claims: 'Indeed, many black women performers have used their Otherness as a weapon of empowerment, as exhibited by the varying degrees of feminism used by Queen Latifah, Erykah Baduh, Lauryn Hill, Missy Elliott, and Lil' Kim.' Other sites of resistance are found in advertising (e.g. the Dove 'Real Beauty' campaign), popular culture (e.g. *The Wire* (HBO) and *Once Upon a Time* (ABC)) and digital media (e.g. social network sites). The resistance of stereotypes, sometimes by deliberate play with stereotypes and multiple intersections, sometimes as a political act, will be discussed more in-depth in Chapter 3. For now it is important to realise that stereotypes are rarely singular or static.

One pressing question raised by feminist scholars is 'Who controls these images?', 'Who is responsible for stereotyping?'. Some suggest that the fact that the majority of people owning the media are men has something to do with it. In Part II we will explore what this something actually entails. However, the sheer number of men owning the media does not entirely explain the presence of gender stereotyping in the media, as the issue is more complex than that. There is no conspiracy of white men (or patriarchal institutions) using their power to insert stereotypes in mass media's content to subjugate women and minorities; other principles of the media industry are at play here. First, media are constantly struggling for audience attention. This is especially visible with regards to advertising. An ad, whether it is in a magazine, on the radio, or on TV needs to grab attention in a split second. To get the message across, stereotypes are ultimately useful, as they are able to communicate a lot in that split second. Therefore, advertising is often considered as a place where researchers can get a glance of contemporary discourses on gender. However, we have to remind ourselves that the ad's purpose is to sell us something, not to convey messages about gender. Second, due to its need for advertising revenue, decision making in the media industry is based on a logic of safety. Producing media, especially popular media, is a risky business as it is hard to predict which products will become successful (and therefore generate revenue) and which will not (and therefore will be a costly affair). Therefore, Todd Gitlin (2000) argues, media industries play it safe and use formulas and themes that audiences have positively responded to before. Partly, we argue, this results in the repetition of existing power structures in the media, including stereotypes.

Stereotypes as discursive practices produce knowledge on the deviant, but also on the normal. They are usually considered damaging to one's sense of the self and one's constructing of identity. When you only encounter yourself in the media as "model minority" you might start to think about yourself as being one, hence limiting other possibilities. So far, we have considered gender representations and stereotypes for femininity. The reason for this is that gender representations work slightly different for men and masculinity.

What About Men?

Up till now we have discussed gender representations in terms of femininity. Again, this is the working of discourse: masculinity has long functioned as the standard to which everything else is compared. For example, when we read a history book, we read the history of men: wars, conquests and discoveries. Hence, we learn a lot about the lives of men in Paris on the 14th of July 1789 (when the Bastille was stormed). We do not know what everyone else was doing that day (did women and children take part in storming the Bastille, or did they stay home and prepare meals?). Similar arguments can be made for the science of medicine (most Western practices are based on research among men), the arts (most famous artists are male) and also the media. Representations of men are rarely researched in terms of their gender. In the previous chapter we have already noted that representations of white, heterosexual men are dominant in all media. However, these results are most often deduced from studies into the representations of women or femininity. As Fred Fejes (1992: 10) argues in his review of studies in American masculinities: 'In most cases the topic of masculinity was not the major, or even a secondary topic of these studies.' Moreover, studies usually discuss the differences they found in terms of masculinity and femininity, even though many (and sometimes more) similarities were found.

The conflation of gender studies with women's studies is not only true for academia in the West, but also for other parts of the world. Yiu Fai Chow (2008) notes that gender studies have been almost synonymous with women's studies in China as well as in the West. Additionally, we face the issue of intersectionality; most studies in masculinities are studies into the intersection of ethnicity and masculinity (cf. Furnham, Mak and Tanidjojo, 2000; Luyt, 2012). In other words, most studies on men and masculinities focus on masculinity that is not "normal", leaving the "standard masculinity", called hegemonic masculinity, unquestioned and unchallenged.

Hegemonic masculinity as a concept was formulated in the mid-1980s as a critique on sex role theory for its disability to account for power structures. Hegemonic masculinity 'embodied the currently most honoured way of being a man, it required all other men to position themselves in relation to it, and it ideologically legitimated the global subordination of women to men' (Connell and Messerschmidt, 2005: 831). Hegemonic masculinity is not so much the most prevalent kind of masculinity in a certain society at a certain time, but the kind of masculinity that is "most wanted" (even though only a small minority of men might be able to perform it).

During the last two decades, research on representations of masculinity has increased. To indicate the multiplicity of masculinity, the term hegemonic masculinity is now firmly attached to most research on the topic (Beasley, 2008) (however, as noted before, studies often concentrate on how non-hegemonic masculinities relate to hegemonic masculinity). Studies on masculinity in advertising serve as a good illustration. The 30-second TV message, with a manifest aim to sell us something, is a compound of information on gender roles. As Lance Strate (1992: 78) argues about beer commercials, 'collectively the commercials provide a clear and consistent image of the masculine role; in a sense, they constitute a guide for becoming a man, a rulebook for appropriate male behavior, in short, a manual on masculinity'. Though Strate (1992) set up his arguments more than 20 years ago, many of his observations are still valid. Masculinity in beer commercials is constructed around a theme of challenge. Men are often pictured outdoors engaging in some activity, faced with a problem they must overcome, et cetera. At the end of the commercial, all is well and problems are solved.

A quick search for recent beer commercials shows that this discourse on masculinity is still in fashion. The beer brand Carlsberg launched a commercial in 2013 that perfectly reflected Strate's ideas. The title of the commercial, "Put Your Friends To The Test", (www.youtube.com/watch?v=8-ikEn3ItQc) already indicates the male bonding principle. The commercial begins with an Asian male face, saying in a gloomy voice: 'Imagine. It's the middle of the night. You're sleeping. Your best friend calls for help. Would you go out and save his ass? Tonight, we put some friends to the test.' In the background we hear the sound of a gong, we see images of a smoky room that hints of an illegal casino. Around the table we see more Asian men, and one Caucasian one. The Caucasian one is the one in "trouble" who calls his best friend to bring him some money. The best friend, also Caucasian, gets up and has to enter the building, the door protected by another Asian male. On his route to the third floor (where the poker room is located according to the doorman) the friend has to conquer several challenges, including a scary elevator, an Asian cook who while flambéing turns his wok into a flame thrower, and fighting Asian men. When he finally meets his friend in trouble and hands over the money a curtain falls and there are lots of other friends (all Caucasian) who enjoy a Carlsberg. The commercial ends with the text, 'Standing up for a friend'.

The ad gives a straightforward idea of masculinity and its intersection with ethnicity. The protagonists, the Caucasian men, are not particularly muscular, handsome or smart. However, they are white males who face the challenge and complete the quest.[2] The Asian men featured are depicted as a threat. They are involved in criminal activities (running the poker game) and in physical aggression (fighting). As an audience we are called upon to identify with the white males who are the good guys. This commercial demonstrates particularly well what can be understood as hegemonic masculinity (the dominant understanding of what "normal" masculinity is), alongside the troubling representation of Asian males in this commercial, which are reminiscent, if not direct copies, of the "yellow peril", a cruel and cunning Asian male.

Similar to femininity, concepts of masculinity are bound to place and time. In that respect we must use concepts such as hegemonic masculinity with caution. The concept suggests that there is one form of masculinity that is hegemonic, however, with a global perspective it is apparent there must be multiple forms of hegemonic masculinity (cf. Beasley, 2008; Chow, 2008). The most honoured way of being a man is culturally specific, while the original concept of hegemonic masculinity, which formulates men as white, middle class, early middle-aged and heterosexual is an explicitly Western masculinity (cf. Kimmel, 1994).

Additionally, we would like to mention that the concept of "hegemonic femininity" is unused in academic research. Some speak of "emphasised femininity" or "hyper-femininity", but hegemonic femininity does not seem to exist. This is an important difference between two research traditions; studies in masculinities take the multiplicity of men and masculinities as a starting point of investigation (for example, Craig, 1992; Moss, 2011), while studies in femininity often position themselves as in difference with masculinities. It is important to note, though, that recent femininity research shows some similarities to masculinity studies' starting point (cf. Holland and Harpin, 2013).

We would like to draw attention to the fact that this multiplicity of subject positions present in the media is largely reserved for white, heterosexual males and females. As soon as any other characteristics come into play such as ethnicity, sexuality or age, the range of subject positions becomes more limited. At least, this is the case for traditional media in the West. We have to wonder how the increasing transnationalisation of media industries and media content relates to gender representations, as well as new technologies, and specifically new media.

Representing Gender in a Global Context

With the increasing globalisation of media content, it is vital to investigate gendered subject positions created in and by the media within a transnational context. As Radha Hedge (2011: 6) argues, '[i]n the global context, questions of culture, subjectivity, and everyday life have to be situated against the ubiquitous presence and proliferation of communication technologies and their ability to transcend time and space'. In Chapter 1 we touched upon the notion that due to the increasing transnationalisation of the fashion industry, gender representations travel across the globe. On a more general level, something similar happens in the media industry. Media industries located in the US being the dominant players, American conceptions of gender are travelling around the globe (Kuipers, 2012). Inspired by Jeroen De Kloet (2008) we argue that these representations of gender are appropriated and indigenised by audiences across the globe while simultaneously producing Western subject positions as desirable. In other words, while these American versions of gender might be exported and conceived as desirable imagery of gender, regional conceptions of gender are and remain equally important. As we have seen in previous sections, geographical location and time are pivotal in the discursive power of representations.

Moreover, De Kloet (2008) also argues for a critical stance towards theoretical conceptions that are developed in the West and their validity for other regions. Western discourses on gender and sex, for example, are not always valid when transported to other localities. De Kloet (2008) shows how the sex/gender distinction that we launched in the introductory chapter of this volume becomes a problematic notion when transported to China. The Chinese notion of sex already provides space for more than one gender performance (including androgyny and gender transgression):

> Epistemological differences between Chinese and Western conceptions of gender and sexuality explain that sex was understood in China not as an irreducible polarity in traditional Chinese cosmology, but as "one principle among many [...] that determined a person's position in the family and in society".
>
> (De Kloet, 2008: 200)

Epistemological differences emerge on a global level. Conducting a multi-layered analysis of the Latinidad – 'the process of being, becoming and/or performing belonging within a Latina/o diaspora' (Valdivia, 2011: 53) – transportation of representations and the theoretical underpinnings thereof is put into question. Angharad Valdivia (2011) points out that representations of the Latina/o, which are arguably as stereotypical as they are rare (*Dora the Explorer* (Nickelodeon) – the exotic one; *Ugly Betty* (ABC) – the lower class go-getter), will be interpreted differently by Latina/o and non-Latina/o audiences as lived experiences (which are regionally different) shape our discursive resources. Valdivia (2011) does not explicitly discuss epistemological differences, but her results and arguments can be interpreted as saying that the notion of the Latina/o in popular culture is a Western construction of the Latina/o, and thus unrecognizable in some cultures. The Latina/o, Valdivia (2011) argues, is constructed as a marker of difference in popular culture, while in some regions this marker of difference does not exist.

So far in this chapter we have explored representations of gender and its intersections, and how these representations relate to subjectivity, subject positions and identity. Some texts produce multiple subject positions for its audiences while others do not. Likewise, some kinds of media texts produce specific gendered subject positions, while others do not.

Gendered Genres

Genres are gendered. As early as 1983, Pam Cook (1983: 17) addressed the hegemonic notion of gendered genres:

There is no such thing as "men's picture", specifically addressed to men; there is only "cinema", and "the women's picture", a sub-group or category specially for women, excluding men; a separate, private space designed for more than half the population, relegating them to the margins of cinema proper. The existence of the women's picture both recognises the importance of women, and marginalises them.

Cook (1983) addresses the gendered identity of the "women's picture" as defined by its character of "not being for men". Apparently, she argues, all other films are for men. Something similar can be said for some TV genres and music genres. In Chapter 1 we briefly sketched out the differences in the representations of women and men for various types of media content (news, popular culture and advertising). In this section we will dive deeper into these differentiations with regard to genres.

Genres and Subject Positions

Genre is a widely used word. For our purposes we follow John Fiske's (1987) understanding of genres as organising principles. Both the audiences and the media industry use genres. It is a simple but effective way to bring order into the welter of different kinds of magazines, TV programmes, music, films, games and so on. This organisation takes place through generic codes called signifiers, such as character types, setting, locations, iconography and plots (Gledhill and Ball, 2013). Genres encompass institutional discourses (production, distribution and criticism) on viewers' expectations and their decoding practices. The audience knows what to expect when sitting down to watch a crime series such as *CSI* (CBS), a sitcom such as *The Big Bang Theory* (CBS) or a documentary like *Planet Earth* (BBC). The media industry, on the other hand, uses genres (and the inherent generic codes) in decision making processes regarding production and distribution (Fiske, 1987). Again, the logic of safety is at work. As Gitlin (2000) phrases it, 'nothing succeeds like success'. This success is necessary, as successful programmes attract advertisers. Advertising, for many broadcasters is the main source of revenue. For example, since the release of *CSI* (CBS) in 2000, we have not only seen two related series (*CSI: New York* and *CSI: Miami*, both CBS) but also many similar, though slightly different, series: *Bones* (FOX), *Criminal Minds* (CBS) and *Cold Case* (CBS). Hence, genres help the media industry to predict which media products will be successful and to avoid financial risks.

Genres are also tools for the media industry to target a certain audience. As media use has increased tremendously over the last decades together with an increase of the amount of media content offered, the battle for audience attention has become more intense. As for most media producers the primary source of income is advertising revenue, with narrow casting being the primary tool. Narrow casting refers to the principle that producers and broadcasters will produce media content that is liked by a specific group of people with a lot of consuming power. As some would say, media industries nowadays sell audiences, not media content (Croteau and Hoynes, 2014). Women are viewed as a group with significant consumer power, as they do the household shopping and spend more money than men on personal care products, clothing et cetera. They are therefore an attractive audience for advertisers (cf. Joyrich, 1996; Shattuc, 1997). Genres such as the glossy and soap operas owe their existence to the fact that these types of shows are excellent ways to reach female audiences. This underlying commercial discourse in the media industry has corollaries for subject positions created by these genres. As Lynn Joyrich (1996: 12) argues, 'television is already quite self-conscious about addressing viewers, already "encoding" presumptions about viewer "decodings" within the text itself [...]'.

Genres balance similarity and difference; we know what to expect, but to enjoy it, we also need to be surprised (Fiske, 1987). This balance is kept through a play with generic codes. The sitcom (situation comedy) *The Big Bang Theory* (CBS) shares its generic codes with the sitcom *Friends* (NBC). The sitcoms revolve around a group of friends who represent different personalities to enable clashes and tensions that generate a certain type of humour (generic code: types of characters). Both sitcoms have an urban setting (generic codes: setting) while a large part of the storyline takes place in the apartment two of them share, while another character lives across the hall. The remainder of storylines takes place in a diner or coffee shop (generic codes: location and setting). Primary themes in the episodes are friendship and romance (generic code: plot). Though both sitcoms share these generic codes, they are unique as well as they are similar. For example, in *The Big Bang Theory* the primary protagonists are four males (*Friends* revolved around three men and three women). Three of the protagonists have obtained PhDs in physics, resulting in jokes that are often "geek related" without making fun of geeks (which is what happens in *Friends* where the character Ross is constantly made fun of). Depending on one's perspective, *The Big Bang Theory* uses or challenges a new stereotype, the nerd, perceived as either a pejorative stereotype or as cool (Kendall, 2011).

This stereotype of the nerd is also gendered. In season three a female character, Amy, who also has a PhD in neurobiology, is introduced. While the male characters are geeky but cool, this female character is far from cool. Amy resembles much more the "to-be-made-fun-off" geekiness of *Friends*' character Ross than the others characters do. However, alongside another blonde woman is introduced: Bernadette. Bernadette is attractive like Penny, but also has a PhD (in microbiology). This shows how generic codes are first of all not fixed, and second of all that they are meaningful in relation to the subject positions created by the text. Due to its palette of personalities, the jokes and the themes of friendship and romance, the sitcom is a genre that caters to both male and female audiences.

Other genres might have a more distinct gendered character. One of the determinants is a genre's position in either the public or private sphere. The private, domestic sphere dominates feminine genres, such as soap operas and drama series, while the public sphere is where masculine genres are often situated, such as news, current affairs and action movies. However, like gender, genres are not stable or static, but dynamic constructs. While the setting and plotlines of soap operas indeed take place in the domestic sphere, the female characters are certainly not all there as passive objects of desire. One of the particularities that make soaps such a pleasurable experience for many female viewers is the fact that soap offers a variety of female characters including business women, single women, mothers, et cetera. By introducing transgressive female characters, patriarchy is challenged and a multiplicity of subject positions becomes available, some of them subversive (Fiske, 1987). Soap opera as a text enables this variety in gender representations, and can thus be seen as a site of resistance (though it not necessarily is for all viewers). Additionally, the scheduling of soap opera has recently shifted from daytime (traditionally a women's time slot, connected to the concept of the housewife) to prime-time, mostly associated with the family, including the man of the house. Christine Gledhill and Vicky Ball (2013) discuss the meaning of these kinds of shifts for the gendered character of the soap genre in terms of their relation with the social circulation of gender discourses.

Clearly, the gendered character of genres is not set in stone. Social developments, like the shifting boundaries between the public and the private, are responsible for this. These social developments have direct and indirect consequences for the media industry, which reflects in media texts. In turn, subject positions created by these media texts are significant for identities. Changes in society are hence related to identities (as they are discursive practice). These changes, in turn, have an impact on the character of the audience as envisaged by the industry (cf. Joyrich, 1996), which, in turn, will have changes on the media text. We will use the talk show as a clarifying example of this circle of impact.

The Femininity of Confessional Talk Shows

Originating from radio, the TV talk show has been part of the TV menu since the early rise of the medium. As a genre it has some very specific generic codes; the show has a host and it takes place in a studio. Sometimes an audience is present and interacting with the guests, and sometimes the topics of conversation are private, sometimes they are public. A talk show can be described as a genre capitalising on a conversation between two or more people in a studio, moderated by one or more hosts and often combined with short reportages on the discussed topic (Biltereyst *et al.*, 2000). The talk show thus indicates a genre category. There are many subgenres, each with more distinct generic codes. For our purposes we will explore the confessional talk show, as this subgenre is usually considered a feminine genre since it focuses almost solely on the private sphere. However, we will show how this genre is transgressing boundaries and how some of these transgressions are intersecting with media industries' desire to get high ratings. These transgressions, though, also have an impact on the subject positions they create. Indirectly, the media industries have an impact on our subjectivity.

When we discuss confessional talk shows, we are referring to shows like the *Oprah Winfrey Show* (1986–2011, Syndication), *Dr. Phil* (Syndication; created by Oprah Winfrey), *Jerry Springer* (Syndication) or *Geraldo* (1987–98, syndicated). These shows have certain features in common. For one, they are scheduled during daytime, deal with issues in the private sphere (often a little sensational), the mode of communication is informal, the audience is somehow involved and their titles reiterate the name of the host. This last feature, the title, is often designed as a handwritten name or signature. In this way a personal bond is created between the host, the audiences and the guests in the show. The generic codes are more or less adapted to the sensational character of the show. While Oprah and Dr. Phil perform the role of a good friend (though Dr. Phil is portrayed more as an expert than Oprah and is thus presented as more paternalistic), Jerry Springer and Geraldo are just as informal but also seek more provocation with their guests and the audience. This "elasticity" of the genre is well exploited by the media industry and within one show we can sometimes spot the changes.

For example, in a detailed description of the evolution of the *Oprah Winfrey Show*, Jane Shattuc (2008) shows how it went from a typical confessional talk show, where individual issues were debated with guests, including interaction with the audience, to a more general talk show, with Oprah promising to go on a 'spiritual quest with moral uplift' (Shattuc, 2008: 168). This turn in focus was largely due to critical comments on the sensationalist character of the show.

One of the most important features of this genre is that the issues they deal with are always located in the private sphere. Family, love, friendship, personal development and many more themes appear over and over in these shows. The subject positions inscribed in these shows, therefore, are relatively limited to stay-at-home parents (mostly housewives and mothers). However, with this focus the genre is also degraded as non-culture and non-political. Shattuc (1997: 90) formulates the general thoughts on the genre as '[t]he nation's picture window onto domestic dysfunction'. This adds another dimension to an already defined subject position; as a housewife your work (that takes place in the private sphere) is not important, it is non-culture and non-political as opposed to other genres. Strengthening this reputation of the talk show and its subject positions, the conversations in these talk shows between host, guests and audiences are often described as gossip.

Yet, many feminist scholars hailed the genre as a new public sphere and stressed the possibilities it has to give women a voice in the public sphere. The second wave feminist slogan 'the personal is political' is embodied by the talk show. Matters that are often considered a purely private matter, such as raising kids, running a household on little money, keeping your family together are now discussed in public and therefore become part of the public sphere. Issues that were considered as individual private affairs are turned into issues of greater, societal relevance. Shattuc (1997: 93) argues that talk shows offer a '[s]ubversive yet gratifying venue for the rare public portrayal of women's struggles'.

Additionally, we would like to add, conversations in talk shows created subject positions for the Other as well. The conversations in these shows are significantly different from gossip. Gossip centres on the Other and is a way to discuss (moral) boundaries between the normal and the abnormal; the pivotal feature about gossip is that it always focuses on someone else who is absent from the scene. Talk shows do the contrary. The conversations are also used to demarcate the normal/abnormal, but do so with the Other on stage. Hence, talk shows create subject positions for the Other.

While conversations may be about private issues, these issues often reveal public issues and are sometimes directly related. Looking at the genre from a non-US point of view, we see the genre's power to transgress this boundary between the private and the public. Sometimes the private issues talked about on talk shows reflect major issues in societies or the transitions a country is going through. Thabisani Ndlovu (2013) for example, shows how in the South African talk show *Relate* (SABC1), the discussions on family and social relations reveal (and obscure) class and racial differentiations and their adherent socio-economic imbalances. Similarly, Jiangnan Zhu and Xueyang Wang (2013) show how, in Chinese talk shows, Chinese politicians have recently started to discuss private issues, but they do this to achieve certain political goals (for example policy adherence). These two examples are far from an all-encompassing account of talk shows on a global level, but they do strengthen the concept of the talk show as a genre that transcends the boundary between the public and the private. The direction of the transgression of this boundary is closely tied to the country or region in which the talk show is produced and broadcast. We have to keep in mind, though, that the first and foremost aim of the talk show is to generate advertising revenue, and therefore mostly deflect heated political debates.

Conclusion

In this chapter we have explored how gender representations in the media function as technologies of gender. We have seen how representations have an impact on our subjectivity and identity. However, we have discussed instances of representation, even though we have argued, with Stuart Hall, Teresa De Lauretis and Erving Goffman, that gender representations are especially important in terms of patterns. Texts are interpreted, and become meaningful within their context. This phenomenon is called intertextuality. Intertextuality is therefore crucial in the understanding of subjectivity and identity, but it also significantly complicates these notions. It is in intertextuality and intertextual play that the fluidity of gender expresses itself. Additionally, increasing media convergence, the transnationalisation of the media industry, and new technology all have an impact on intertextuality. Digital media, for example, offer a site not only for self-definition and resistance against stereotyping, but they also create a new environment for the interpretation of subject positions. In the next chapter we will therefore examine the concept of intertextuality and what it means for subjectivity and identity. Developments in the media industry (convergence and transnationalisation) and media technologies will be discussed in later chapters.

Further Reading

Interested? There are many books (and journal articles) available that discuss gender representations in the media. We would like to highlight two recent ones:

- Moss, M. (2011). *The Media and the Models of Masculinity.* Lanham/ Boulder/New York/Toronto/Plymouth: Lexington Books.

Mark Moss's volume offers a useful exploration of contemporary discourses on men, masculinity and the media. He explores several popular domains, such as sports, television and domestic space, showing how the media have an impact on masculinities.

- Mazzarella, S.R. (Ed.) (2013). *Volume III: Content and Representation. The International Encyclopaedia of Media Studies.* Malden/London: Wiley-Blackwell.

This edited volume gives a detailed insight in contemporary representations in media content, discussing Persuasion and Information (advertising and news), Entertainment (popular culture) and Interaction and Performance (new media).

Notes

1 Recently, this practice has been adapted in some countries. In Australia people can choose a third option (crossing an X) and in Germany parents can choose to leave the field 'sex' blank on the birth certificate of their child.
2 Interestingly enough, in the commercial one of the "friends" is female who, like the others, is victorious in her quest. She does challenge the undemanding notion of masculinity present in the commercial. However, interestingly, she is called upon by the only black "friend in trouble".

Chapter 3

Intertextual Representations

In previous chapters, we have discussed many examples of gender representations – Lady Gaga, Marilyn Monroe, and Dior adverts, to name a few. Occasionally, we indicated that these meanings are part of a pattern of representations. In this chapter we will dig deeper into these patterns and how they are pivotal to our understanding of gender representations. Representations get meaning within a context of other representations. This context, pivotal to meaning construction, is referred to as intertextuality. Intertextuality complicates the discursive meanings of gender representations in relation to subjectivity and identity in multiple ways.

First, representations are often contradictory. The two *The Big Bang Theory* characters, Amy and Bernadette, discussed in the previous chapter, are almost each other's opposite. Adding to that the third female character of the show, Penny – another blonde who is intelligent (though not as intelligent as Bernadette and Amy, or the men in the series), pretty and in the possession of great social skills, *The Big Bang Theory* as text can hardly be accused of creating a singular subject position for its female audience or to promote a stereotype of women who have obtained a PhD. This contributes, we would like to argue, to a more fluid conception of gender than the conventional dichotomy discussed in Chapters 1 and 2.

Second, no one only watches *The Big Bang Theory* and nothing else. Amy, Penny and Bernadette get meaning in the context of all other media content an audience member has consumed. The already contradicting subject positions created are hence further complicated.

Third, often media industries consciously employ intertextuality as a strategy for both attracting an audience and to endorse their products commercially. In *The Big Bang Theory* multiple jokes include references to other TV programmes such as *Star Trek* (CBS/Paramount), *Doctor Who* (BBC), and *Red Dwarf* (BBC). Hence situating the programme as suitable for a certain audience, creating specific subject positions. Also, many media products are produced and distributed at multiple levels. We will explore this last form of intertextuality, called convergence, in Chapter 6.

In this chapter we will investigate intertextuality as a concept and its potential to articulated fluid notions of subjectivity and gender.

Intertextuality

As a concept, intertextuality refers to fact that meaning construction of any given text does take place within a wider context. Etymologically, intertextuality refers to a text within texts. Julia Kristeva (1986) coined the concept intertextuality in contemporary academia. It indicates that a text is not a fully autonomous entity but that its meanings are also produced by other texts. Grounding her thoughts in Mikhail Bakhtin's theory, Kristeva states that '[a]ny text is constructed as a mosaic of quotations; any text is the absorption and transformation of another. The notion of intertextuality replaces that of intersubjectivity, and poetic language is read as at least double' (Kristeva, 1986: 37). A text can thus be seen as a multidimensional space in which other texts are present (or, as Kristeva emphasises, the text exists out of other texts). The meaning of the texts are thus co-constructed by other texts, thus, intertextuality appears in the space *between* texts (Fiske, 1987). For the reader, this means that the text is always interpreted in relation to other texts and a 'range of textual knowledges is brought to bear upon it' (Fiske, 1987: 108). However, this new interpretation, which is co-constructed by previous interpretations, also adds to future meaning constructions. As Andrew Edgar and Peter Sedgwick (1999: 198) argue, '[t]here can then never be a definitive reading of a text, for each reading generates a new text, that itself becomes part of the frame within which the original text is interpreted'. From this perspective, one could claim that the author of the text, the identifiable creator such as a media industry, does not really exist (Barthes, 1977). This notion of an absent author is intimately tied to post-modern or post-structural thinking about media representations.

Intertextuality marks an important shift from the relation between author and reader to the relation between text and reader. Intersubjectivity, where meaning is negotiated in the interaction between author and reader of a text, is replaced by intertextuality, where meaning is negotiated in the interaction of the reader and the text, invoking a network of other texts.

In media there are many, many examples of intertextuality. Some media products are even famous for it. For example, cartoons *The Simpsons* (FOX) and *South Park* (Celluloid Studios), musicians like Madonna, "Weird Al" Yankovic and Lady Gaga, and the movie cycle *Scary Movie* (Wayans Brothers) each employ intertextual strategies and are well known for it. An example of intertextuality is this still from *The Simpsons*' episode 19, season 10, which immediately calls into memory Salvador Dali's painting *Persistence of Memory* (1931).[1]

Intertextuality in *The Simpsons* can often be viewed as a parody or pastiche, as is often the case in popular culture. Pastiche (meaning that a media text is solely constructed out of a variety of other, identifiable texts) and parody (meaning an imitation of an existing media text that intends to mock, comment or trivialise the original) are the best-documented forms of intertextuality in media studies. Sometimes this kind of intertextuality is called "camp", especially when it transgresses the boundaries between high and low culture. Products

Figure 3.1 Still from *The Simpsons* ('Mom and Pop Art')

that are usually assigned to the low culture domain are appropriated by audiences from the elite. However, camp has a more general meaning and refers to a combination of things that actually do not fit together (Van Zoonen, 2004). For example, *The Simpsons* combines a cartoon with art elements. This mix-up of styles is both appreciated and mocked by the same audiences. Camp in that sense combines opposites: highbrow and lowbrow culture, old and young, 'but in particular femininity and masculinity' (Van Zoonen, 2004: 33). The drag queen is camp *par example*, who performs an exaggerated femininity which sheds an ironic light on conventional femininity (and thus critiquing heteronormative conceptions of gender). Therefore, camp is also considered as a queer political weapon, used to reassign and deconstruct heteronormative notions of gender (Pisters, 2011). We will return to the notion of queer politics later in this chapter.

Some scholars criticise the emphasis of intertextuality in academia and the suggestion that the author is absent. Linda Hutcheon (1989, 2000) argues that in parody and pastiche especially, there is a manifest intent of the author to parody something or some meaning. Hutcheon (2000) has a point here, though we would like to suggest that maybe this is the case for parody and pastiche, however, there are many other forms of intertextuality that are not so intentional.

Intertextuality can be found on different levels in the media and is formulated in various ways. Fiske (1987), for example, distinguishes *horizontal* and *vertical intertextuality*, while simultaneously distinguishing primary, secondary and tertiary texts. While primary texts refer to media products, secondary texts refer to texts about the products (such as professional reviews and critiques), which are also often mediated. Tertiary texts refer to the level of the audience and texts about their interpretation (for example, a letter to a celebrity, fan fiction, or an interpretation of a song, music video or other media text on YouTube).

Horizontal intertextuality refers to the relation between primary texts that are explicitly linked to one another. One of the most widely discussed forms of horizontal intertextuality is genre, often focusing on the similarities between different media texts and their conventions, and referring to a "formula" to pinpoint the generic characteristics of a media text. Vertical intertextuality indicates the relation of primary texts with secondary and tertiary texts that specifically refer to it (Fiske, 1987). The primary text, the media product at hand and the subject positions it creates, gets meaning in dialogue with other primary, secondary and tertiary texts, each of which articulate subject positions.

Fiske's notion of intertextuality sketches a web of references around one central primary text, even though Kristeva's formulation of the concept seems wider (any text is built up from other texts). There are other ways to distinguish or categorise forms of intertextuality, some of which encompass the broader meaning proposed by Kristeva. Guy Cook (2001) defines intrageneric (between genres) and intergeneric (within genres) intertextuality. All of these forms are marked by another distinction that is valid in all cases, the difference between "intended intertextuality" and "inescapable intertextuality" (Gray, 2005).

Inescapable intertextuality is the kind of intertextuality that authors such as Kristeva (1986), Barthes (1977) and Fiske (1987) describe; the intertextuality that is inherently and inevitably part of any text. Think, for example, of our analysis of Benny Benassi's music video discussed in the previous chapter. We can hardly claim that our interpretations of such a video are new and unrelated to previous music videos and other media texts we have consumed before.

Intended intertextuality refers to a "business strategy" of the author or producer of the text as explicitly and purposely referring to other primary texts to evoke certain connotations. Famous examples are films that poke fun at other films such as *Scary Movie* (1 to 5), *Epic Movie* (Friedberg and Seltzer), and *Not Another Teen Movie* (Gallen).

Box 3.1 Exercise: Intertextual Characters

Choose a fictional TV series you enjoy watching and pick one of the primary characters.

1. Reconstruct the inescapable and intended intertextuality in one episode of the programme.
2. How do both kinds of intertextuality relate to the gender of the chosen character?
3. Which subject positions does this create?

Debashish Panigrahi and N.D.R. Chandra (2013) argue that this kind of intertextuality also serves to keep the audience captivated; they puzzle to find out how to connect the references in the movie to other movies they might have seen.

Another, more common form of intended intertextuality is closely related to convergence culture (Jenkins, 2006). Conglomerates use different types of media to promote certain products in multiple ways. For example, promoting a movie by using your magazine sections for advertising and interviews with cast members, your cable channel for commercials, et cetera. This kind of intended intertextuality is common practice. A good example of such an approach is the TV series *Heroes* (NBC). The series itself runs over four seasons (a fifth is announced for spring 2015) and can be watched like any other television show. However, next to the series, running not only parallel but also adding to the narrative of the show, were 'webisodes' (starting with *Going Postal*), an online game and graphic comic books. Though it is unclear whether this strategy was successful (did NBC indeed reach a larger audience than it would have without this strategy?) it is easy to understand how such a strategy has an impact on the meanings in the text; people who followed the web series did literally follow a slightly different narrative than people who only watched the TV series. Hence, the subject positions created in the *Heroes'* narrative were intentionally constructed in more than one place.

In an increasingly globalising world, we might add another dimension to intertextuality. As David Hesmondhalgh states:

> Cultural texts originated in one country are increasingly seen, heard, and so on in other countries. Because of this increasing flow of cultural texts, audiences and symbol creators can, in many places, draw on texts from many other different places. Texts, genres and even technologies (such as musical instruments) will be often reinterpreted and adapted by symbol creators in other contexts.
>
> (2007: 219)

Due to increasing digitisation of media texts and increasing global distribution, it becomes easier for all kinds of producers to practice what we might call *global intertextuality*. This kind of global, intentional intertextuality is especially visible in advertising. A study by An Kuppens (2009) on the use of English in TV advertising in Belgium and the Netherlands (where the primary language spoken is Dutch) and a similar study by Slobodanka Dimova (2012) about TV ads in Macedonia (where Macedonian is spoken) show how the use of English is an intentional strategy used by the industry to evoke certain meanings and connotations. Another form of global intertextuality is elements of TV programmes that refer to non-US originating material. In the Netherlands, the immensely popular infotainment programme *De Wereld Draait Door*[2] (Vara) has an item called *De tv draait door* (meaning *The TV Goes Crazy*) in which bloopers seen on screen are broadcasted. Often, the bloopers are derived from foreign channels. These kind of international references are also a form of global intertextuality.

Developments in media technology, globalisation and convergence in the media industry each account for gendered subject positions to become

increasingly intertextual. On the one hand, these complicated and often contradictory meanings provide a space for the reader to produce counter-hegemonic
meanings, while on the other hand, we have to be aware that despite the
optimistic notion of polysemy of media texts, the discourses of particular
examples of media content are 'often designed or inclined to control, confine
or direct the taking of meaning, which may in turn be resisted by the reader'
(McQuail, 2005: 238). The emphasis on the readers and the meanings created
by them will be investigated in Chapters 8 and 9. We will now explore how
intertextuality enables more fluid conceptions of gender.

Disrupting Gendered Representations

Intertextual representations disrupt subject positions in various ways and on
different levels. Opening up the possibility for counter-hegemonic meanings of
gender and gendered subject positions, intertextuality can be considered as a
tool to disrupt conventional gender representations (as were discussed in
Chapter 1). This complex dynamic is best illustrated by an example. We will
explore Lady Gaga as an intertextual media text, as she forms an excellent
example in multiple ways, as Lady Gaga herself, her music, her clothing et
cetera all show intertextual complexity.

As a singer, Lady Gaga herself can be seen as an intertextual icon of contemporary Western pop culture. Her continuous play with her own appearance,
culminating in showing up at the 2011 *MTV Music Awards* as her male alter ego
Jo Calderone, is reminiscent of Madonna. During the 1990s, Madonna's play
with appearances was seen as a post-modern representation of femininity, as
she showed many forms of femininity, many imitations and exaggerations of
feminine stereotypes, without an essential femininity being behind it. Exactly
the same can be said for Lady Gaga. Sometimes Lady Gaga shows an intentional
intertextuality with Madonna. For example in the music video *Alejandro*
(2010) Lady Gaga imitates Madonna and copies parts of Madonna's videos
Vogue (1990) and *Like a Virgin – In Bed With Madonna* (1991). By her imitation
of another grand pop icon, Lady Gaga herself becomes intertextual.

Second, Lady Gaga's music videos are often highly intertextual. Discussed in
media and academia and a topic of many student papers, *Telephone* (2010) is
exemplary for the notion of intertextuality in different dimensions. The music
video is nine minutes long and offers a linear narration directed by Jonas
Åkerlund (a famous director of music videos). There are many examples of
intended horizontal intertextuality. For example, there are references to the
work of film maker Quentin Tarantino, pop art aesthetics and a lot of references to cartoons. On top of that, the music video is positioned as a sequel
building on the narration of the previous video *Paparazzi* (2009) in which Lady
Gaga is arrested for killing her boyfriend. The video *Telephone* starts with a
shot of barbed wire on top of a wall indicating a prison, which becomes visible a few moments later. Some opening titles are screened, reading 'Streamline

Figure 3.2 Still from *Telephone* (Lady Gaga feat. Beyoncé)

Presents, A Serial Pictures Fix, Telephone, Starring Lady Gaga and Beyoncé, and Tyrese Gibson' mimicking the opening of a television episode or movie.

The mise-en-scène in this music video is a North American society, with props like a women's prison, motel rooms, the American union jack, diners, et cetera. Lady Gaga's outfit refers to the comic super heroine *Wonder Woman*, an icon of popular American comic culture of the 1940s often read as a feminist icon in popular culture. Beyoncé, as a North American pop star, is featured in the video and evokes connotations to her own music, while Tyrese Gibson, an American actor and singer evokes further connotations to movies and his own music. Further references to visual culture are aplenty, and can be found for example in the representation of a *Pussy Wagon* out of Tarantino's film *Kill Bill*, or the naming of Beyoncé as "Honey B" as in the movie *Pulp Fiction* (Tarantino).

References towards women rights or the representation of women are multi-present in *Telephone*; the video's plot is about how one woman helps the other to get rid of an abusive boyfriend, the song that plays on the radio when Lady Gaga is in prison is her own song *Paper Gangsta* of which the lyrics refer to women's empowerment, and the finale of the video shows Lady Gaga and Beyoncé gripping hands in a reference to the movie *Thelma and Louise* (Scott and Khouri), generally perceived as a feminist film. These intertextual references subvert a hegemonic representation of women and femininity and may have repercussions on the mediated discourse of gender.

There is much more that can and will be said about Lady Gaga, her performances, and her music videos. While we have just deconstructed the video *Telephone* as a feminist reading, there are many who think the video is not that profound at all and the excess of sexuality in the video is a way to sell more music. The debates over Lady Gaga – positioning her as either a feminist or a sex kitten; an icon for the LGBTQ community[3] or an icon for young girls under 13; a Madonna imitator or someone inspired by Madonna – are endless and underscore our point. As a pop icon that plays with intertextuality on several levels she opens up space for both hegemonic and counter-hegemonic readings and an endless amount of subject positions.

We might say that Lady Gaga and her music have a high polysemic potential. As explained in Chapter 1, polysemy refers to the multiple meanings a sign can have; as the signifier can relate to multiple signifieds. Polysemy then can be understood as a form of inescapable intertextuality. This multiplicity of meanings is further enhanced by intended intertextuality, as it can add to the number of possible readings. This is because the reader of the text has to have the knowledge and skills to understand the references. For example, Lady Gaga's outfit in the music video *Telephone* that refers to *Wonder Woman* will almost always be recognised as a superhero outfit, by some it will be recognised as the outfit of *Wonder Woman*; some will be able to connote *Wonder Woman* as feminist icon, while others yet will connote *Wonder Woman* as a sexy superhero. In Part II we will discuss these reader's skills more in-depth. For now it is important to understand that intended and inescapable intertextuality both open up the possibility for the construction of a variety of subject positions by and in media texts. This is important because multiple subject positions also impact politics. Media as technologies of gender relate subject positions to power. Intended and inescapable intertextuality can disrupt the conventional femininity/masculinity dichotomy upon which patriarchy is founded. Inter-textuality has the potential to open up spaces for more fluid conceptions of gender and relate them to power structures governing gender discourses. The articulation of subject positions by media texts hence is related to politics. The politics of representation in relation to subject positions has been a topic of interest in the field of queer theory.

As Queer As

The word queer is defined as "strange", "weird" or "peculiar" and in earlier days was used as a term of abuse for homosexual people. During the '80s the word has been re-appropriated by the LGBTQ community and has been adopted as an honorary nickname. Queer now functions as an umbrella term for 'those who do not consider their sexual identity and/or desires as strictly heterosexual, and/or articulate sexual and gender identity positions that are considered as diverging from the heteronormal' (Van Bauwel, Dhaenens and Bil/tereyst, 2013: 226).

As an official academic field of inquiry, queer theory was coined by De Lauretis when she introduced the term at a conference in 1990. De Lauretis's aim was to critically evaluate all categorisations of gender and sexuality and to complicate these notions with intersectionality (hoogland, 2007). Queer studies' scholars concentrate on non-normative representations of sexuality and gender. However, as Butler (1990) has argued, this seems to create a new category, contradictory of the discipline's aims. In practice this leads sometimes to conflicting opinions. While, according to some, Lady Gaga is an icon for the queer community, some queers say this is impossible as Lady Gaga is a heterosexual. Who is right and wrong here does not matter. More interesting to queer theorists is that both these subject positions are feasible (and, they would add, more positions than these two can be imagined). Queer theory emphasises a retreat from binary thinking (McIntosh, 1997: 365), embracing all "non-normative" identities relating to the need to revise societies' assumptions about gender and sexuality (Hayward, 2000: 309). In queer theory, texts are approached from multiple perspectives unravelling multiple signifiers such as context, intertextuality and different subject positions in addition to the text itself (Hayward, 2000: 362).

Queer theory was first integrated into film studies where practices of queer reading became common (e.g. Cover, 2000; Gittings, 2001; Rich, 2004; Wallace, 2000). One of the first queer studies in popular media, located by Angela McRobbie (2011), was Richard Dyer's *In Defense of Disco*.[4] In this text Dyer (1979: 21) describes disco and the readings thereof by the audience as subversive: 'It is a "contrary" use of what the dominant culture provides, it is important in forming a gay identity, and it has subversive potential as well as reactionary implications.' Other landmark texts for the conceptualisation of queer theory are the study by Caroline Evans and Lorraine Gamman (1995), revisiting the gaze theory in relation to queer theory, the work of Alexander Doty (2000) who locates queer readings in movies that are mainstream (or classics), and the work of Butler (1990) who introduced the idea of gender performativity.

Queer theory is closely related to politics and activism (cf. McRobbie, 2011). Sometimes this link is obvious and the boundaries between scholarship and activism are blurred. At other times, these ties are less clear. Queer theory emphasizes an anti-essentialist notion of identity and the construction of identity. Both notions are of vital necessity for identity politics (Creekmur and Doty, 1995; McIntosh, 1997; Stein and Plummer, 1996). Steven Seidman argues:

> Queer theorists argue that identities are always multiple or at best composites with literally an infinite number of ways in which "identity-components" (e.g. sexual orientation, race, class, nationality, gender, age, ableness) can intersect or combine. Any specific identity construction, moreover, is arbitrary, unstable, and exclusionary. Identity constructions necessarily entail the silencing or exclusion of some experiences or forms of life.
>
> (1996: 11–12)

For queer activists this notion translates to the political desire to experience gendered and sexual identities as constructed by the individual but evaluated by society as being all-equal (for example, similar rights and plights regardless of gender and or sexuality but also things like being able to kiss one's lover in public without being harassed or arrested for it).

However, according to Seidman (1996), this anti-essentialist and constructionist notion also undermines the opportunity for political activism. Activism is usually based on shared elements: things people have in common with each other. Both notions from queer theory undermine a shared identity that is a necessary base for activism. However, we believe that beliefs, communal desires or aims, can form a firm grounding for activism.

Important to note is that the queerness of a text is not necessarily tied to obvious markers such as gay characters. According to Corey Creekmur and Alexander Doty (1995: 4), reading practices can vary from revealing queerness in popular culture to re-inscribing queerness at the margins of popular culture. Queer, like camp, is in the eye of the beholder. The practice of queer reading should not be interpreted as making texts queer but rather as trying to understand how texts might be understood as queer (Doty, 2000). So while the text might not be inherently queer, representations might be read as non-normative and resisting hegemonic conceptions of gender and sexuality. However, these representations are incorporated in mainstream popular culture and mostly stick within the realm of "normality", being constructed within the normative boundaries of contemporary mainstream popular culture (Van Bauwel, Dhaenens and Biltereyst, 2013).

Queer Subject Positions

As of the late 1990s, popular media, especially popular television, has been marked with a slow but steady increase of LGBTQ representations. While Hollywood movies have always represented queer characters (Dyer, 1990), it is a more recent development for media such as television, popular music and magazines. TV series that predominantly represent queers are entering the transnational television market (Van Bauwel, Dhaenens and Biltereyst, 2013). Simultaneously, research that focuses on such alternative readings and the multiple subject positions available in popular media has increased. As stated, the importance of these queer (and oftentimes intertextual) representations lies with their relation to power structures and therefore in their political meaning. In our view, three notions are explicitly useful to look into to answer this question: the disruptive power in heteronormative discourses with regard to gender roles; the tightening up of the relation between gender and sexuality; and the disruption of the gender character of media genres, as discussed in the previous chapter.

Disrupting Gender Roles

Gender roles and gender socialisation are interestingly disrupted by intertextual and queer representations. We learn from a variety of sources, of which media form a significant portion, how to behave like a man or a woman, what to look like, et cetera. In other words what is normal and what is deviant in terms of gender. While media texts are never inherently queer and queer readings of media have always been possible, the deliberate play with gender representations in current TV shows disrupts gender roles in a different way. While some texts incorporate an intentional queer reading (movies such as *The Adventures of Priscilla, Queen of the Dessert* (Elliot), *TransAmerica* (Tucker) and *Boys Don't Cry* (Peirce)) and hence make a statement about homosexuality or transgender people, contemporary TV shows seem to incorporate the play with representations to make the narrative more interesting. In other words, the political aim seems to lack (and maybe a more commercial aim took its place). Nevertheless, this does not mean that these shows do not have an impact on gender politics.

For example, in the TV series *Once Upon a Time* (ABC), characters from different story worlds come together. They live in a small village called Storybrooke, which is under the spell of an evil witch. In the village, characters from the Grimm Brothers' fairy tales, such as Snow White and Little Red Riding Hood, are mixed with characters from children's books such as Peter Pan, Pinocchio and the Mad Hatter, characters from horror stories such as Dr. Frankenstein, and characters from Chinese folklore such as Mulan. Next to this intricate web of story-universes colliding, most characters are not what they seem. For example, Little Red Riding Hood is also the Big Bad Wolf (as she is a werewolf), Rumpelstiltskin is also the crocodile Hook is chasing and the Beast (of the French fairy tale *Beauty and the Beast*). The mother of the evil queen, Snow White's stepmother, is also the Queen of Hearts who is originally featured in Lewis Carroll's *Alice in Wonderland*. On top of that, some character traits that we do not encounter in the original stories, are taken up by the producers to give extra twists to the series. Snow White is featured to have excellent hunting skills (she had to survive in the woods, after all), while Mulan is in love with Sleeping Beauty, Princess Aurora. Interestingly enough, characters that have symbolised femininity for decades are now presented with ultimately masculine character traits (hunting, being a predator).

The series is received with mixed reviews (Metacritic, 2014). Though generally positive, the intricate storylines are confusing for some people and the added character traits not always welcome. Mulan's gay character, for example, caused some noise on Twitter and the internet. Some people loathed this addition, yet others hailed it as Hollywood's confirmation that true love goes beyond the heteronormative frameworks. Obviously, the twists that the producers weaved into the narrative provide for multiple subject positions and alternative readings of the text. However, there seems no deliberate aim to highlight debates on gender issues or to transgress heteronormative discourses. In other words, the show does not seem to have a political aim at all. Other current TV shows that display a play with gendered notions do have a political aim, however, and they tend to address issues around sexuality more often.

Gay – Straight – Queer?

As we have seen, queer theory has been used as a theoretical interrogation and interpretation of gender and sexuality in media texts (Dhaenens, Van Bauwel and Biltereyst, 2008). The political element of queer studies arises as a concept of resistance, resisting dominant, often heteronormative, discourses. Authors such as Larry Gross (1998) claim that sexual minority audiences read media texts "as if" and continuously reverse hegemonic meanings (i.e. they read against the grain and produce counter-hegemonic readings). Note the emphasis on sexual minorities in Gross's claim; queer theory relates sexuality more explicitly to gender than other academic strands that focus on representations. Sometimes, queer representations are understood as the representation of LGBTQ characters in media texts (Joyrich, 2014). The increasing appearance of LGBTQ characters in mainstream media (Glyn and Needham, 2009) in TV shows such as *Buffy the Vampire Slayer* (WB), *Modern Family* (ABC), *The New Normal* (NBC), *True Blood* (HBO), and in movies such as *As Good as It Gets* (Brooks) and *American Beauty* (Mendes) has evoked mixed reactions. Positive reactions, as representation in numbers is important (see Chapters 1 and 2), and negative, as these mainstream representations often set a standard for how to be a "normal queer" (cf. Joyrich, 2014; Battles and Hilton-Morrow, 2002).

Others perceive queer representations as a broader pallet of representations, though the connection between sexuality and gender remains. In general, queer representations refer to characters whose gender and sexual identities are blurred, paradoxical and undefined. These explicit queer representations are preoccupied with alternative representations of identity and sexuality (Van Bauwel, Dhaenens and Biltereyst, 2013), disrupting heteronormative conceptions of gender.

The show *True Blood* forms an interesting example of this wider conception of queer representation. The show's main plot revolves around the people in the (fictional) village of Bon Temps, Louisiana. Japanese scientists have invented synthetic blood releasing vampires from their dependence on human blood. Some of these vampires now try to integrate into society. One of the main characters, Sookie Stackhouse, a telepathic waitress, gets involved with vampire Bill Compton. Their relationship evolves over several seasons, falling from one catastrophe into another. As the story evolves, more creatures of the night, such as werewolves, shape-shifters and fairies (HBO, n.d.) appear. Making use of mythical characters such as vampires and werewolves, the show develops a variety of plotlines around the classic Other. The danger of *True Blood*'s characters generates a high erotic potential (Novak and Krijnen, 2014), while the integration of vampires into mainstream North American society parallels the integration of gays in contemporary society (Dhaenens, 2013).

Box 3.2 Queer Vampires

The vampire has always been more or less queer. In Bram Stoker's *Dracula*, usually considered as the mold for contemporary vampire narratives, this relation is implicit, though Stoker (1897) gives us some hints. On page 47 Dracula chases away the female vampires attacking Jonathan, exclaiming: 'How dare you touch him, any of you? How dare you cast eyes on him when I had forbidden it? Back, I tell you all! This man belongs to me!' Though the homoerotic potential is often received positively, it also positions homosexuality as a monstrosity.

As is usual in the vampire genre, in *True Blood* vampirism is explicitly connected to homosexuality (Beck, 2011). Frederik Dhaenens (2013) points out that the debate in the vampire community in *True Blood* mirrors the debate in the gay community. In that way, *True Blood* opens up multiple gendered subject positions in relation to sexuality, disrupting the heteronormative framework. In other words, the relation between queer studies and activism is still of relevance. However, we want to emphasize this reading is one of many possible readings. As Bernard Beck (2011) shows, a similar argument can be made for the multicultural society.

True Blood's queer representations do not stop at these dichotomous positions (assimilate to "normal society" or entirely resist) as the show also features characters that question fixed gender and sexual identities (Brace and Arp, 2010). For example, the character Lafayette Reynolds embodies a flamboyant gay character. While Lafayette wears outspoken and flamboyant outfits and make-up, he simultaneously performs a stereotypical masculinity, for example by showing his masculine strength and his ability to fight. The combination of femininity and masculinity in one character simultaneously reifies and reassigns normative notions of gender and sexuality.

In other media formats queer representations are increasingly present. Rosalind Gill (2007a) uses the notion of "queer chic" to stress the changes in the last decade in advertising in the way lesbians and gays were represented. She points to the way the queerness becomes part of a specific contemporary visual culture when stating that 'what is striking is the way in which queerness is aestheticized and fetishized in advertising, rather than being treated as merely a different sexual identity' (Gill, 2007a: 100). Still, there are very few advertisements were queer is normalised or even mainstreamed. Gill (2007a) links this evolution to the emergence of "hyper-sexualised chic" and "lipstick lesbianism", which represent an eroticised imagination of heterosexual males and refer to codes of pornography, and she (Gill, 2007a: 103) concludes:

> Overall, then, while homosexuality is much more visible in advertising than it was ten years ago, it is signified through highly specific, highly

sexualized codes. Queer chic can seem to add edge, risk and sexiness to products that are often associated with straight men and traditional sexism. It is for this reason that adverts for beer, alongside more predictable products like fashion and fragrance, have increasingly deployed this style.

While queer chic as an aesthetic style might open up more subject positions, it also reifies the tie between gender and sexuality: gay masculinity is presented as hyper sexual.

Box 3.3 Sexualisation/Pornofication?

Sexualisation and pornofication are two contemporary buzzwords that are often used interchangeably. The concepts do mean something quite different, however. While sexualisation refers to turning everything into something sexual, pornofication refers to the use of aesthetic elements of the porn industry for non-porn media products.

Another reason to employ a queer chic style is found in the "discovery" of the queer market for advertising in the West. Gay couples are thought to have higher education (and therefore more spending power) and more time (because they often do not have children) which makes them an attractive target group for advertisers (Himberg, 2014). So while the industry adds queer chic style to give their products some edge, they simultaneously target a new market. Instead of narrowcasting, Julia Himberg (2014) argues, we should think of multicasting.

Multicasting is not contradictory to ideas on how the industries aim their products at audiences we have discussed in previous chapters. It is within the transaction between industry and advertisers that gender is an important signifier. Differentiation seems to be the key element in a business plan of the media industry today. Offering different identity representations provides attractive content for different audiences and target niches, but accumulate in the end to a larger audience.

This tightening up of the relation between gender and sexuality is also cause for many debates that go beyond the notion of queer representations. These debates do not concentrate on queer representations as such but on the sexualisation of representation and the portrayals of hyper femininity and masculinity. These issues are part of heated debates, especially when the content is targeted at young audiences. In Part III we will go deeper into these debates, as they focus on the relation between media and their audiences.

Queering Genres

A last issue that arises when looking into increasing intertextual and queer representations is the idea of gendered genres, as we discussed in the previous chapter. Media genres often have a masculine or feminine identity. Depending on the content relating to the private or public sphere and its audience, a genre is more or less gendered. Using soap opera and the confessional talk show, we viewed how this gendered character is constructed. However, genres are increasingly transmedial, hybrid and global. The gendered character of media genres become difficult to identify due to changing norms and standards in the production.

An interesting case study on the hip hop genre in Sweden by Kalle Berggren (Berggren, 2014) is illustrative. Hip hop music, a genre usually identified as masculine, is adopted more and more by female musicians. These female hip hop artists challenge, negotiate and re-appropriate gender norms. A similar line of thought is valid for some TV programmes. Though the drama series *24* (FOX) appears masculine, Brenda Weber and Karolyn Steffens (2010) argue that the narrative could be considered feminine. The violence performed by the main character, Jack Bauer, is contextualised in the series by 'an endless repetition of threat, constant crisis, and evasiveness of closure' (Weber and Steffens, 2010: 863) that can be defined as a feminine textual body. Intended intertextuality and the play with queer representations further add to the diffusion of gendered character of genres, making them queerer.

Some genres, we would like to argue, are historically queer, such as the vampire genre (Beck, 2011). Other genres have become more queer by employing a queer chic style, or because they have integrated elements of a large variety of genres and so they are hard to identify. The talk show, as discussed in the previous chapter, is increasingly queer. Elements such as the focus on the private sphere and non-rational topics are increasingly diffuse and sometimes even used for exaggeration and parodying of genre (Cragin, 2010). *The Jerry Springer Show* could in this sense be considered as camp, as its overt exaggeration of moral outrage and its obviously fake guests at some times are surely used as a parody. However, it also transgresses traditional notions of the gender characters of genres, and enables producers to multicast.

Conclusion

Exploring intertextuality, we have discovered that gender representations are rarely articulating a singular subject position. Sometimes these intertextual (and queer) representations are obviously a business strategy, at other times the intertextuality is in the eye of the beholder. Both form the content of the next two parts of this book. Historically, in the study of gender representations, the texts always formed the core of the analysis. We have to be careful of textual determinism though (see also Chapter 1). Representations are part of patterns that should be understood within their contexts. The production of media texts forms one part of the context in which representations should be understood. In Part II we will delve into questions of media production and its relations to gender. The other part of the context for representations is formed by audience consumption. The presence of gendered stereotypes in media texts does not have a one-on-one relationship with audiences' interpretations thereof. In other words, content does not predict meaning making. In Part III we will engage with audiences' consumption practices.

Additionally, globalisation and media convergence create a different context for the production and consumption of representations. We have seen how multicasting is a viable notion to understand the adaptation of queer chic in contemporary media. We would like to raise awareness to the locality of the notion of queer chic, as there is some tension with the notion of globalisation. Obviously, queer chic is not popular, nor adopted on a global level. As a business strategy it is therefore only useful in an exclusive part of the Western world. Further analysis of queer chic – when it is used, by whom and for whom – could highlight the possibilities and limitations of the political potential of queer representations.

The global and convergent context of media representations is also pivotal for the audiences who interpret them. Audiences are aware of (some) of the industries' strategies and in many ways have become more active prosumers that not only interpret but also produce representations. This context should be taken into account when exploring media audiences. Therefore, in Part III we will investigate different notions of media audiences, what they do with different types of media and how to understand these activities.

Further Reading

- Dyer, R. (1990). *Now You See It: Historical Studies in Lesbian and Gay Film*. London/New York: Routledge.

Dyer's book is considered as ground-breaking work for students of queer theory. In the volume Dyer explores films about and by gay and lesbian people. Taking a historical approach (from WWI to the present) Dyer highlights films and historical contexts.

- Glyn, D. and Needham, G. (2009) (Eds.) *Queer Television: Theories, Histories, Politics*. London/New York: Routledge.

This book engages with queer theory in-depth, exploring the most important concepts of queer theory. The authors do this while focusing on TV in all its complexity (including industry, production, audiences, texts, et cetera) in relation to queer theory.

- Butler, J. (1990). *Gender Trouble: Feminism and the Subversion of Identity*. London/New York: Routledge.

Though relatively recent, Butler's *Gender Trouble* is more or less "a classic" in media studies that engage with gender performativity and queer studies. It is in this volume that Butler argues against an account of patriarchal culture, as developed by feminists, as she feels this reconstructs a gender dichotomy. Instead, Butler argues, gender is a fluid concept that changes over time and in different contexts. You might find this book hard to read as the writing style is very dense. However, there are many "reading companions" to be found on the internet.

Notes

1 A painting that more often is used as intertextual reference, we find it not only in popular culture like *The Simpsons*, but also in children's books, like Anthony Brown's *Willy the Dreamer*, and other art works.
2 The title encloses two meanings: *The World Keeps Turning* and *The World Goes Crazy*.
3 LGBTQ stands for Lesbian, Gay, Bisexual, Transgender and Queer.
4 Dyer's text was not published as a scholarly publication but in a magazine, *Gay Left*. According to McRobbie (2011: 140) 'this itself says a good deal about the blurring of the boundaries between university research, pamphleteering and activism of that moment'. The article should therefore not be read as a non-scholarly publication, but as an illustration of the close ties between queer studies and activism.

Part II

Producing

Chapter 4

Who Produces What?

In the previous chapters we have examined gender representations in the media and how they relate subjectivity and identity. We saw how women are under-represented in general in comparison to men. Furthermore, representations of gender often intersect with ethnicity, age and class, resulting in women and men of colour often being represented in stereotypical ways. As a result, these representations promote essentialist notions of gender. As technologies of gender, gender representations often limit subject positions available to its audience. An important question raised is: 'Who is responsible for these representations?' Often the media are accused of misrepresentation of gender (and ethnicity). However, we should wonder who "the media" are. As such, we argue we cannot speak of "the media", as there is no coherent, monolithic power block inserting essentialist notions in media content.

The question on media production and how gender is related to it is, however, incredibly important. The rationale for the vast amount of research on gender and media production is based on the assumption of reaching critical mass. Critical mass is a metaphor derived from the field of physics; it indicates the amount of radioactive material necessary for a nuclear reaction to take place. In the social sciences, the term critical mass is used to signify 'some relatively small subset of a group interested in the provision of a public good to make contributions of time, money, or other resources toward the production of that good' (Oliver, Marwell and Teixeira, 1985: 546). Hence, for our purposes, critical mass is understood as the idea that once enough women take part in media production (with an emphasis on managerial positions), media content will (ideally) become unbiased with regard to gender representations.

Indeed, some studies show a relationship between the number of female or male characters portrayed onscreen and the number of females or males working behind the scenes. Different studies (e.g. Glascock, 2001; Lauzen, Dozier and Cleveland, 2006; Lauzen and Deiss Jr., 2009) show that the higher the number of female executive producers for a TV programme in prime-time, the higher the number of female characters in that programme. However, Martha Lauzen, David Dozier and Elizabeth Cleveland (2006) and Lauzen and Douglas Deiss Jr. (2009) also note that there are differences between genres. In scripted (i.e. fiction) programmes the relationship between women in the production team and the portrayal of women is clear, in reality shows however, it was not. Lastly, in news media (radio, TV and newspaper) it is also true that 'stories by female reporters are visibly more likely to challenge stereotypes than those filed by male reporters and are also less likely to reinforce stereotypes than those reported by men' (GMMP, 2010: ix).

So, there is a relation between the number of women in production and the representation of gender in the media produced. However, as the examples above show, this relationship is not straightforward. The concept of critical mass should not be understood as a free floating idea, disconnected from all factors impacting production. The shape of the production process and the distribution of interest and resources are pivotal for the effects that critical mass might have (Oliver *et al.*, 1985). In other words, how media production is organised, its historical roots, convergence of media industries and the dynamics of technology do not only have repercussions for the relationship between gender and media production, but also for the content of production and hence for the representations of gender. In this chapter we will investigate what we can understand as media industries and how gender is presented in them. In Chapter 5 we will investigate the power structures that impact the presence of gender in media industries. In the last chapter of this part we will look into the dynamics of technology and globalisation and how they impact the relation between gender and media production.

Media Industries

Media are produced by an uncountable number of people working in an uncountable number of media organisations. The roles of these people in these organisations vary tremendously, from managerial jobs, such as creative directors, to more practical jobs, such as typesetters. Organisations themselves vary just as greatly as the jobs they provide. Size, location, organisational structure and the type(s) of media they produce are just a few variables to be taken into account.

In a certain sense, the media industry is like any other industry; they produce something, they aim to make a profit, and they are subject to rules and regulations. Media content is seen as a product within a highly competitive market. However, Hesmondhalgh (2007) points out one important difference between media and other industries: the media do not just produce content; they produce content with symbolic value. The media industry is therefore widely acknowledged as an important contributor to the shaping of knowledge, values and beliefs of people and institutions in modern society (Hesmondhalgh, 2006a). It is this relationship with society that instigated academic inquiry into who is involved in production. Many believe that there is a relationship between media ownership, media production and the symbolic value of media content, arguing that media content serves the interests of their owners (Hesmondhalgh, 2006b).

With regard to this ownership, white, affluent, heterosexual men have an over-whelming presence in the media industry. Women, ethnic minorities, sexual minorities and other minorities are less present or simply excluded. Because of this (gender) disparity, media are thought to promote male-biased interests. This perspective, though, suggests a direct relationship between media owner-ship and media content. As argued earlier, this would be an oversimplification of media production as other factors, such as organisation structure, historical roots and technological changes are also of importance. That the relationship between ownership and media content is very complex, however, does not mean that it is irrelevant.

Box 4.1 Exercise: Producing Your All-Time Favourite

Think of your all-time favourite media product. It can be a movie, TV show, music album, video game, et cetera. Try to find out which company produced your product. Usually, this is written on the product somewhere. Next try to find out which company distributed it? Is it the same company as the producing one? Are the two companies owned by one 'parent company'? Now, find out who the members of the executive board of the company (or companies) and the people in higher managerial positions are.

Reflect on what this structure of ownership means for the content of your product in relation to gender.

At the time of writing we can distinguish five major media companies, owned and directed by only a few people. According to the Fortune 500 list, an annual ranking of America's largest corporations, the largest conglomerate is The Walt Disney Company, followed (in order) by 21st Century Fox, Inc., Time Warner, CBS Corporation and Viacom (CNNMoney, 2011). Alongside US-based giants, a small number of larger western European media companies are listed as global players as well (Trappe, Meier, D'Haenens, Steemers and Thomass, 2011). Most of these corporations are not owned by a particular person, but by anonymous shareholders, meaning the exact owners are unknown, since there are many shareholders (and they might be women as well as men). However, we do see gender disparity of board members in the companies' boards of directors. The Walt Disney Company has the most female representation, with three female members out of ten (30%). Other corporations have less female representation; 21st Century Fox, Inc. has only one female member out of twelve board members (8.3%), Time Warner and CBS Corporation have two female members out of respectively a total of twelve (16.6%) and fourteen (14.3 %) board members, and Viacom has four out of thirteen (28.6%) female board members. These numbers form an impression of who owns and directs media production. They are significant numbers because the gender of owners and directors is presumed to have an impact on media production.

Of course we cannot simply state that these directors steer all their employees into the direction they prefer. That would be a neo-Marxist view on the media (Downey, 2006) and flawed, as research has proven repeatedly that media producers do have agency. However, the autonomy that producers often claim to have is also not the entire truth (Hesmondhalgh, 2006b): the environment of production, including social values, norms and institutions, do have an impact on the production of media content. For example, a journalist's work is structured by the kind of news organisation she or he works in, the hierarchy in the company, the conventions of what is newsworthy and what is not, and many other things. On the other hand, the journalist has the agency to choose, for example, whether he or she wants to fulfil a critical role as a journalist or a more descriptive one, how to deal with the conventions of the daily process of news gathering, and whether or not to comply with the organisation's hierarchical structure. Each of these decisions has an impact on the final product.

Taking these factors into account, John Downey (2006) proposes three competing approaches to understanding the relations between media ownership, media production and media content: 1) political economy approach; 2) liberal approach; and 3) social-liberal approach. The first approach, political economy, refers to an economic way of thinking in which the economic sphere is explicitly related to social and political phenomena (Hardy, 2014). 'The allocation of resources is recognised to involve political, not merely economic, decisions whose moral consequences permeate social life.' (Hardy, 2014: 4). In a sense, from a political economy approach, media owners do have a large influence on media production (as they allocate the resources) and we could argue that media products reflect and serve the interests of the owners. Since the owners are mostly white, affluent, heterosexual men, media supposedly reflect only their ideas and serve their interests. This determinist view on media production is not entirely true. This is clear when we look at the context of the media industry as explained above, and also when we look at media products themselves. For example, TV series such as *True Blood* (HBO) and *GLEE* (FOX), cartoons such as *The Simpsons* (FOX) and *South Park* (Comedy Central), or artists such as Lady Gaga and Kanye West can hardly be said to serve the owners' interests, since these programmes or people often criticise the powerful elite (Downey, 2006). However, this political economy approach is often underlying the work of feminist scholars who explicated more nuanced and related dynamics that are either the consequence or the cause for this relationship between production and ownership. We will discuss these dynamics in Chapter 5.

The liberal approach states that the media industry is profit driven and produces exactly that which sells, or what the audience wants to consume. This would imply that media owners and producers listen carefully to their audiences in order to give them what they want. This approach is called upon often to explain the mainstream media and the abundant presence of sex and violence in media products. Along with the fact that the context of production needs to be taken into account (and hence the impact of social values, norms and institutions on the production process), research shows that this approach is also insufficient. For example, although TV ratings show that audiences all over the world prefer nationally produced content, the US dominates the TV market (Straubhaar, 2007). Many European countries import high quantities of American TV programmes. Due to the high costs of producing TV programmes, it is cheaper to buy them in. European audiences therefore watch a large number of programmes that were not made for them but for an American audience. This dynamic has another interesting consequence. TV programmes are sold in packages, meaning that if a broadcaster wants to buy a hit series, like *Modern Family* (ABC), they are forced to also buy other shows, some of which are not even produced yet (Kuipers, 2011). This means that audiences are offered shows simply because the broadcaster had to buy them and surely not always because the broadcaster thought the audience would like it. This part of the trade in TV programmes has some consequences in relation to gender that we will discuss in Chapter 5.

The third approach proposed by Downey (2006) is the social-liberal approach. This approach is 'on the one hand wary of the degree of control that states may wish to exercise over the operation of the media. On the other, it recognises the threat that media markets may pose for pluralism' (Downey, 2006: 17). This approach covers the middle ground and advocates a dual system, one with private and public media (cf. Curran, 2002). Social-liberalists would argue for governmental regulations on public media granting media access to all groups in society, while also maintaining space for private media with a more profit-driven profile. This approach combines the political economy approach with the liberal approach and proposes solutions for the most important points of critique that each approach suffers from. Granting access to the media for all groups in society means that media content does not serve the interests of a particular owner, but those of different groups present in society, including women, ethnic minorities and sexual minorities.

These three approaches on the media industry in general and the relationship between ownership, production and media content hint at some interesting issues regarding our principal question for this chapter: 'Who produces what?' Therefore, we will now focus on the individuals working in the media industry. There is such a large variety in jobs and positions, so we will first focus on some general dimensions of how gender relates to the concept of the media professional. Next, we will sketch out how women and men are present in the production of mass media.

The Media Professional

There are many professionals in media production: writers, editors, production assistants, costume designers, actors, sound technicians and so on. Every media product comes about through an intensive collaboration among people fulfilling these roles (Bielby and Harrington, 2008). An important distinction should be made in these professions: "below-the-line" and "above-the-line", which are terms used to distinguish the "creative professions" and the "craft professions" (Banks, 2009). The terms are derived from 'a particular worker's position in relation to a bold horizontal line on a standard production budget sheet between creative and technical costs' (Banks, 2009: 89). In general, we can state that in all different media industries (film, TV, music, newspapers, radio, magazines) women are more often found below-the-line than above-the-line.

Many countries have legislation against direct discrimination of women as professionals. This does not mean that we find a gender balance in media production. Media production is still marked by vertical and horizontal segregation with regard to gender (Van Zoonen, 1994; Torkkola and Ruoho, 2011). Vertical segregation refers to the idea that women are found in, for example, managerial or editor-in-chief positions less often than men. Horizontal segregation refers to specialisations within a certain field. For example, if we look at the newspaper business, we see how women are more present as journalists in human-interest topics and men more as sports commentators.

Vertical and horizontal segregation exist in all countries and in all media industries. In general, we could say that women are under-represented in all areas of media production. The importance of this under-representation is emphasised by Carolyn Byerly and Karen Ross (2004). Not only does the "who" in production matter for media content, and hence the ability of media to contribute and maintain the status quo, but also if the media can contribute to new and more egalitarian arrangements in society. TV creators themselves also strongly believe in this. For example, Barbara Hall, a writer on shows such as *Family Ties* (NBC) and *Judging Amy* (CBS), explains in an interview her view on the importance of women in the TV industry: 'I think it's a combination of more women getting involved in the workplace, and also women *and* men getting a little bit more fearless about what they want to do.' (Longworth, 2002: 193).

Over the past decades the presence of women in media production has gradually increased, though coherent overviews are not available. According to Byerly and Ross (2004), this increase has contributed significantly to a shift in the media agenda. There are, however some significant differences to be noted in the various media industries and, equally important, in various regions around the world. These differences are partly due to the status of a certain medium and partly due to regional social norms. First, we will discuss these differences for the news media, taking into account three medium types: newspapers, news radio and news television. The reason is pragmatic; research reports usually investigate all three media at once. Second, we will look into the magazine, radio, television, film and music industry, focusing on everything except the news branch of these industries.

News Media

Studies in news production and gender are ample and seem to show similar trends. There seems to be an increase in women in news production. However, the increase of female journalists is much higher than the increase of female editors-in-chief. This increase of women in the field should not be over-estimated. In 1995, Margaret Gallagher sketched a clear picture based on a comparative study of 239 media organisations in 43 countries, providing a global scope of women in (news) media. The research is extensive and gives a nuanced insight into differences between regions and media types. Calculating a crude average percentage of women's and men's share in employment, 31.4% of media employment is women, 68.6% is men. More than 15 years later, an even larger but similar study (containing 522 companies in 59 countries) by the International Women's Media Foundation reports that women represent 35.1% and men represent 64.9% of the workforce in news production (IWMF, 2011). So, while it is justified to speak of an increase, it is slight.

In both studies we find an interesting gendered division of labour (in terms of vertical segregation) and regional differences. With regard to vertical segrega-tion, women fulfilled 26% of the governing and 27% of the top management jobs in 2011. Though this still means that men outnumber women in these jobs by three to one, compared to Gallagher's study in 1995, where women fulfilled just 12% of the top management positions, this is a solid increase. Besides top management positions, women and men have many other roles in the news media. None of these studies show that men and women are present in equal numbers, though women are more present as a "senior level professional" (41.0%), and in "sales, finance & administration" (35.6%). This average number of managerial positions in the news media obscures regional differences.

In the IWMF research project, 59 countries were studied and were divided among seven regions: Middle East and North Africa, Sub-Saharan Africa, Americas, Asia and Oceania, Eastern Europe, Nordica Europe and Western Europe. Details on gender balance in the workforce in each country were studied in the report. One major observation can be made: in countries from the East and Nordic European region, women fulfil more top management positions than in other regions (43% and 37%, respectively) (IWMF, 2011). Reasons for these regional differences are diverse. Sometimes social norms that hamper women's access to the workforce, or the "glass ceiling", should also be taken into account. The underlying causes of vertical segregation and regional differences in the presence of women in news production will be discussed in Chapter 5.

News production is also horizontally segregated. While men tend to cover topics such as the economy and sports, women are more often found in human-interest and entertainment (cf. Claringbould, Knoppers and Elling, 2004). The status of each area determines this horizontal segregation. Investi-gative journalism, for example, is considered as high quality journalism and therefore has a high status. It is also the case that most investigative journalists are men (Djerf-Pierre, 2007). This status of the profession and area of interest has to do with a dynamic called "feminisation of the media", which will be discussed in Chapter 5. Whether this kind of horizontal segregation is common globally is unknown.

We now have roughly sketched an impression of who produces what in news media. Such an overview is rare: news media have been researched for decades and always have been a primary topic of feminist enquiry. For all other media, global studies such as the IWMF project do not exist. Numbers are scarce and scattered over a multiplicity of case studies that focus on a specific genre or country. Still, some general trends can be described for each medium type.

Magazines

Let's start with one of the oldest media in which women are part of the workforce: the magazine. Sammye Johnson (1995) reports that the first magazine – *Gentleman and Lady's Town and Country Magazine* – targeted a female readership starting in 1784, and to do so included women in their production force. Ever since, women have been part of the magazine industry as editors, writers and publishers. We can distinguish four professional roles in the magazine industry: editorial, advertising sales, circulation and production. These professional roles include a plethora of job titles, complicating the task of creating an overview of the apparent gender gap: the share men and women take in each role and in (top) management positions (Johnson, 2007).

In the US magazine industry women are regularly found in management positions. Vertical segregation is indeed less in this branch of media than it is in others (Johnson, 2007). Derived from 2010 statistics, The US Bureau of Labor Statistics (2011) reports that, of the total number of employees in periodical, book and directory publishing 48.5% are men, while 51.5% are women. Simultaneously, wage disparity seems to have decreased as well (Johnson, 2007). Together these figures indicate a gender balance for the magazine industry in the US; whether this balance exists in other regions of the world as well is unknown. As explained, exact figures on who produces what in the magazine industry are rare, and often based on small case studies.

Despite the gender balance in other areas, horizontal segregation in the magazine industry is commonplace. Women are top managers and editor-in-chief when we look at women's magazines, such as *Vogue*, *Cosmopolitan* and *Marie Claire*. The magazine industry recognises a few very powerful women, like Martha Stewart, Oprah Winfrey and Anna Wintour. However, these women are in charge of "women's magazines" while men still dominate "men's magazines" about computers, current affairs, cars, sports, et cetera.

With regard to the print industry, we can note a major difference between the different print media of magazines and newspapers. While in the magazine industry a gender balance seems to be in place, in the newspaper industry a gender imbalance exists. Why this difference exists between these partly comparable media types, we will address in Chapter 5.

Radio

Compared to magazines and newspapers, radio is a fairly young medium. Radio broadcasting began worldwide in the early years of the twentieth century, while scheduled broadcasting became regular around the 1920s. As in all industries, women have been part of the workforce, though horizontal and vertical segregation play a larger role in the radio industry than in the magazine industry. However, it is even harder to find figures on how many men and women work in which roles in the radio industry. The US Bureau for Labor Statistics, for example, shows only numbers for radio *and* television broadcasting (stating that in 2010 34.4% of the total number of employees in these industries were women, 65.6% were men). In an overview of the radio industry in the US, Judith Cramer (2007) shows how throughout the history of radio gender disparity has barely changed. In terms of vertical segregation, men held most management positions in 2003 (74.1%). Women hold positions like interviewers and coordinators. Though there are no figures available, we can expect that men form the majority of below-the-line professions such as sound technician and sound editors. According to Cramer (2007), this vertical segregation has always existed in the radio industry. However, we need to make an important observation here. Cramer (2007) discusses the radio industry in the US and focuses primarily on commercial broadcasting. When we expand our view to other regions of the world and different types of radio broadcasting, such as community radio or alternative radio, the picture changes.

Community radio usually indicates small, non-profit broadcasters owned and produced by the communities they serve. These stations encourage the local community to share experiences and information. Community radio seems more accessible to men and women of all ages and classes. For example, Ammu Joseph (2004) describes several examples in India of small projects in which women of the lower casts take the lead in producing community radio, which has an empowering effect. Likewise, Carmen Ruíz (2004) describes a similar project among native Aymara women in Bolivia. Both authors show how regular media production is almost inaccessible for these women, and how these small-scale projects function 'to enable members of the disadvantaged majority, especially women, to access, participate in, and make decisions regarding media and communications' (Joseph, 2004: 143). These projects seem promising. Yet, we need to take into account that they are very small scale experiments with limited reach that need a change in structure and sensitivity to become more successful. Additionally, community radio stations often reflect the gender stereotyping of mainstream radio stations in staff and volunteer roles (Mitchell, 2004). In most regions, women are still under-represented in the production staff of community radio (Basnet, 2010). In the Asia Pacific region for example, women are present in all positions within community radio: 28% of leadership positions and the technical staff is made up of women, while 44% of the administrative staff, program producers and volunteers are women (Migrioletto, 2010). These numbers are promising, but men still hold the majority of positions. In other words, horizontal and vertical segregation also exist in community radio.

One clear exception is a specific variety of community radio: women's alternative radio. While community radio aims to serve a certain community (such as universities and cities), the term alternative radio usually indicates small broadcasters aiming to serve a certain political goal. Maybe the most famous example is the internationally accessible, weekly, one-hour programme called Alternative Radio, featuring interviews with intellectuals. The title on the website www.alternativeradio.org is followed by the subtitle 'Audio Energy for Democracy'. Alternative radio is often described as a medium that is highly accessible to women (Mitchell, 2004), though this is limited to women's or feminist alternative radio. Women's alternative radio serves to create room for the female voice, dealing with women's issues that have been ignored in the mainstream media, but also music produced and performed by women (Engstrom, 2010). Many of these stations originated in the 1960s and 1970s to voice the (mostly radical) feminist political agenda that was largely ignored by mainstream media. Women exclusively ran most of these stations. Today, most women's radio stations aim to be inclusive, meaning that they operate as a mixed-gender station and attempt to reach a male audience as well (Mitchell, 2004). This last development counters the most important critique on women's alternative media in general. Linda Steiner (1992: 126–27) eloquently explains: 'Women's media often alienate potential sympathizers with their highly particularized version of their cause and their audience; this provides an easy opening for ridicule and accusations of self-ghettoizing.' This point of critique relates to gender discourses on media production in general, which we will address in Chapter 5.

The variety of horizontal and vertical gender segregation for community and alternative radio outlined above teaches us an important lesson: within a medium there are differences with regard to gender. We should therefore not only be mindful about horizontal and vertical segregation, but also about what "a medium" such as radio or television is, exactly. The complexity of the concept of medium with regard to production will be discussed in Chapter 6.

Television

As one of the largest cultural industries on a global level, it is surprising how little data can be found on who actually works in this industry. The data that are available either concentrate on television news or focus on the American sector of the industry. For example, in 2012 the Writers Guild of America (WGA) reported that women have a 27% share of positions in television. There is also an earnings gap in television; the median earnings for women in 2012 were \$112,081, while the median earnings for men were \$120,242 (WGA, 2014). The earnings gap is slowly decreasing, though, in comparison to earlier years. Comprehensive data for other parts of the world seem absent and therefore it is impossible to create any sense of horizontal and vertical segregation, or below- and above-the-line employees and a possible gender inequality.

It is also important to distinguish between commercial and public broadcasters. Commercial broadcasters are profit driven and have advertising as their primary source of revenue. Public broadcasters are regulated by the government with the explicit aim to grant access to the media for all groups in society (Croteau and Hoynes, 2014). The trends described above are valid for the US, but also only reflect the commercial broadcasting system of that region.[1] A quick glance at the numbers of the public broadcasters in the Netherlands, for example, show us that they employ an equal number of women and men (169 women and 170 men). Men seem to earn slightly more; 41 (24.1%) men are found in the highest salary categories, as opposed to 33 (19.5%) women (NPO, 2014: 131). This is especially interesting when we consider the fact that the number of years employed by the NPO is higher for women than for men (NPO, 2014: 136). Women have a slower career growth than men, indicating that there is still a gender gap (even though it is a much smaller one than the one reported by the WGA). The annual report of the British Broadcasting Corporation (BBC) supports this notion. In 2011, women made up half (49.2%) of the BBC's total workforce and over one third (36.0%) were employed at senior management levels (BBC, 2011: 2–42).

Though the figures for the BBC and the Dutch NPO are not representative of other regions, the fact that these are public broadcasters is what we want to draw attention to. The dynamics that cause gender inequality and salary gap in the American commercial TV industry seem to have less impact for public broadcasters. One of the main reasons for this is the organisation structure. As Denise Bielby (2009) argues, the commercial character of the American television industry causes decision makers to follow a logic of safety. This logic of safety results in, among other things, hiring people who look the most like the predecessor in terms of age, gender, ethnicity, et cetera. This logic of safety is, of course, not entirely absent in public broadcasting, but financially they are more secure and often have a specific mission formulated by the country's government. Additionally, both the NPO and the BBC deliver similar statements in their annual reports: 'A fundamental commitment to serve our audiences drives the BBC's equality and diversity agenda: we aim to reflect the variety of the world we live in through our workforce, who directly and indirectly make rich, meaningful content which delivers quality and value back to all UK audiences' (BBC, 2011: 2–42). We will pay more attention to how the organisation of the media industry has an impact on gender inequality for each branch of the media in Chapter 5.

Film

The film industry, one of the oldest mass media industries, and its relation to gender disparity has been under-researched, similarly to the TV industry in general. However, there is slightly more knowledge regarding contemporary facts and figures on the presence of women and men in the film production process than there is for the TV production process. Denise Bielby and William Bielby (1996) note that, despite some differences, there are few reasons to assume that the dynamics at work in the TV industry with regard to gender are different for the film industry. The authors suggest that the gender inequality might be slightly less in the film industry than in the TV industry when they note that, in 1990, one third of highly ranked executives in the film industry were women. Whether this is still the case today is unknown.

The most interesting aspect of the film industry is its history. As Bielby and Bielby (1996: 252) state: 'Film writing is one of the few professional occupations in which a labour force with a substantial female presence has been displaced by men'. Apparently, in the era of silent films (1895–1929), the number of female writers is estimated to be between 50% and 90%. The boundaries between various roles in the production process – writer, editor and producer – were easily crossed, and women moved from one position to another. By the mid-1930s the number of female writers had decreased to 15%. The status of the industry had changed, and also visibly changed the attractiveness of certain professions for men and women.

The transformation of film writing from a female dominated profession to a male profession can be explained, according to Bielby and Bielby (1996), by the same dynamic as for news production as described by Gaye Tuchman. With the invention of sound movies, the film production process was rationalised. As Janet Staiger (1983: 34) argues, 'American studio filmmaking developed from its attempts to minimize costs and to provide efficiency, regularity, and uniformity of production'. Large corporations became dominant in financing and producing feature films. Writing film scripts became an institutionalised part of film production.

In the 1950s independent film production became a trend, though this had little impact on the presence of women. Bielby and Bielby (1996) point out that the number of women in the film industry reached a historical low in the period from 1960 to 1970. From 1970 onwards there has been an increase of women in the profession, though numbers are still relatively low. In 2012, only 16% of the screen writers were female (Writers Guild of America, 2014). Why the presence of women increased from the 1970s onwards is unknown. Bielby and Bielby (1996) indicate that the women's movement might have had impact. The women's movement put women's issues on the agenda and women started organising themselves into interest groups. These developments might have encouraged women to enter the industry. On the other hand, the authors note that the 1970s also mark the start of the blockbuster era. Increasing the financial risk of film production, studios put more emphasis on hiring established writers, producers and the like, hence making it more difficult to enter the field.

This latter dynamic is also associated with the cause for the gender gap in salary (Bielby and Bielby, 1996). Working only with established professionals (following a logic of safety) also increased the salary of a small elite group in the film industry. With the industry dominated by men for about half a century, a gender salary gap was created that still exists today. While male screen writers earned on average $78,000, female ones earned only $61,776 on average (WGA, 2014). Notable, the earnings gap for film writers is much larger than the one for TV writers.

Music Industry

As is the case with the other media industries, statistics on gender in the music industry are scarce; perhaps even scarcer than other media industries. Nevertheless, the few studies that can be found paint a similar picture of gender (in) equality as seen in the other industries. Similar dynamics such as "status of the job" and "patriarchal structures" can be defined.

In a study on the presence of female artists in the billboard charts in the US in the period between 1997 and 2007, Marc Lafrance, Laura Worcester and Lori Burns (2011) show how male artists dominate the Top 40 charts. The authors make a distinction between the charts for singles bought and charts for singles played on-air. Male artists dominate both charts. Interestingly enough, the difference between male and female artists in records sold appears to be smaller than the difference between how frequent songs are played on-air. On average, from 1997 to 2007, 54.1% of Top 40 sales were by male artists while 41.4% were by female artists (the remaining 4.5% of sales was made up by a combination of male and female artists). For air play, these numbers are quite different: 61.6% of Top 40 air play was made up by male artists, while 34.3% was by female artists (again, the remaining 4.1% was made up a combination of female and male artists) (Lafrance et al., 2011).

These numbers not only show a gender disparity, but also suggest other mechanisms. First, though audiences seem to buy the records of female artists, Top 40 DJs seem to play more records of male artists than female artists. Second, these numbers only tell us something about the performers of music. We do not know who has produced the music, written the lyrics, or who the sound technician was, et cetera. In other words, it is uncertain whether horizontal and vertical segregation in the music industry exists, and if so, how. Like radio and TV, we can expect below-the-line professions, such as sound technician, to be mostly occupied by men, while women mostly occupy positions in the administrative staff. Third, these figures are based on Top 40 charts and therefore represent a certain music genre, namely mainstream and popular music. However, studies in other genres, though rare, do show similar male dominance (Valdez and Halley, 1996). Fourth, this study, and most others we found, focus on the music industry based in the US. Regional differences may be a factor. As Marc Verboord and Amanda Brandellero (2013) show in their comparison of hit charts in nine different countries, over time these charts have become more "global" (i.e. they contain music by artists from other countries than the US). Their study indicates some shifts over time in terms of country of origin; we might expect that there are also regional differences in this regard.

With regard to horizontal and vertical segregation, William Roy and Timothy Dowd (2010: 195) state: 'Compared with men, women musicians have historically faced a narrow range of instruments and responsibilities [...], unstable employment [...], limited commercial success [...] and disgruntlement from fellow instrumentalists when their presence in symphony orchestras moves from token numbers to a sizable minority [...]'. Horizontal segregation in the music industry refers to a smaller range of instruments and responsibilities, while vertical segregation refers to the more unstable careers and limited commercial success for women.

Conclusion

In this chapter we have provided an overview of who produces what in media. Clearly there are differences between the various media industries, although women are generally under-represented in media production. There are many reasons and theoretical perspectives explaining this under-representation that will be discussed in Chapter 5.

Additionally, there are three interesting trends to note: the better part of research on gender and media production does not discuss gender, but sex. Numbers of female and male producers, editors, writers, directors, performers and the like are carefully scrutinised, proving over and over again that women are under-represented in most, if not all fields of media production. Insights into the sex/gender dichotomy of the last few decades force us to be critical about this distinction.

The second trend we want to draw attention to is the overwhelming focus on what is called "hard media", or rather, news production. While news production is the only field investigated thoroughly in terms of gender, this kind of research also primarily focuses on one specific role in the field: the journalist. We have also seen that within a particular media industry, horizontal segregation is often dependent on the status of a certain genre (for example, women screen writers are hired to write for women's genres likes soap operas). The status of the medium, an important element to explain the differences between the media with regard to gender disparity, can be extended to explain the differences within media. In Chapter 5 we will explore the relationship between the status of media, genres and gender.

The third trend we want to call attention to is the fact that all studies we encountered focus on a singular media industry. This enabled us to draft a (limited) overview of 'who produces what' in which industry, indicating that the gender disparity in some industries (for example the magazine industry) is smaller than in others (for example the TV industry). However, this approach suggests we can speak of separate industries, while in reality the industry is horizontally integrated. The major companies mentioned in the introduction of this chapter do not concentrate on magazines or radio or TV or films, but on all types. For example, Time Warner encompasses four major divisions: Turner Broadcasting System (managing TV stations such as CNN and Cartoon Network, cable networks), Warner Bros Entertainment (producing and distributing television series such as *The Big Bang Theory*, home videos, comic books and films), Home Box Office (better known as HBO, producing television series such as *True Blood* and *Game of Thrones*, and movies), and Time Inc. (managing and producing magazines such as *People*, *Time* and *Entertainment Weekly*, and online activities such as *CNNMoney* and *InStyle*). Next to the multiple media types integrated in one conglomerate, some segments are partnered with segments from other major conglomerates. For example, Warner Bros TV group, a sub-segment of Warner Bros Entertainment, is a 50/50 partner with the CBS TV group (Time Warner, 2012). We can only guess what the consequences of the integration of the media industry are in terms of gender disparity. However, integration also has important repercussions for perspectives on media texts and production thereof. We will discuss these repercussions in Chapter 6.

In the next chapter, we will discuss the question of how the concept of gender relates to the under-representation of women in the media industry, and also how the media industry is gendered itself.

Further Reading

Media production is an interesting and developing field of media studies. For a general introduction to media production we recommend:

- Hesmondhalgh, D. (Ed.) (2006). *Media Production*. Maidenhead: Open University Press.

In this highly accessible volume Hesmondhalgh brings together a collection of essays that discuss globalisation, the media professional and discourses on audiences within the media industries.

For a more specific take on gender and media industries, we suggest to read:

- Creedon, P. J. and Cramer, J. (Eds.) (2007). *Women in Mass Communication* (3rd edition). Thousand Oaks/London/New Delhi: Sage.

This edited volume provides a wonderful collection on women working in print, advertising and broadcast media in the US. For a more international perspective we recommend:

- Ross, K. and. Byerly, C. M. (Eds.) (2004). *Women and Media: International Perspectives*. Maidenhead/Malden: Blackwell.

Chapters 6 to 9 of this edited volume discuss gender and media production on an international level, sketching a nuanced perspective on women in media production.

Note

1 For the US the term public broadcasting often refers to something else than described here. As (McQuail, 2005: 179) states, 'the term "public broadcasting" in the United States generally refers to the minority network mainly financed by viewers and listeners voluntarily and choosing to pursue certain cultural goals'.

Chapter 5

Power and Gender in the Media Industry

A rather bleak picture of the representation of men and women in the media industry was sketched in the previous chapter. The overview is a brief one and therefore limited, but it shows how women are under-represented in the media industry in general (though there are noticeable differences between media) and how horizontal and vertical gender segregation exists in all media industries. However, the relationship between gender and media production does not stop solely at the number of males and females working in these industries. As discussed in Chapter 4, numbers of female producers have slowly, but steadily, increased. Popular music artists like Lady Gaga and Taylor Swift, TV producers such as Lena Dunham (*Girls* (HBO)) and Shonda Rhimes (*Grey's Anatomy* (ABC)), and the editor-in-chief of *Time Magazine* Martha Nelson, are just a few examples of successful women in media production. They not only show that women can take up top positions in production, but they also function as role models. Their position as producers, however, is not uncontested and is still considered an exception to the rule. Lena Dunham, the writer of the increasingly popular TV show *Girls,* is accused of not being feminist enough and that she is only successful due to her privileged background; critics personally attack Lena Dunham: 'Sometimes a fat pig is just a fat pig, no matter how prettily you write it' (AL.com, 2013). In a similar vein, the appointment of Julie Larson-Green as the new head of Xbox, department of Microsoft, was met with negative comments from gamers stating that Green will create baking and knitting games, and that she is not a gamer even though she has 19 years of experience working for Microsoft (Greenfield, 2013).

Contradicting these fierce, sometimes aggressive, criticisms is the applause these women also receive, but still, these kinds of controversies seem to only revolve around female producers. Undoubtedly, there is something else at play here in addition the under-representation of women in media production. In this chapter we will dig into the relationship between sex and gender for two reasons. First, this relationship explains vertical and horizontal segregation. Second, this relationship has specific consequences for the media industry itself. To follow Marjan De Bruin (2000: 225), we will 'go beyond the "body count" and to start looking at specific social practices, embodied in conventions and rules, formally and informally, based on history and tradition, sustained by people working in the media organizations'.

In other words we will connect the concept of power to under-representation of women in media production and the media industry itself, asking questions such as why women occupy managerial positions in the media industry less often than men (vertical segregation), and why these positions are limited to certain types of media or genres (horizontal segregation). To do so, we will first look into the concept of the glass ceiling from a macro level, answering the question: 'How do we understand the "glass ceiling" and what does the concept explain?' Second, we will investigate the glass ceiling on a micro level, investigating how this glass ceiling is both caused and maintained by the organisation of the media industry. Third, we will look into the status of media in society and the consequences this image has on the questions of power in the media.

What is the Glass Ceiling?

The glass ceiling is the most commonly used concept to explain the vertical segregation of gender in media production. The glass ceiling is also a rather vague concept, making it hard to define. For example, the Federal Glass Ceiling Commission (1995: iii) in the US states the following: 'There seemed to be an invisible – but impenetrable – barrier between women and the executive suite, preventing them from reaching the highest levels of the business world regardless of their accomplishments and merits.' Although this Commission has produced several reports on the glass ceiling, they still carefully formulate that there "seems to be" rather than there "is" a barrier.[1] This caution marks the debate over the glass ceiling. Over the years, the glass ceiling has been a topic of heated debates. The question 'Does the glass ceiling (still) exist?' has characterised headlines of many newspaper articles and research/discussion papers. Some authors simply state the glass ceiling does not exist. A quick search on the internet easily turns up contributions that deny the existence of the glass ceiling directly. In a contribution called *The Myth of the Glass Ceiling*, by someone who calls himself Novaseeker (2009), the glass ceiling is discarded as a blatant lie fabricated by feminists (we assume the author is male, as the contribution is found within a website dedicated to men's issues).

Other authors are more nuanced, but in the end conclude something similar. For example, Anthony Delano (2003: 273) refers to an ongoing British study (started in 1990) in which the authors state that, '[w]omen journalists have become so completely assimilated into the journalistic workforce that they need no longer be regarded as a separate group'. Yet other authors point out that it is time for women to take heart and to stop complaining about inequality (Van Hintum, 2013). This opinion is not only held by outsiders to the media industry, but is also voiced by female journalists themselves. As Maria Hardin and Erin Whiteside (2009) show in their study on female journalists, young female journalists are convinced that sex and gender are a non-issue in their professional context. However, as we have shown in Chapter 4, gender inequality in the media industry remains a fact.

Trying to deal with the facts, many researchers have investigated the mechanics underpinning the glass ceiling. Topics of investigation are ample and vary. For example, Wiji Arulampalan, Alison Booth and Mark Bryan (2007) show how the salary gap between men and women has decreased in general but still exists. Others investigate how some women manage to break through the glass ceiling and others do not. Alice Eagly and Linda Carli (2007) prefer to speak of a "labyrinth" instead of a glass ceiling, since some women manage to find their way through. Another issue regarding the glass ceiling is that studies show the glass ceiling takes different shapes and forms in various countries and regions (Arulampalan *et al.*, 2007; Pandian, 1999; Zuiderveld, 2011).

The reason the glass ceiling is glass is due to its invisibility: the ceiling is transparent; you never notice it until you bump into it. The term is often used loosely to explain various types of gender inequality in the workforce: the salary gap between women and men in the industry; the number of women and men in managerial positions; or any other difference between men and women in the work force. This loose use of the concept is regrettable in our opinion: once a concept is thought to explain everything, it usually explains nothing. Therefore, a more nuanced formulation of the glass ceiling is necessary. David Cotter, Joan Hermsen, Seth Ovadia and Reeve Vanneman (2001: 657–61) formulated four criteria to distinguish glass ceiling effects from other mechanisms causing gender inequality. These criteria are:

1. 'The glass ceiling represents a gender difference that is not explained by other job-relevant characteristics of the employee';
2. 'A glass ceiling inequality represents a gender or racial difference that is greater as higher levels of an outcome than at lower levels of an outcome';
3. 'A glass ceiling inequality represents a gender or racial inequality in the chances of advancement into higher levels, not merely the proportions of each gender or race currently at those higher levels';
4. 'A glass ceiling inequality represents a gender or racial inequality that increases over the course of a career.'

The glass ceiling is thus understood as gender inequality that is hierarchically organised; the inequality increases towards the top and cannot be explained by any other characteristic of the employee or the profession (for example, working in the media industry does not require specific physical abilities). According to the four criteria, the glass ceiling is not only causing gender inequality but also ethnic inequality. Here, it is essential to note that other factors in addition to gender and ethnicity are also of importance. As discussed in the introduction, age is also a relevant factor. Hence, we can logically deduce that many other features such as class, disability, sexuality, et cetera also have consequences for climbing professional ladders and also intersect with one another.

Next, we would like to speak to criterion 2. This criterion states that when we discuss the concept of the glass ceiling, we refer to gaps in salary and the number of women holding higher managerial positions in the industry. However, this does not mean that a salary gap does not exist on lower levels: unfortunately for women, it does. In this case however, we do not speak of a glass ceiling but of a "sticky floor". The sticky floor indicates a situation in which 'women are promoted as often as men, but receive lower wage gains consequent upon promotion. In firms with formal wage scales, women remain stuck to the lower wage points on the wage scale of their new, higher job grade' (Booth, Francesconia and Frank, 2003: 296). In other words, women tend to earn less than men for similar job performances.

The glass ceiling inequality is different than plain sexism, even though, as we will see, sexist ideas sometimes form the underpinnings of the glass ceiling. In the report from the Federal Glass Ceiling Commission (1995: 28) one businessman comments: 'It's always going to be tough to figure out how to treat the women, but now it's worse and I'd rather not be in a mentoring relationship with them [women].' As the glass ceiling is an issue of power, it is hard to put one's finger on what constructs and conserves the glass ceiling, since the barriers are invisible and it's hard to single out actors, mechanisms and structures. In studies on the media industry and particularly studies investigating news media, many mechanisms are described and analysed. Each of these mechanisms has a specific contribution to the existence and sustenance of the glass ceiling. First, we will discuss the ideas and perspectives that are specifically tied to the organisation of the media industry. Second, more general perspectives and ideas aiming to explain the construction and preservation of the glass ceiling found in society at large are discussed.

The Organisation of the Media Industry

To discuss the organisation of the media industry and its consequences for the low number of women in managerial or higher positions, we revisit the previous chapter where three perspectives on the relationship between ownership and media production were discussed. The political economy, the liberal, and social-liberal perspective each have their own dynamics and postulate particular ideas on why there are fewer women than men in high positions in the media industry.

As was explained in Chapter 4, a political economy perspective underlies many feminist works on the media industry. Political economy explains how the majority of media owners are wealthy, white, heterosexual males who desire that their interests are reflected by "their media" (hence excluding women and other groups). This perspective most directly explains the glass ceiling: it is simply not in the media owners' interest to hire women, and they actually benefit from not doing so. However, this view assumes that men purposely and explicitly exercise the exclusion of women and others (such as Afro-American men). In conflict with non-discriminatory legislation in many countries, it is dubious whether this kind of deliberate exclusion actually exists. For example, the Federal Glass Ceiling Commission (1995: 31) states: 'Corporate leaders say that they want to remove the barriers that obstruct access to the top. Rare, indeed, is the white male high-level executive who publicly opposes the principles of inclusion.'

However, this does not mean there are no direct or indirect consequences of the fact that most media owners are white, affluent, heterosexual males. These consequences are simply not as direct as discrimination on the basis of sex. A better explanation of the significance of the features of media owners on the number of women in high-level positions is what Gallagher (1995) calls "the old-boys'-network". The old-boys'-network refers to an informal system of friendship and mutual assistance through which men who are acquainted with each other through, for example, student fraternities and private schools exchange favours and connections. A common expression used is: 'It's not what you know, it's who you know and in the old-boys'-network the connections that lead to wealth are often decades in the making' (Gamba and Kleiner, 2001: 102).

For women, this informal and exclusive system also exists, but the favours and contacts do not relate to the public sphere (i.e. business and politics), but to the private sphere (i.e. care for the elderly, fundraising). Nevertheless, when we search the internet for "old-girls'-network" we find quite a few professional organisations founded by and for women to enhance women's professional lives. However, they often call themselves "new girls" instead of "old" (e.g. www.newgirlsnetwork.net/). This change in name can be perceived in a couple different ways: a play on words, as it is a new development in society, but also as not wanting to be old. In Part I on representation, we already saw why old in connection to women is different than old in connection to men. Women present in the media are generally much younger than men, and their age is more often paid attention to.

Additionally, new media gave rise to a "new-boys'-network" that is young and trendy. Michelle Gamba and Brian Kleiner (2001: 102) define it as '[a] new boys' network through which companies form, contacts meet, investments flow and deals happen'. New media, specifically the internet, were viewed as potentially more egalitarian than old media in terms of gender and ethnicity. However, this egalitarian potential of new media has been proven wrong by many authors. As Gamba and Kleiner (2001) argue, the new-boys'-network shows remarkable similarity to the old-boys'-network. In the next chapter we will further explore the relationship between new media and the dynamics that construct the glass ceiling.

From a political economy perspective, the old-boys'-network as a major organising principle forms a direct explanation for the preservation of the glass ceiling. However, the principle of the old-boys'-network does not explain all underpinnings of the glass ceiling. An indirect explanation can be derived from the liberal perspective on the media industry. The idea of the free market in the media industry and the enormous increase in the number of TV channels, magazines, movies, et cetera, has made the "search for the audience" ever more important. Commercial broadcasters have to attract advertisers, as they are a major part of earned revenue. To attract advertisers, audiences are categorised and broken down into groups to be "sold" to the broadcasters (cf. McQuail, 2005). One of the most common breakdowns of audiences is gender (Kuipers, 2012). In her research on cultural intermediaries, the people who trade in TV programmes and formats, she shows how notions of gender influence the categorisation of programmes along the lines of gendered audience groups. As discussed in Chapter 4, media types and genres that aim for a female audience hire more women in professional roles. The feminine media types and genres (also referred to as soft media and genres) have lower status than masculine, or hard media types and genres. Women can reach top managerial positions in soft genres, but not so easily in hard genres. The liberal perspective thus explains the glass ceiling indirectly. The distinction between hard and soft genres also has to do with the status of male and female production.

The direct and indirect explanations for the glass ceiling similar to those found in the political economy and liberal perspective are much harder to find by reviewing research that takes a dual-market perspective. Of course when we consider private media, the explanations are still relevant. For the public media however, many postulate that gender equality in mission statements is often reflected in the numbers of female and male employers. Nevertheless, in these organisations where the number of women and men hired are similar, gender inequality still exists in salary and positions men and women occupy that cannot be explained.

Glass Ceiling and Societal Structures

The general principles tied to the organisation of media we discussed in the previous section only partly elucidate the construction and maintenance of the glass ceiling. Other structures that are believed to form the glass ceiling's underpinning are of more societal character. Research into these "other" structures is manifold. Research concentrating on the news room and journalism discuss these underpinnings best, however, as Van Zoonen (1994: 60) argues, although most studies concentrate on news production in general,

> studies have illustrated that gender takes on a specific meaning in particular organizational contexts (although not necessarily a new meaning), but the extent to which this happens or is allowed to happen, and its specific sources, expressions and consequences differ from case to case.

In other words, in general we can identify some mechanisms that together form the foundations for the glass ceiling. These mechanisms are not the same in each industry, on each level, for each individual. The structures most crucial to the glass ceiling are: the status of labour and, consequently, genres and different media types; the relationships between media professions and the private life; the historical roots of media production; and the male values inherent to media production. We will discuss these four structures and highlight regional differences where relevant (and possible), as the major part of these studies is still situated in the Anglo-Saxon region.

The Status of Labour and Media Types

A distinction was made in Chapter 4 between below-the-line and above-the-line professions in the media industry, and how this division in labour reflects a difference in women and men present in the industry (Banks, 2009). While below-the-line professions are usually articulated as craft-professions, above-the-line usually refers to creative professions.

> ## Box 5.1 A Room of One's Own – Virginia Woolf
>
> A famous essay on the status of women's crafts and their position in society was written in 1929 by Virginia Woolf. In the text, narrated by fictional characters, Woolf argues that female writers are excluded from the world of literature dominated by patriarchy. Women, Woolf says, are in need for a room of one's own (plus some money) in order to write.

Women are more often found in below-the-line professions and men in above-the-line professions. Implicitly, this also situates women's production as craft more often than creativity. This is not an unusual observation, neither is it very new or contemporary. As Mary Celeste Kearney (2006: 25) argues:

> Largely utilitarian in nature, the domestic arts of girls and women have long been disparaged as "handicrafts", products of manual household chores that allegedly do not require much intellect, reflection, or creativity to produce, and thus do not hold the same cultural status as the non-utilitarian artistic objects created by wealthy individuals.

This distinction in the status of what men and women produce runs through one of the major dynamic underpinnings of the glass ceiling: the distinction between hard and soft genres or media types.

Tuchman first introduced the notion of hard and soft news in relation to gender in 1973 in a discussion on news production. Tuchman (1973) describes how the selection of events that become news is not only dependent on the contents of the event, but also on the way the event happens. While hard news is defined as unexpected events that are factual and interesting for humanity (Tuchman calls these unscheduled events), soft news concerns events that focus on human interest and do not evoke urgency for publication (Tuchman calls these events non-scheduled). Male journalists are mostly involved with the production of hard news, while female journalists are mostly involved with soft news. Since then, a large body of research focusing on these two concepts has been accumulated (Reinemann, Stanyer, Scherr and Legnante, 2012).

Soft news and hard news have become related to quality (hard news is quality news, while soft news is not) and to gender, hence relating quality to gender. Hard news is considered to be of high quality with features such as serious, factual, important and urgent, and is tied to masculinity. This kind of news is considered to have more prestige and earns more societal respect. Conversely, soft news is considered not serious, non-factual (i.e. emotional), does not evoke any urgency and is tied to femininity (Ziamou, 2000). As we have shown in the previous chapter, horizontal segregation of men and women largely follows the boundaries marked by this distinction. Though the distinction is originally made for news production, the hard and soft dichotomy is extended to media types and genres (cf. Beasley, 1993; Van Zoonen, 1994).

Horizontal segregation of gender in the workforce is noticeable on the level of genre. Women are not only assigned to take care of the human interest (soft) sections of the newspaper, women also more often take care of the soft genres of popular TV. Marxist feminist writers have attached this notion to the high/low culture distinction, what they call the 'gendering of cultural forms' (Gledhill, 1997). While popular media genres such as soap opera, the romance novel and popular music have been viewed as a mass culture of low quality, genres such as current affairs programmes, literature and classical musical have been branded as high culture, connoting high quality and masculinity.

Historical Roots of the Organisation of Media Industry

Jeremy Tunstall (1993) describes how the British Broadcasting Company emerged in the 1920s from the post office, staffed by men who had survived World War I, and later in the 1950s was staffed by men who served in World War II. This history of civil service and military tradition defined the role of producer as a masculine one from the onset. In his research in the 1990s, Tunstall (1993) concluded that horizontal and vertical segregation are still practiced in the BBC, even though they have an equal opportunity policy. These historical roots are important for most European broadcasting systems, though the consequences of both wars and historical roots differ per country. In the Netherlands for example, the compartmentalisation of society caused religious groups, Catholics and Protestants, to form the first public broad-casters (Bakker and Scholten, 2005). Here, religious concepts result in defining roles as masculine.

Box 5.2 Exercise: Gendered History?

Choose a national newspaper and trace its organisational structure (Who owns it? Is the newspaper part of a multinational or not? Who are the members of the executive board?). Try to gather data on the number of women and men employed by the newspaper (often this information can be found in year reports). Next, find out the historical roots of newspaper businesses in general (and your newspaper in particular). Now reflect on what the organisational structure and the history of newspaper businesses might mean for the current state of affairs with regard to gender.

The historical roots of the organisation of the media industry have defined the role of producer by masculine qualities. As a consequence, characteristics such as objectivity, leadership ability, desires and responsibility were considered to be necessary for managerial positions. Stereotypically, men were thought to have these qualities in larger quantities than women (Heilman, 2001). As Virginia Schein (2007: 4) argues, '[t]o "think manager" was to "think male", and this view worked against women seeking to enter and advance into management positions'. New developments in ideas on management appear to place a greater emphasis on female skills such as emphatic capacities. However, as Romy Fröhlich (2004) shows, these developments turn into a "friend-liness trap", indicating the vicious circle that traps women upon arrival in the media industry. First they are praised for their so-called feminine skills, but these skills are simultaneously the obstacle as they try to climb the social ladder, as masculine traits are still considered to be desirable in managerial positions.

Male values revolving around the media profession are also articulated on a more indirect level. Byerly (2004) explains how the newsroom is marked by masculine hegemony. Power is not asserted as a direct authoritarian control of the news room, but

> through institutional hiring and promotional practices that privilege white men over others, and that rely on nineteenth-century criteria to determine which events should be covered (and from what perspective), which facts and sources should be included in a story (and which not), and how headlines should be written and pages laid out (or, in broadcast industries, how stories should be sequenced and given time allotments).
>
> (Byerly, 2004: 114)

As Cynthia Carter, Gill Branston and Stuart Allan (1998: 141) argue, 'often subtle, taken-for-granted strategies in and through which journalists, knowingly or not, routinely define "what counts as reality" in alignment with patriarchal renderings of the social world'. This means that the historical roots of media industries have had and still have a major impact on the continuation of the glass ceiling. As we have seen, it is not entirely clear what exactly the repercussions of the masculine hegemony of the media industry on content are. The few studies that are available show indeed that the number of female producers has an impact on media content, but that these effects vary with genre and media type.

Next, the definition of professional roles as masculine does not only have consequences for how media production is organised, it also has consequences outside the media industry and specifically to the intersection of the public and the private sphere.

Media Professions and the Private Life

Men are expected to operate in the public sphere, while women are bound to the private sphere. Media are *de facto* part of the public sphere. This intersection of media production with the public sphere has had some very concrete consequences. Media jobs were not defined as 9-to-5 jobs, requiring more than 100% dedication and commitment (Tunstall, 1993). The scheduling of after-hours work activities intersects with obligations towards the family in general but also with social norms of what was and is appropriate for women (Joseph, 2004). As Katie Milestone and Anneke Meyer (2012: 45) argue, '[t]he lifestyle and habitus of the cultural producers was far removed from the reach of most women. This was in addition to the social mores of the time, which presented powerful behavioural expectations of the "happy housewife heroine"'.

Family structures and social norms sometimes require women to deal with disapproval from their families or significant others. Of course, these cultural norms are regionally diverse. As Joseph (2004) explains in a case from India (pointing out that India is a large country and that regional differences within India should be taken into account), social class, or rather the old caste system, shapes aspects of social life including expectations for women and their families. Social class has always had consequences for the balance between the private and the public, as women of lower social classes are more often forced to enter the workforce than women of middle and higher social classes (for the simple reason of need for income). As social class intersects with race and ethnicity, vertical and horizontal segregation in the media industry should be understood not only as gendered but also as intersecting with ethnicity and social class.

In most cultures women are still carrying the largest share of responsibility for the family. Female employees in the media industries are particularly aware of this complexity. In a study on creative labour, David Hesmondhalgh and Sarah Baker (2011) argue that the definition of creative careers (in this case media careers) as non-traditional conflicts with women's life cycles. Since women are frequently the primary caretakers of children, it is difficult for them to meet the requirements and demands of a profession that is 24/7. Media industries have profited from this complexity. Female media professionals more often have part-time contracts and work flexible hours for a modest salary to balance their professional and private lives (cf. Ross, 2004; Ziamou, 2000). These practices result in what Tunstall (1993: 174) calls 'the unintended results of retarding women's promotion'.

An additional consequence of the difficult balance between family and creative labour is "the revolving door effect". The revolving door refers to the stagnation in reaching critical mass when the number of female journalists, or other professionals, entering the field is equal to the number of females leaving it (Barret, 1984; De Bruin and Ross, 2004; Hardin and Whiteside, 2009).

The revolving door and the complex balance between private and public life form sustenance for the glass ceiling. In addition to defining various roles as masculine and the repercussions for the balance between the professional and the private life, the historical roots have also had an impact on audiences. We will discuss audiences in more detail in Part III, but for now it is interesting to look into the intimate relationship between production and audiences, as the male values in the production process have shaped the perception of some genres as feminine or masculine and have also produced gendered audiences.

Male Values in Production and Audiences

Soap operas, soft rock and glossy magazines are all media genres that have been defined as feminine or soft genres. Conversely, the evening news, heavy metal and scientific magazines have been defined as masculine or hard genres. Drawing either female or male audiences, the "gendered character" of these genres seems rather natural: they aim for female or male audiences, and that audience is exactly who consumes the media. This, however, is an over-simplification of the dynamic. As we already have seen, producers of feminine genres are more often women than in other more masculine genres, but the mechanics of the glass ceiling are still at work. The historical definition of the role of the media professional co-constructed the distinction between the soft and hard genres of today and the appropriate audiences for these genres.

Milestone and Meyer (2012: 49) discuss the historical roots of rock and roll in the 1950s and how these roots defined audiences: 'Rebelliousness and overt sexiness were at odds with the categories defining the femininity of the time, which were connected with domesticity and demureness.' The character of rock and roll, defined as rebellious and sexy, were unsuitable for the tender female disposition of the time, hence defining the rock musician as male and the rock fan as female. Music producers became more and more important, and male rockers were designed to be adored by female audiences. Milestone and Meyer (2012: 50) claim that '[s]o potent and strong was it that a relationship between gender and popular music based on extreme binary oppositions became established. This was exploited by the music industry, which saw the benefits of the gendered fan/consumer relationship'.

Music producers in this case can be viewed as cultural intermediaries, and it is their role that is of interest here. Cultural intermediaries define what is legitimate and illegitimate culture, what is desirable and by whom it is desirable. Jennifer Smith Maguire and Julian Matthews (2012: 552) define them as follows:

> They construct value, by framing how others – end consumers, as well as other market actors including other cultural intermediaries – engage with goods, affecting and effecting others' orientations towards those goods as legitimate – with "goods" understood to include material products as well as services, ideas and behaviours.

Though Smith Maguire and Matthews (2012) do not discuss gender specifically, from their definition we can understand how cultural intermediaries have an impact on the gendered character of hard and soft genres. This is particularly illustrated by the work of Kuipers (2012), which shows how cultural intermediaries in the TV industry – TV buyers and sellers – not only trade TV programmes but also gendered conceptions of the audiences. Kuipers (2012) describes how during yearly organised conventions[2] audiences are framed by traditional conceptions of masculinity and femininity, sometimes even by colour-coded leaflets (pink ones for programmes aimed at female audiences and blue ones for programmes aimed at male audiences). Narrowcasting, a practice where production of media focuses more and more precisely on audience segments, produces a side effect of trading in gender conventions. As the US is still the largest exporter of TV programmes, it is also American gender conventions that are broadcasted widely across the world (Kuipers, 2012).

The industry profits from the relationship between gender and consumption: by creating gendered subject positions in their texts, they get to sell two products rather than one (one to a female and one to a male audience). This dynamic is seen in other industries as well, having an impact on the content of the media products sold (cf. Milestone and Meyer, 2012; Bielby and Bielby, 1996).

Aside from the economic relationship between masculine role definition and gendered audiences, there are other reasons for the exclusion of women in media production that might be ridiculed and laughed at in contemporary times, but still have had a major effect on the representation of women and men in the industry. For example, Mitchell (2004) discusses how in the early days of radio, producers claimed that audiences preferred to hear male voices. Though this suggestion might seem laughable by some, it still inspires research today. Emma Rodero, Olatz Larrea and Marina Vázquez (2013) show how male voices are still used more often than female voices in radio advertising, and also demonstrate that this is based on convention and is unrelated to advertising effectiveness.

Conclusion

In this chapter we have viewed how gender and power are articulated in and sometimes by the media industries. We distinguished various mechanisms that construct and maintain the glass ceiling. So far we have circumvented the discussion of increasingly important media, namely what are called new media (social network sites, the internet, smartphones, apps, videogames, et cetera). These media raise important questions regarding the industry, which is increasingly harder to define as professional roles are much harder to distinguish. Furthermore, new media also raise questions about what production actually is. The term prosumer (a contraction of producer and consumer) is illustrative of this. We will address these questions in Chapter 6 together with the consequences of the gendered conceptions of audiences, products and consumers as discussed in this chapter.

Further Reading

For an insight into the practices of media professionals within the media industries, we refer to:

- Caldwell, J. T. (2008). *Production Culture: Industrial Reflexivity and Critical Practice in Film and Television*. Durham/London: Duke University Press.

In this volume Caldwell investigates cultural practices and beliefs within media industry and analyses the texts created by these professionals. Caldwell's employment of an ethnographic approach offers rich insights into how to consider media production as a cultural activity. For an approach more directly connected to gender we recommend:

- Milestone, K. and Meyer, A. (2012). *Gender and Popular Culture*. Cambridge/Malden: Polity Press.

This book forms one of the rare occasions of researchers engaging with the production practices of popular culture and how they relate to gender. In relation to other chapters on representation and consumption the authors create a valuable account of production, content and consumption of popular culture and the relations to gender.

Notes

1 The title of the report is interesting though – 'Good for Business: Making Full Use of the Nation's Human Capital' – indicating that the research into gender inequality is economically driven as it causes financial loss.
2 Examples are NATPE (National Association of Television Program Executives) and MIPCOM (organised by Reed Midem Organisation in France).

Chapter 6

Blurring Production

Studies in the production of media are divided into two separate fields. One field focuses on the media industry and how production is organised within that industry. The other field focuses on the consumers and how they produce media content. In this chapter, we will focus on the second field, unravelling the gendered consumer as a producer of media and the relationships with and consequences for the media industries. We will argue that the changing meaning and context of media production, caused by technological developments and globalisation, has consequences for production's relation to gender. First we will discuss the concept of "new media", which is closely tied to the idea that the media consumer becomes a producer in a convergent media sphere. Next, we will place this development of new media in the context of the media industry, which has, as we will see, responded to these developments. Lastly, we will explore the concept of the produser/prosumer, both concepts used to describe consumers as producers, and their relation to gender.

New Media?

For over two decades the term "new media" has come into vogue, referring to a multiplicity of definitions that each tries to characterise the newness. Often this characterisation contrasts new media to old or traditional media. For example, Croteau and Hoynes (2014) show how new media differ from old media by naming a few characteristics: many-to-many communication, sender and receiver are often both known, and the line between producer and the receiver is blurred. Yet, other authors define new media as digital or interactive (requiring audience participation), as opposed to the analogue nature and passive uses of traditional media. All of these elements (and more) are of relevance when defining new media. Recently, authors have attempted to formulate definitions encompassing all these aspects. For instance, Leah Lievrouw and Sonia Livingstone (2006: 8) define new media as 'infrastructures for communication and information that comprise particular types of artefacts, practices and social arrangements; they are socially shaped in distinctive ways and have characteristic social consequences'.

Their definition is broad and addresses many features of new media that are relevant to understanding the relations between gender and the media. The broadness of the definition is also its weakness: it includes traditional media like TV and radio, which also comprise things, ways of usage and social arrangements. Therefore, we would like to emphasise that their definition also contains a new understanding of media in general, and new media such as the internet, Web 2.0 and smartphones specifically. In previous chapters we understood media in a material sense – products audiences can consume, be it movies, TV programmes, newspapers, radio broadcasts or magazines. Lievrouw and Livingstone (2006) formulate new media as comprising of artefacts, practices and social arrangements. Not only the material product itself, but also the social aspect is now part of understanding the media. Social network sites (SNS) illustrate this point. They are as much media artefacts as they embody social practices. This expanded conceptualisation of (new) media allows us to grasp media production in different terms and in different dimensions than we did in previous chapters. This understanding allows for a more dynamic and fluid understanding of the production, content and reception of media.

We would like to take a moment to consider the "new" in new media. New media and their technologies have become part of our everyday lives and we now live in an era where a significant part of the population in the Western world are considered digital natives. A digital native is a person who has been interacting with media technologies from the day they were born. Using new media technologies therefore comes rather natural to them, as it has always has been part of their lives. Others, like the authors of this book, had to learn how to utilise new media technologies, and are therefore digital immigrants (Prensky, 2001). Therefore, while some media might still be new for digital immigrants, this distinction between new and old media is less logical for digital natives.

Though digital natives can be found all over the world, the centre of gravity lies in the West. Access to new media technologies is not equally distributed in the world, not over regions nor social groups. On a micro-level the consequences of this unequal distribution of access to digital media is studied in terms of the consumers who produce media content. For example, Kearney (2006) discusses intersectionality of class and gender in this perspective. Creating new media content, she argues, is also a costly affair; therefore, most girls who produce new media content are white and affluent. On a macro level, this unequal distribution of access to digital media is referred to as the digital divide, as some people have access to new media and can benefit from them while others do not. The International Telecommunication Union (ITU) reports that in 2013, 77.7% of households in developed countries had internet access while only 28.0% of the households in developing countries had access (ITU, 2014). This access coincides with the percentage of digital natives in such countries. On a global level, 5.2% of the population (or 30% of the young population) are considered digital natives. The proportion of digital natives in developed countries is much higher than in developing countries, ranging from 0.1% in

Timor to 14% in Iceland (ITU, 2014). The digital divide does not so much indicate a gap in economic measures, but a gap in information access and competencies to read, create and produce media content (called media literacy). Later in this chapter we will explore the digital divide in terms of gender.

In contrast to these developments on a micro and macro level, we will now look more closely into the consequences of new media developments for the media industries. We will focus on two development concepts: intermediality and convergence culture.

Convergence Culture

The ascension of new media technologies brought many significant changes to media industries and audiences alike. Digitalisation, meaning the creation of traditional media in digital form while using 1 and 0 of computer code, meant that formerly distinct media products could now converge (as in digital form they do not differ). For example, most smartphones now carry music, photos and videos. Production and dispersion of media products became less expensive, while technological possibilities increased (i.e. special effects, 3D movies and Blu-ray). Simultaneously, it was possible for audiences to use media devices in multiple ways and to become more interactive. The smartphone, for example, does not only allow us to call our friends and family but also to play games, watch TV, mail, chat, shop, et cetera, anywhere and at any time. This confluence of media production technologies for both media industries and audiences has been named "convergence culture" by Henry Jenkins (2004, 2006):

> Media convergence is more than simply a technological shift. Convergence alters the relationship between existing technologies, industries, markets, genres and audiences. [...] Convergence is taking place within the same appliances [...] within the same franchise [...] within the same company [...] within the brain of the consumer [...] and within the same fandom.
> (Jenkins, 2004: 34)

While media industries use multiple outlets for one and the same media product, audiences consume these products in multiple and varied ways. For example, the popular TV series *GLEE* (FOX) is produced on several levels (Edwards, 2012). Next to the TV show itself, there is an app (*GLEE* Experience), which gives you the ability to produce your own karaoke-versions of popular *GLEE* songs and mix them with other people's from all over the globe, CDs and iTunes songs, sneak peeks on YouTube, a Twitter feed that gives away snippets of the story, the 3D Concert Movie, a spin off called *The GLEE Project*, which is a talent show where the winner gets to be a character on the TV show *GLEE*, and *GLEE* games for Wii and Xbox. *GLEE*'s narrative is developed on many different platforms and on some of these platforms fans contribute (as in the app and the talent show).

This convergence of technologies, producers, audiences and media content has an impact on culture in a variety of ways. Jenkins (2004) indicates several fields of tension between producers and consumers, such as the way audience ratings are measured and rethinking the media aesthetics. However, the term convergence culture is used so often in academic studies that its meaning has become diffused. James Hay and Nick Couldry (2011) show how convergence indicates at least four areas of inquiry: synergy in the media industries; multi-plication of platforms for news and information; technological hybridity; and media aesthetics. The involvement of the audience, as indicated by Jenkins (2004), has disappeared from this understanding of convergence culture. Yet, other authors such as Juha Herkman (2012) argue that the term convergence is misleading in itself because it implies a coming together of things, though the trends show that there is an increase in gadgets, technologies and uses, and thus the trend is divergence rather than convergence. Therefore, Herkman (2012: 370) prefers to use the term "intermediality" instead:

> Communication takes place by increasing the number of media channels and communication technologies, which are inherently linked to each other, but which also have histories and traditions of their own – traditions that cannot be reduced to a single concept of convergence.

Hence, convergence is an umbrella term (Spielmann, 2007). Nevertheless, we are interested in what convergence culture means for the relationship between the media industry and audiences, more precisely gender specific audiences. Mark Deuze (2007: 244) formulates this change in relationships thusly: 'The blurring of real or perceived boundaries between makers and users in increasingly participatory media culture challenges consensual notions of what it means to work in the cultural industries.' In other words, convergence culture indicates a shift in the power relations between industry and audiences, between producer and consumer. Some consider this as an ultimate victory for the audiences. In 2006, on his blog Pressthink, Jay Rosen writes about the people formerly known as the audiences, using this concept to inform traditional media that the era of passive consumers has passed and that audiences are now in control. This shifting of power relations finds expression in the terms "prosumer" or "produser".

Produser

Though the term produser is intimately tied to digital media, its predecessor, prosumer, was coined by Alvin Toffler in 1971 in a book called *Culture Shock,* of which the first sentence reads: 'This is a book about what happens to people when they are overwhelmed by change.' Toffler (1971) predicted a change in the needs of the consumer, wanting an ever more customised pro-duct, and an industry having to respond to this change. However, Axel Bruns (2006: 2) cautions us, as the term prosumer still indicates an industry that produces, and a consumer who consumes. He therefore proposes to use the term produser: 'These produsers engage not in a traditional form of content production, but are instead involved in *produsage* – the collaborative and continuous building and extending of existing content in pursuit of further improvement.' This produser, as a concept of academic interest, was further developed by Jenkins (2006) in his book on convergence culture. In Jenkins' (2006) view, the produser is not an average consumer but rather an active fan. Fans have always produced art works based existing (often popular) cultural products. In convergence culture, these fans have turned into conversation partners for the media industry. We have to note here that this is a very specific view on the produser as it only includes fans. The extent and limits of who is and who is not a produser will be answered later. First we will further explore the power shift between industry and audiences, as Jenkins (2006) also emphasises that the industry always has infinitely more power than any aggregate of consumers, however, the industry cannot ignore consumers any more, nor think of audiences as passive consumers. In that sense, Toffler's (1971) prediction makes sense and the industry has to respond.

The power shift has hailed a new way to view the audience (Bird, 2011; Curran, Fenton and Freedman, 2012) and their activities. This sense of an active audience, however, is not new and, above all, not all audience members should be considered as produsers (Bird, 2011; Van Dijck, 2009). As José Van Dijck (2009: 43) notes, referring to a journalist for the *Guardian* named Arthur, a rule of thumb suggests that 'if you get a group of 100 people online then one will create content, 10 will "interact" with it (commenting or offering improvements) and the other 89 will just view it'. This phenomenon has been long known in "earlier" new media as news groups. In these groups, the majority of users read the discussion and rarely, if ever, contribute to the ongoing discussions. These people are usually labelled as lurkers and contrasted with posters (Nonnecke and Preece, 2000). Nowadays, lurkers are viewed both positively and negatively. Some would say that lurkers only take and give little, benefiting from public goods and the collective intelligence found on the web. Others would say that lurkers are simply an audience (and provide a good reason for advertisers to be active on the site).

More important, Van Dijck (2009) continues, is to understand the media industry not as a dichotomy of producers and consumers, but as trio of producers, consumers and advertisers.

Box 6.1 Exercise: Test Your Profile

To get some personal experience with the ties between advertisers and the web, try changing some features of your SNS profile such as your gender, age, religion, et cetera. View in the days after how this affects the ads you get to see.

The concept of participatory culture that celebrates an emancipated consumer tends to disregard an important pillar of media production: the need to raise advertising revenue (see Chapters 4 and 5). In that sense, Van Dijck (2009) argues, produsers not only produce media content, but also produce data that are of interest for the advertising industry (cf. Curran *et al.*, 2012).

This notion of data-producing audiences is different from the idea of narrow-casting we presented in the previous chapter. Not only is a share of audiences' attention sold, incredibly detailed data on individual users are collected and combined into profiles enabling, for example, customised advertising through the use of cookies and the data-mining of IP addresses. For example, Facebook's market value was an estimated $100 billion dollars when it first went to the stock exchange. This value is not generated by the content produced by over a billion users, but by the data connected to these users. The possibility for direct marketing based on data from your profile, sites and comments you liked, et cetera, is of tremendous value for the advertising industry. While Facebook doesn't necessarily require a very active participation of its users, as many users do not post much and only "like" other people's posts, we might rethink whether Facebook's users are actually active participators that shift the power relations between consumers and the media industry.

This political economy perspective on the relationship between produsers and the media industry has another node. Media industries have developed strategies to co-opt the labour of produsers for their own benefits, reducing the produser to a material benefactor (Bird, 2011). On one hand, this can be viewed as part of the renegotiations of power between the consumer and the media industry (Jenkins and Deuze, 2008). On the other hand, some studies show that the industry has already appropriated discourse on fan activity, and developed strategies to use these activities to expand (Sundet and Ytreberg, 2009). Interviewing Norwegian media executives, Vilde Sundet and Espen Ytreberg (2009) show how these executives have appropriated words like activity, emotional engagement, audience experimentation and participation in their discourses on how they view the audience. These appropriations obscure the way decisions are made within the industry. For example, Sundet and Ytreberg (2009) state that an emphasis on an experimentation as a motivating factor for an audience to interact and participate with media, promotes a focus on gadgets and a young, male target group. In other words, the media industry seems to have developed strategies for disciplining audience activities and the surveillance thereof (Bird, 2011).

Furthermore, these accounts of the emancipated produser run the risk of separating the produser and her or his activities from the structuring conditions of everyday life (Driscoll and Gregg, 2011). First, the authors show how Jenkins' application of subcultural theory's principles ultimately amounts to 'the overwhelming function of Jenkins' perspective in the book is to offer insight into fan behaviour' (Driscoll and Gregg, 2011: 569). Fan activities have to be placed in a situated context. As Catherine Driscoll and Melissa Gregg (2011) argue, feminist scholars like Janice Radway (1988) have always positioned fans and their activities within a context of identity politics. In the account of the produser, who is (in Jenkins' account) actually a fan, this vital connection to politics and identity has disappeared, stripping the conceptualisations of the produsers of the legacy of feminist scholarship. Fans should not be considered as 'free-floating agents who fashion narratives, stories, objects and practices from myriad bits and pieces of prior cultural productions' (Radway, 1988: 363). How the media relate to identities will be discussed in following chapters. For now we will concentrate on the production of new media content.

We are curious to find out who these produsers are, even if they only make up 1% of the active audience on the web. Overviews of who produces what in digital media are harder to find than those of more traditional media. This is not only due to the fact that the concept of produser is relatively ambiguous, but also because digital media are more dynamic and more volatile than traditional media. Mostly, research reports show numbers on how many people have an account on a social network site. For example the 2012 report of the Pew Research Center[1] show that 50% of people in the US use a social network site, however, only 34% of Lebanese people do, while 3% of people in Pakistan used a social network site (Pew Research Center, 2012). Though these numbers give us insight into the number of people who have signed up to the sites, we do not know whether this also means these people are produsers or that they just have an account.

Sometimes we catch interesting glimpses, such as on the website Information is Beautiful (2009). Here we find that only five people in a 100 create 75% of the tweets. Of those five people 32% are bots. We also find that of all people with a Twitter account, 55% are female, while 45% are male (Information is Beautiful, 2009). In a gender comparison of SNS, women use these sites more often than men do. However, while the top five SNS dominated by female users are Instagram, Facebook, Habbo, Yelp and Docstoc, the top five dominated by men consist of YouTube, LinkedIn, Flickr, Stumble Upon and Last.fm. The female top five contains two private information sites (Instagram and Facebook), one game site (Habbo), one restaurant-finding site (Yelp) and one professional site (Docstoc). The male top five has two video and image hosting sites (YouTube and Flickr), one professional networking site (LinkedIn), one music site (Last.fm) and one plug-in that is used to "stumble upon" the best internet sites (Stumble Upon) (Information is Beautiful, 2012). So, while women's sites focus more on the private, men's sites tend to focus more on public.

The above figures are based on users in the US. Other overviews, such as those found on the site Social Bakers (2013), show that celebratory accounts of women dominating SNS should at least be nuanced in terms of region. Social Bakers (2013) shows that in Europe, North, South and Middle America, Canada, Japan and southern Africa, the ratio of male and female users is close to 50/50, with slightly more female users (1% or 2% in many countries). In the rest of the world, however, the percentage of male users is much higher. In northern and middle Africa and Indonesia, the gender ratio of users is about 70% male and 30% female; in China 60% of the users are male, while 40% are female. In Afghanistan, Pakistan, and India, 70% of the users are male and 30% are female, and in the Middle East 75% of the users are male while 25% of the users are female. These numbers should make us aware that reports and accounts on new media shifting the power balance of the media industries' relations with their audiences and the balance with regard to gender equality should be carefully positioned and are relative on a global level.

One caveat is that many of the overviews are created by commercial companies who want to sell a service to other companies. For example, the company Social Bakers is a marketing company aiming to sell e-marketing to other companies, and therefore create overviews to report the most popular Facebook pages in all countries of the world. It is unclear how the data are generated, and therefore interpreting them as fact should be done with caution.

What does Produsing Mean?

So far we have discussed the industry, a potential power shift in the production of media content, and who the produsers are in terms of their perceived gender. A seemingly simple question that proves itself difficult to answer is 'What does production or producing actually entail?' in the contemporary trends of media convergence, globalisation and mediatisation. Can we consider the texting of 140 characters a form of producing media content? Thus far there is no consensus on when to consider audience participation as media production. James Hamilton (2014) suggests that common conceptions of audiences' production underestimate the variety and diversity of this production. Furthermore, he states, many contemporary studies on the prosumer show negligence towards the fact that audiences have been quite productive for some time. In general we can distinguish two lines of work: one focusing on the media industry, while the other is focused more on the user, including fans but also the broader concept of User Generated Content (UGC) (cf. Blank and Reisdorf, 2012).

User Generated Content

User Generated Content (UGC) is a common term used to indicate the new media content produced by what we formerly knew as audiences. UGC includes a wide range of applications such as news sites, blogs, web shops, photo sites, SNS, file sharing sites, open access software, et cetera. Grant Blank and Bianca Reisdorf (2012) argue that there is little empirical work on the motivations and thoughts of prosumers.

Box 6.2 Early Produsers

Authors of fan fiction are known to be female more often than male. Fan fiction is not a recent phenomenon. Charlotte Brontë for example wrote fan fiction in her early years, and Lewis Carroll's *Alice in Wonderland* was a popular object of fan fiction in its time of appearance. A more recent example is *50 Shades of Grey* by E.L. James that started as fan fiction of the *Twilight* series.

However, in the area of fan art there is quite a large area of work instigated by Jenkins' (1992) work on textual poaching. Poaching means that one illegally uses someone else's ideas. Jenkins (1992) bases himself on the work of Michel de Certeau, who frames audiences' activity as a struggle for the possession of the text. In Jenkins' (1992) view, poaching should be seen as fans taking bits and pieces from existing texts and re-appropriating them, focusing his work on the creations of fans such as fanzines, fan art, fan fiction and fan music. According to him, the majority of these producers of fan fiction are female, but we are uncertain whether this also indicates all types of fan artists to be female more often than male.

Fan art is a small portion of the UGC in general. Looking into UGC, most studies show that men form the majority of creators. The Organisation for Economic Co-operation and Development (OECD, 2007)[2] reports in 2007 that 86% of the creators (i.e. people who produce online content) in Europe are male. Moreover, the majority of these male creators are 16 to 24 years old. As of now, UGC is male dominated. These numbers are relatively surprising. At the dawn of the internet, the medium was expected to be more egalitarian in terms of gender, age, ethnicity, sexuality and so on in the opportunities it offered to its audiences and its usages. Though it is now commonly accepted that gender and technology 'are multidimensional processes that are articulated in complex and contradictory ways which escape straightforward gender definitions', as Van Zoonen (2002: 6) eloquently formulates, the gender disparity is hard to understand.

Some of the explanations for this gender imbalance in UGC, we feel, might be found in what the OECD (2007) calls drivers of UGC: the technological, social, economic, institutional and legal drivers. These drivers should be considered as clusters of mechanisms that underlie the increase of UGC. Each of these drives has a distinct relation to gender, though the OECD does not indicate this specifically, and each of the drivers should, in our opinion, be understood in relation to the other three drivers.

Technological Drivers

The OECD report (2007) suggests that technological development enabled the increase of UGC. The availability of broadband access to the internet, the capacity of hard drives, and the development of software that makes it easier to design and publish content on the web are all technological drivers. Though the OECD (2007) positions these technological drivers among social, economic and legal drivers, the point they develop does breathe a technological determinist air. Many authors have argued against this view on (new) media technologies (MacKenzie and Wajcman, 1999; Williams, 2003), stating that technologies do not instigate social changes. On the contrary, as Leah Lievrouw (2006) postulates, technology is socially shaped. She then continues to define this "social shaping of technology" (SST). According to Lievrouw (2006: 248), SST diverges attention towards the 'importance of human choices and action in technological change, rather than seeing technology as politically and ethically neutral, an independent force with its own inevitable logic and motives, or as a mysterious black box that cannot be analysed socially'. SST then focuses its attention to 'the content of technology and the particular processes involved in innovation' (Williams and Edge, 1996: 865). What this conceptualisation means in terms of gender is further developed in the field of Science and Technology Studies (STS) which incorporates an important feminist node.

Within STS one of the central questions is how new media, like other media products, incorporate barriers against certain groups of users. In other words, some media products are more attractive to certain audiences than others (Oudshoorn, Rommes and Stienstra, 2004). Reasons for these barriers are sometimes sought in the processes of technology design. As Nelly Oudshoorn et al. (2004) show in their research, design teams imagine a user for the new technologies they develop. It is here that a strong alignment between hegemonic masculinity and the technology exists. This dynamic is very similar to the ones discussed in Chapter 5. Hence, we might view media technologies, and the production and use thereof, as forming an environment (what Neil Postman (2000) would call a media ecology) in which a heteronormative, male dominated symbolic order is reproduced.

Other studies that account for the barriers in new media products build upon these notions of hegemonic masculinity in the designing processes of new media by discussing how these have direct impact on the content of these media. Mel Stanfill (2014) for example, shows how web interfaces reinforce and reproduce social logics. For example, when creating a profile on an SNS, you are often offered two options when filling in gender: male or female. Most of the time, male is the default option in these lists. This reproduction of hegemonic masculinity hails the male user as the imagined one (by interpellation, see Chapter 1). Gender is thus mediated by the software architecture of the platform (De Ridder, 2013). For example, when Facebook changed their gender settings in February 2014,[3] allowing its users to choose from 56 different options, it was controversial, but was also celebrated as Facebook transcending dichotomous gender notions. We might wonder how many people actually will scroll down the whole list to find something that actually suits their perceived gender. Unless the options are listed alphabetically, the social logic is not overthrown.

These interface structures allow for certain actions while simultaneously disallowing others. New media, then, are thought of as offering certain affordances to practice agency in comparison to other media (Humphreys and Vered, 2014; Stanfill, 2014). Following Sal Humphreys and Karen Vered (2014) we would like to emphasise that new media offer *different* affordances than older media. Though recent research shows that 'new media have actually *not* radically altered the traditional ideal of passive consumers who should grin and take what they're sold' (Stanfill, 2014: 11) and we can easily spot the association of hegemonic masculinity with technology in the design and the imagined users of new media, some affordances do allow for a more fluid conception of gender. Facebook's multiple gender options are an example, but so are the possibilities to choose an avatar that is gendered differently than the player, or the possibility in the *Sims* to pursue homosexual relationships (cf. Van Zoonen, 2002; Van Doorn, 2011). So while new media reproduce and reinforce more conventional gender logic, simultaneously they allow for more varied gender performance due to their interactive nature.

Social Drivers

The next set of drivers behind the increase of UGC named by the OECD (2007) is of social character. In their report they signal an increased willingness of users to share content and an increased desire to express oneself online. This willingness, however, is mostly shared among those under 25 years of age (OECD, 2007). These social drivers are also related to gender. As we have seen, women are active on different sites and create content for different outlets than men do. Additionally, in Chapters 4 and 5 we have seen that women are historically excluded from media technologies. Women are under-represented in the production of TV, film, newspaper and magazines, which additionally is vertically and horizontally segregated in terms of gender. Many studies show how a similar trend can be viewed for Web 2.0[4] (Ji and Skoric, 2013; Blank and Reisdorf, 2012). To create content a user needs technological ability, to feel comfortable revealing personal data, and a sense of confidence in using Web 2.0. As Pan Ji and Marko Skoric (2013: 224) show: 'Men and women excel in different domains of social networking. Women were found to be more sociable with friends and family members than were males both in cyberspace and in real life.' Linda Jackson, Yong Zhao, Anthony Kolenic, Hiram Fitzgerald, Rena Harold and Alexander Von Eye (2008) refer to this difference as the "new digital divide". The digital divide, they argue, is not so much about access to new media any more, but about the intensity and nature of the use of new media. What we see developing in new media use is not only that women use new media less intensely than men do, but also that this use is vertical and horizontal segregated.

Different to the structures inhabiting new technologies, ability and confidence are based on the users' experiences, background and many other features. As discussed in the previous chapter, girls from an early age are less encouraged to develop technical skills than boys, hence their skills and familiarity with technology later in life are less advanced than boys' skills and familiarity. Along with decreased stimulation to develop these skills, social notions of what it means to be a girl are also at play. Grounding herself in the work of Angela McRobbie and Judith Halberstam, Mary Celeste Kearney (2006) argues that to understand girls' production, a traditional conception of femininity as a master discourse organising girls' and women's lives is not sufficient any more. We must recognize the new gender *habitus* in which girls have access to masculinity. Girls' activities are not confined to the private sphere any more and they are more and more involved in cultural activities that are traditionally male dominated (for example, playing football and creating art). However, Kearney (2006) also notes that girls and women are still scarce in numbers with regard to creators of UGC. This scarcity is not only linked to gender, but intersects with class, which directly relates to the third driver: economics.

Economic Drivers

The third driver indicated by the OECD (2007) is economic in character and points to the decreased costs of internet access, availability of tools for creation and an increase in commercial interest in UGC. OECD then uses this driver to explain the increased production of UGC. However, this driver also features a specific gender dimension.

On a global level, women have lower education and lower wages and hence less access to the internet. Not only will they therefore develop less familiarity and skills with new technologies, but this will also create new gender gaps. In their report *Doubling Digital Opportunities,* the UNESCO Working Group on Broadband and Gender of the Broadband Commission (2013) shows how there is not one, but several gender gaps. Women have less access to new technologies in general, and the consequences of limited access reflect in diminished access to the labour market and in choices and opportunities for education (resulting in different options career-wise). Economic drivers do not only make access easier, as the OECD report mentions, they also create barriers. Though in the West economic drivers work in the advantage of media access for all, in other regions economic drivers form a disadvantage for media access in terms of gender. Similar to the dynamics on underlying the relations of gender and power in the media industries (explored in Chapter 5) that showed that most of these dynamics are historically and socially situated, the drivers in OECD's (2007) report should be thought of as explaining the Western perspective on UGC, not a global one.

Institutional and Legal Drivers

Lastly, the OECD (2007) demonstrates how legislation on copyrights and licensing has become more flexible, allowing for more UGC. It is unclear so far if and how this driver is gendered. Most legislation is formulated gender neutral, but that doesn't mean the consequences of such legislation are. However, at this time, it is unclear how new legislation affects gender and UGC.

Conclusion

In this chapter we have further developed our understanding of media production. Due to a variety of developments, not only in the media industries but also on a technological, social and global level, the concept of production has changed itself. The notion of the prosumer and participatory cultures challenge traditional relations between the media industries and their audiences, offering exciting opportunities for both audiences and industries. However, an all too celebratory account of convergence culture and the power shift it could bring about seems ahistorical and neglecting the commercial character of contemporary media. Though we are attracted to the rebellious idea of the cumbrous industries not being able to catch up with the swift, edgy prosumers and grass roots organisations, we are afraid it is often an illusion. Sadly, there seems to be more and more evidence of the contrary, that media industries incorporate prosumers' activities in their discourses and production.

Technologies are not inherently female or male. While their development and design is usually considered to reify a male symbolic order, consumption and uses of technology are often framed as more feminine (for example for SNS) (cf. Van Zoonen, 2002). However, production and consumption are not separate activities and they mutually construct each other. In between production and consumption we find the text itself, or the media content. As (new) media indeed offer a diversity of affordances for gender play, or contain certain barriers for female users, we are curious to find out how media products do this. In other words, it is time to explore the content of media and how gender practices of consumption have an impact thereon.

Further Reading

Fascinated by the blurring of boundaries within media and media production? For a general introduction we suggest:

- Jenkins, H. (2006). *Convergence Culture: Where Old and New Media Collide*. New York/London: New York University Press.

As discussed in this chapter, Jenkins gives a detailed account on how convergence culture and the prosumer relate to each other and to society. For a more general account of new media we recommend:

- Lievrouw, L.A. and Livingstone, S. (Eds.) (2006). *Handbook of New Media: Social Shaping and Social Consequences of ICTs*. Updated Student Edition. London/Thousand Oaks/New Delhi/Singapore: Sage.

This edited volume offers a multitude of essays on social shaping and social consequences of new media, touching on topics such as youth, power and globalisation. An investigation of how new media production relates to gender can found in:

- Kearney, M. C. (2006). *Girls Make Media*. New York/London: Routledge.

Kearney's book offers a detailed study of what girls produce in terms of films, zines and websites. The social context within which this production takes place is a strong part of her analyses.

Notes

1 The Pew Research Center conducts public opinion polling, demographic research, media content analysis and other empirical social science research. Though its research focuses on the US they also offer some insights into global trends.
2 The (OECD, 2007) speaks of User Created Content instead of User Generated Content. For the purposes of clarity we stick to one term in this chapter.
3 Facebook so far has only introduced these options in the US and the UK; it is unknown if and when these options become available on a global level.
4 Web 2.0 is difficult to define precisely; however, it refers to the possibilities it offers for interactivity, enabling users to contribute content. Grant Blank and Bianca Reisdorf (2012: 539) define it as: 'Using the Internet to provide platforms through which network effects can emerge'.

Part III

Consuming

Chapter 7

Who Consumes What?

Efforts producing media content have the ultimate aim of reaching audiences. Throughout the previous chapters we have employed various concepts, audience, audiences, users, readers, consumers, viewers and so on. But what do all these terms actually mean? Do developments like the rise of convergence culture and increasing globalisation have an impact on notions of the audience? Before embarking on the adventure of exploring the relation between gender and media consumption, we must first answer these questions.

Let us stand still first at the meaning of the word audience. In a recent volume, Richard Butsch and Sonia Livingstone (2014) attempt to disentangle different understandings (discourses) of audiences. In an increasingly global world, we, as media scholars, must be cognizant that conceptions on audiences can be "distinctive" or "native" in specific cultures. Moreover, discourses on the audience are always laden with politics (as discourses incorporate a notion of power, see Chapter 6). Discourses on audiences are both public (i.e. they take place in the media themselves, among friends, but also are part of the industries' ideas on media) and academic (i.e. theories on what audiences entail are formulated among scholars). The latter is especially of interest for us. Due to globalisation, the rise of "new media" and, consequently, convergence culture, the validity of the notion of "audiences" is increasingly debated (see for example De Valck and Teurlings, 2013; Lotz, 2007; Morley, 2006). In Chapter 4, we visited part of this debate when we problematised the notion of media production. Media production is not only in the hands of the industries any more, but in those of the audiences (accumulating in the term prosumer, see Chapter 6).

However, with regard to audiences, the results of these current developments constitute a dichotomous perspective: either the audiences are sitting back and enjoying "old media" or the audiences are active participants and co-creators of new media content. As David Morley (2006) argues, such a conception of "old media audiences" also connotes an extremely negative view of media users as a homogeneous mass of couch potatoes, even though audience research itself has shown the opposite. In this part of the book we will employ the word audiences. Audiences are viewed as producers of meanings at the moment of media consumption: 'Cultural representations and meanings have certain materiality, they are embedded in sounds, inscriptions, objects, images, books, magazines and television programmes. They are produced, enacted, used and understood in specific social contexts' (Barker, 2012: 8). We use the plural audiences to emphasise the multiplicity of the audience as there is no single mass of people passively receiving media texts (cf. Croteau and Hoynes, 2014). However, we would like to ask you, the reader, to bear in mind the multiple meanings of the word audiences and various perspectives on what "audiencing" entails.

A second point of attention is the general meaning of audiences within media studies. In Chapter 6 we have seen how the rise of new digital media fostered new understandings of media production. However, it simultaneously fosters (or forces) new understandings of media reception. Joke Hermes (2014) proposes two paradigms, the "mass media paradigm" and the "Web 2.0 paradigm". While the first refers to a concept of the audiences as a mass with a centralised source and a multitude of dispersed viewers, the latter refers to audiences who match with the prosumer as described in Chapter 6. Using two case studies, Hermes (2014) shows convincingly that the Web 2.0 paradigm is attractive but the mass media paradigm has lost 'little of its heuristic potential in everyday life' (Hermes, 2014: 36). Instead, academic thought within the mass media paradigm is proto-professionalised, meaning that it has become part of everyday understandings about audiences among audiences. However, this does not mean that the mass media paradigm is satisfactory to understand the new developments in media audiences. In Chapters 8 and 9 we will engage more in-depth with the discussion of audiences and their relations to new media.

Third, we would briefly like to visit the notion of audiences in the context of globalisation. Increasing globalisation accounts for many changes in the production and (hence) content of the media. Unquestionably, these changes relate to the concept of the audiences. Production, content and consumption of media need to be understood in relation to each other. Perspectives on media audiences in a globalised media environment are mostly developed with regard to identity. Audiences all over the globe consume more and more international media products (though, as we have seen in Chapter 4, the majority is of Western origin). Many have thought about how this development relates to senses of belonging (Morley, 2001), imagined communities (Anderson, 1983), cultural proximity (La Pastina and Straubhaar, 2003) and more. For example, Asu Aksoy and Kevin Robins (2000) discuss how diasporic audiences (in their case Turkish immigrants living in Germany) negotiate their identities using both homeland media as well as guest-land media. Though these approaches are interesting, it is beyond our aims to discuss them comprehensively. However, we will take globalisation and its meaning for gendered identities into consideration in Chapter 8.

Lastly, we want to draw attention to the difference between the concept of media audiences and the concept of media users. Media user usually refers to overviews of who uses which medium and in what circumstances: 'The actual media habits and uses of media as objects in the context of everyday life, including the spatial and temporal context within which audiences encounter the media' (Siapera, 2010: 181). Often, an ethnographic approach is adopted to study the meanings of media use in everyday life. Studies are usually small in scale and employ participatory observation methods. Morley, one of the progenitors of ethnographic audience research (Press, 2006), postulates that the baseline of this ethnographic approach (Morley, 1986) is that the way we watch television tells us a lot about our views on gender, the family and society. For example, Lynn Spigel's (1992) work on television and the domestic space shows how television was positioned as a "home theatre", placing it within the private sphere of the home. The domestic space, a women's domain, was reorganised to accommodate the new medium. Other studies that focus on media use pay attention to gendered patterns, or sex differences, in media use. According to Julia Wood (2011), there are general differences between women and men and their media use. However, as Fien Adriaens, Elke Van Damme and Cédric Courtois (2011) point out, there is no consensus on media use and its relation to gender. Some studies argue that there is no gender difference (e.g. D'Haenens, Klokhuis and Van Summeren, 2001), while others argue that boys watch more television than girls, play more videogames or listen to different music genres (e.g. Roe, 2000). What is important, though, is not how large the differences between women and men, or boys and girls are, but that media use forms an important context for media consumption.

Studying Audiences

Audience research aims to inform us about what audiences actually do with media texts in everyday living. An interest in what audiences do with the media they consume exists as long as media exists.

Box 7.1 Techno-Panics

Concerns about new technologies are as old as technologies themselves and remarkably similar. Bell Rooney (2011) mentions that, at the advent of the train, there were worries that women's bodies wouldn't be able to travel at 50 miles an hour, as their uteruses would fly out. Generally these concerns are called techno-panics, indicating that people who worry about the consequences of technologies are panicking (an irrational and emotional state). Techno-panics are usually attributed to older people.

> Anything that is in the world when you're born is normal and ordinary and is just a natural part of the way the world works. Anything that's invented between when you're fifteen and thirty-five is new and exciting and revolutionary and you can probably get a career in it. Anything invented after you're thirty-five is against the natural order of things.
>
> (Douglas Adams, 2005 [1999]: 95)

With the advent of the printing press, and books evolving from exclusive hand-copied exemplars into an easily reproducible commodity and hence cheaper information carriers, thoughts on the impact of such a development have been formulated. Increasing literacy and the availability of ideas (other than those preached by institutions like the church) were thought to corrupt the mind. Conrad Gesner (a Swiss biologist, doctor and linguist) wrote in 1545 that too many books are 'confusing and harmful to the brain.' Others celebrated this new freedom of information. In other words, some worried, some saw the dawn of a new era of civilisation. These positive and negative views of the impact of media on audiences are recurring perspectives. Heated debates surround the dawn of each new medium, some predicting the downfall of human kind, others the rise of a new civilisation. Contemporary debates focus mostly on new media, with similar arguments flying around. In 2008 Nicholas Carr (2008) argued something similar to Gesner, stating that the internet scatters our attention, while the book promotes contemplativeness.

Gender is of importance in these debates. In an interview Genevieve Bell, the director of Intel Corporation's Interaction and Experience Research, puts forward the idea that one of the first push backs in debates on new technologies is the vulnerability of women and children to the effects of this technology (Rooney, 2011). Within current debates on new media this notion is exceptionally visible. For example, the internet is thought to be dangerous, especially for girls, as they can fall prey to internet predators who will lure them into sexual practices (see Chapter 9).

Interestingly enough, these debates and arguments are usually not based on research (Hermes and Reesink, 2003). Conclusions about the audience are drawn from assumptions, and contribute to a gendered discourse on media audiences. Popular media are especially subject to criticism. From the 1970s onwards, out of interest in subcultures and partly as a critique on textual determinism, scholars from the CCCS focused attention on subcultures describing boys and men and their practices with popular culture. In 1976 Angela McRobbie and Jenny Garber (also members of the CCCS) drew attention to this "biased" focus on boys and men, or rather the absence of girls and girls' practices within the CCCS's work. In their essay, they postulate that because girls are subordinated in society, their experiences differ from those of boys and call for research on the experiences and practices of girls. Their work and the overall work of the CCCS instigated academic interest in the media as they 'are understood by audiences' (Lewis, 1991). With regard to gender, the signifying practices of gendered audiences around the world were researched. However, other traditions, like effect studies, did not disappear from the field of studying media.

Beside the rich academic field of audience studies, the industry always had a particular interest in audiences and their gender. Media products were always targeted at specific gendered audiences. For example, when magazines entered the market, women's magazines were also produced involving women in its production force (Chapter 4). Similarly, when radio became a mass medium, it was not long before the radio soap targeting women (as they were responsible for the purchase of washing detergents) was invented (Gledhill and Ball, 2013). Broadcasters and production companies invest tremendous amounts in audience research as they want to know audiences and market shares and profile them in order to sell their products to advertisers. Advertisers, then, are mostly interested in finding out how to reach their target audiences, with gender being one of the most important markers. Studies into media use sometimes answer to the industry's request for knowledge. Rating companies like the American *The Nielsen Company* (take a peek at www.nielsen.com/us/en.html) exist in many countries. The technological developments in media cause these processes to become more complicated. How does one measure, for instance, who has (illegally or legally) downloaded and binge-watched the latest HBO hit series, for example?

With regard to audiences, there are many questions to raise: 'Who are they?'; 'Why do they consume what they consume?'; 'How do audiences construct meanings with regard to the media texts they consume?'; 'Are audience members all the same, or are they all individuals with specific and unique interpretations?'; 'Is there some middle ground?'; 'How does the concept of audiences relate to production practices of the media industry (and of audiences themselves)?'; and 'What has the content of media have to do with that?'. To explore possible answers to these questions and their relation to gender we will construct a brief sketch of the different academic lines of thought on media audiences and their consumption. The most important are effect theories, cultivation theory, uses and gratifications theory, and the encoding/decoding model. Though we discuss each of these disciplines separately, we would like to note that some of these disciplines share thoughts and ideas, while some criticise each other. Our separation of these disciplines is therefore somewhat artificial. In Chapters 8 and 9 we will focus on why people consume what they consume and how we can understand audiences within their context. We will discuss how the characteristics of media representation and the specificities of the medium itself interrelate with the social context and competences of the audiences and the context of consumption (Van Zoonen, 1994).

Effect Theories

Perhaps the most famous study in media effects is Hadley Cantril's (1954) study of the effect of the broadcasting of the radio play *War of the Worlds*, based on the book by H.G. Wells and directed by Orson Welles. The narrative concerns an invasion of England by aliens from Mars. In the primary character's neighbourhood, a meteor crash turns out to be the crash of a metal cylinder from which Martians appear. The Martians build machines, tripods, and try to conquer the world, while feeding on human blood. In the end the Martians die because of the earth's microbes and bacteria to which they have no resistance. Orson Welles directed the radio play, which was broadcast on October 30th,

1938 (one day prior to Halloween). As Welles wanted the play to be as realistic as possible, many "news flashes" were incorporated into the play. As the story goes, many people listening to the play thought it was interrupted by a genuine news flash. A wave of panic swept over the country. Within a month, stories of this panic had spread to 12,500 newspaper articles all over the world. The broadcasting of the radio play might well be the first global mass media event, and it is famous, as it is also one of the first mass media studies that focuses on effects.

Box 7.2

You can listen to the radio play of *War of the Worlds* at www.mercury theatre. info/.

Hadley Cantril was interested in mass behaviour, and trying to answer the question of '[w]hy this broadcast frightened some people but not others' (Cantril, 1954: 413). Though in later years Cantril's study has been criticised for its over-dramatisation of the size of the effect (all in all not that many really panicked, and no real serious events took place), his explanations of the effect are still in vogue. For example, media use and people's distracted attention (one reason is that some people missed the announcement at the beginning of the radio play that it was a fictional play) is now commonly known as selective perception (McQuail, 2005). Cantril's study is usually positioned as an example of the hypodermic needle/magic bullet theory (media injecting content in audiences). Lately voices argue that the *Invasion from Mars* should be considered a text bridging the era of the hypodermic needle perspective and the era of limited effects, therefore marking the paradigm shift in media effects studies (Pooley and Socolow, 2013). The limited effects model that evolved within the field of media effects is usually credited to Paul Lazarsfeld. The model explains and explores the many reasons why the media do not have such a large effect on audiences (McQuail, 2005). However, the basic assumptions remain intact: audience members are considered to be passive consumers who absorb media content. Media are thus considered to be structuring, or limiting, an individual audience member's agency.

Studies on media effects come in many forms and shapes, and the concept of effect itself is hard to define. We might, for example, view dressing up as Darth Vader, Jack Sparrow or Daenerys Targaryen during the carnival or Halloween as a (harmless) media effect, while the violent play of children imitating *Pokémon* fights on the playground could also be viewed also a media effect. In general, media effects can be understood as a causal relation between media content and individuals' behaviour or perspectives on the world. As became clear in the discussion described earlier, most media effects are assumed to be ill natured.

Over the decades much research has been devoted to effects, especially effects of violent and sexual media content. This content is assumed to have a causal relationship to individuals' behaviour in terms of violence or sex (deviance). Playing a lot of video games such as *Grand Theft Auto* and *Assassin's Creed* is thought to have many effects including disinhibition, imitation and de-sensitisation (cf. Goldstein, 1998). Nevertheless, most causal relations shown in studies are rather weak and it is very difficult to isolate an effect and prove a causal relationship. However, this does not mean that effects are absent (cf. Croteau and Hoynes, 2014). On the contrary, researchers within this discipline generally agree that there is some effect (although opinions vary widely about the size of it).

It is important to note that effects from this perspective are always considered bad. As Staiger (2005: 19) states: 'I seriously doubt that all the hoopla about media would have occurred if people thought only what they judged to be good effects were coming from an experience with media.' All the hoopla is not instigated only by the media themselves, though, but public opinion in general leans towards a conception of the media as having a causal effect on individuals and society as such. Current debates on sexualisation, discussed in Chapter 9, are illustrative.

A fair share of studies on media effects has an experimental set-up and most of the time gender is part of the design (at least the ratio male/female of the participants is noted, whether researchers study gender or sex differences is up to the reader of these studies to decide). For example, current research on the effects of violent video games shows not only that these games are more attractive to men (or male adolescents), but also that men have a greater need for sensation and aggression in video play, they are better at justifying the violence they use in the game and they are less emphatic (Hartmann, Möller and Krause, 2014).

Box 7.3 Ten Things Wrong

David Gauntlett (1998) is a well-known critic of the "effects-model". In a famous article he describes the 'ten things wrong with the effects-model', criticising the methods and the assumptions of this academic tradition. You can find this text at www.theory.org.uk/david/effects.htm and form your own opinion.

Though studies like these partly explain why men play more violent video games than women, they do not explain why men are better at justifying aggressive acts. Experimental effects research can answer some questions, while it leaves others unanswered.

Another contemporary strand of effect studies is concentrated on media use and its effect on body images. These studies almost exclusively focus on women. They claim that exposure to media has an (negative) impact on body satisfaction of female adolescents (e.g. Knauss, Paxton and Alsaker, 2007; Knobloch-Westerwick and Romero, 2011; Shooler and Trinh, 2011) and women (e.g. Tiggeman and Pickering, 1996; Want, 2009). Most research is done on the exposure to television and magazines, but recently new media are a topic of investigation (Tiggeman and Miller, 2010). The key notion in these kinds of research is socialisation, or sex role theory (see Chapter 1). It is argued that media socialise (young) women in a gendered perception of the ideal body and thinness. Sometimes this argument is taken to the extreme, mostly in public debate, and media are blamed for the increasing number of girls that suffer from eating disorders.

These, and other effect studies, have received a fair share of criticism. Typically, these studies use an experimental design taking both the research subject as the media exposure out of a naturally occurring situation. People do not watch commercials on a computer and then answer questions about their perceptions of what they just have seen. Rather, commercials form a break in between the programmes we want to watch. Questions are raised about these and many other aspects of the experimental design, such as the validity of media responses in such unnatural settings, whether the media exposure can be isolated from peers and parents, and whether it is just to treat audiences as inadequate and passive "dupes" (cf. Gauntlett, 1998). More important, though, is the underlying assumption of gender. These studies talk about gender, but measure sex. As Van Zoonen argues:

> Audience reaction is conceptualized as a dichotomous activity of accepting sexist messages or rejecting them. Either audiences can accept media output as true to reality, in which case they are successfully socialized, brainwashed by patriarchy or lured into the idea that what they see and read is "common sense", or they see through these tricks the mass media play on them and reject the sexist, patriarchal, capitalist representation of the world.
>
> (1994: 35)

This mechanic idea of gender audiences is also notable in another discipline: cultivation theory.

Cultivation Theory

Similar to socialisation is cultivation theory (aka cultivation hypothesis, cultivation thesis), perceiving media – specifically television – as a symbolic world that sustains values and norms upon which humans act and base their behaviour. The task of television, as the most important public storyteller, is the cultivation of social realities,

All societies have evolved ways of explaining the world to themselves and to their children. Socially constructed "reality" gives a coherent picture of what exists, what is important, what is related to what, and what is right. The constant cultivation of such "realities" is the tasks of mainstream rituals and mythologies.

(Gerbner and Gross, 1979: 367)

Arguing that television is notably different from earlier media (it is free of charge, it enters the home, it visualises), George Gerbner and Larry Gross (1979: 364) present television as the most important public storyteller: 'Television is likely to remain for a long time the chief source of repetitive and ritualized symbol systems cultivating the common consciousness of the most far-flung and heterogeneous mass publics in history.' Indeed, time spent with the TV (be it a traditional TV set, or live streaming on a tablet) is still very high in comparison to other media. For example, in the US half of the leisure time for adults (2.8 hours per day) is spent on watching TV (US Bureau of Labor Statistics, 2014), while in the UK adults watched 3 hours and 52 minutes of TV each day (Ofcom, 2014).

There are important differences between cultivation and socialisation. The first difference with socialisation theory is that in cultivation theory the symbolic world is thought to reinforce already existing worldviews, values and norms (the word cultivation also points to this). Socialisation proposes that new norms and values are incorporated by audiences. The second difference is that cultivation theory aims its arrows on what Gerbner and Gross (1979) call the basic assumptions and perception of the facts of life, instead of on displayed behaviour. A third important difference is that cultivation theory aims for longitudinal effects of the whole of the media diet, instead of the experimental set-up that shows short-term effects of individual instances of media content (and generalisation to long-term effects have to be assumed). Lastly, Gerbner and Gross (1979) position cultivation theory as a critique on traditional effects studies and their centralising of the disruptive power of the media. They argue that this view is anachronistic, as they state on page 369: 'Once the industrial order has legitimized its rule, the primary function of its cultural arm [TV] becomes the reiteration of that legitimacy and the maintenance of established power and authority.' So while media effects researchers fear that violent media content instigates aggressive behaviour of what Gerbner and Gross call the "lower orders" (poor people, ethnic and racial minorities, children, and women), cultivation theory views the symbolic world as ruled by violence as 'cultivating uniform assumptions, exploitable fears, acquiescence to power, and resistance to meaningful change'. This is very similar to a Marxist view on the impact of media, as discussed in Chapter 4.

The concept of media exposure lies at the heart of cultivation theory; how much media are actually consumed by the audiences under research?

Box 7.4 Exercise: Media Diary

Track your own media use for a full week. Write down each day which types of media you have encountered. Try to not only think of 'regular' media such as TV, radio, YouTube, Facebook, et cetera, but also try to trace your encounters in the public space, such as billboards, adverts in public transports and so on. Be as precise as possible about the kind of content in terms of genre. At the end of the week, reflect on the amount of time you have been in contact with media content, and what kind of messages were prevalent. What kind of messages were cultivated?

A distinction is made between heavy viewers and light viewers. Gerbner and Gross (1979) show how heavy viewers give a "television answer" more often than light viewers. Heavy viewers overestimate their chances to get involved in some type of violence (these viewers estimated 10% in a regular week), while in reality this number is much lower.

In Gerbner and Gross' original article, heavy viewers watch 240 minutes of television or more per day. Nowadays, this number might be too small, as the average viewing time has increased over time. For example, in the Netherlands, the average viewing time was 120 minutes per day in 1990. In 2000 this number had increased to 163 minutes, while in 2013 Dutch viewers watch an average of 195 minutes per day (SKO, 2014).

This study has its critics. First, Gerbner and Gross discuss the distinction between heavy and light viewers within the American context of their research (cf. Van Zoonen, 1994). Viewing habits diverge tremendously on a global level. The Economist reports that in 2007, people in the US watch more than eight hours of television per day on average, while the Swiss only watch a little over two hours per day (Economist, 2009). Compared to the numbers of the Bureau of Labor Statistics in the US, who report only 2.8 hours per day devoted to television, the numbers used in cultivation theory should at least be assessed critically. Additionally, the distinction between heavy and light viewers also pushes other relevant social background elements from the scene. Why are the heavy viewers heavy viewers? This issue underlies a more methodological critique. Though a correlation can be shown, this correlation does not indicate the direction of the relationship or the nature of the relationship.

Within this tradition, Nancy Signorielli has specifically focused her research on gender. She explored the image of men and women in prime-time network drama television and the relationship between television viewing and maintaining sexist views (1989, 1997, 2009; Signorielli and Bacue, 1999; Signorielli and Morgan, 2001). She concluded that sex role images have been stable, traditional and conventional over the years. Additionally, she concludes that viewing a lot of TV may be related to having more sexist views of women's role in society.

Current research focuses more often on digital media and seems to confirm Signorielli's results (cf. Dill and Thill, 2007).

Within cultivation theory audiences are still passive, though they are already different from the empty vessel approach that typically underlies media effects studies. From 1970 onwards we find a new conceptualisation of audiences as more active, and media consumption is understood as taking place within the context of the audience.

Uses and Gratifications

In 1959, Elihu Katz responds to a then current debate on the viability and vitality of the study of mass media. Some, with Bernard Berelson leading, declared the field of mass communication to be dead. In his paper, Katz argues that a certain strand of this research that focuses on communication as mass persuasion might be dead, but there is a part that survives and thrives as well (Katz, 1959). Katz then proposes a new direction for mass media research called "Uses and Gratifications" (U&G). Instead of 'What do the media do to people?', research should be geared towards 'What do the people do with the media?' (Katz, 1959: 3). One interesting remark Katz (1959) makes is that this approach broadens studies to include popular culture, something usually within the domain of humanities (Katz, 1959: 2): '[I]t represents a new kind of interdisciplinary coalition which, although unfashionable, may prove fruitful [...].' The perspective on the audiences takes a turn from passive to active, but also the perspective on mass media research takes a turn from looking into "serious media" as weapons of persuasion, to looking into popular culture. Though Katz argues this might be promising, still today a full integration of both disciplines has not taken place.

The U&G perspective was still relatively new in 1959. One of the earliest (perhaps even the first) research within this tradition was Herta Herzog's study on radio soaps.

Box 7.5 Out of the Question: A documentary movie

The movie Out of the Question: Women, Media, and the Art of Inquiry investigates the role of women in early media research. The movie is accompanied by a website (www.outofthequestion.org) which 'provides biographical and bibliographical information about a group of pioneering women in the fields of communication and media research'. The site contains a welter of information of women's roles in media research. One pressing issue they want to address is what we might call the 'symbolic annihilation of women from academic media research'.

Herzog (1944) argued that as the daytime radio serial took up a large share of the audience, it was worthwhile investigating that audience. In her study she identified multiple uses and three major gratifications: emotional release, opportunities for wishful thinking and obtaining advice. In studies that followed, more gratifications and uses were defined.

Important to note in the U&G approach is that it poses media content as offering certain options to the audience. The audience is active and acts on a certain need, seeking to gratify it with media content. Differences between audience members are attributed to psychological and personal differences. Currently, new media's U&G are investigated. Journal articles with titles like 'Gender and the Internet: Women Communicating and Men Searching' (Jackson, Ervin, Gardner and Schmitt, 2001) emphasise the differences between the use of online communication by men and women. Some authors argue that new media offers different options than traditional media (Sundar and Limperos, 2013).

As with all models, the U&G approach has been subject to critique. First, the approach is still somewhat mechanistic (Van Zoonen, 1994). A rather function-alist assumption underlies the activity of the audience members who show rational behaviour when choosing which medium and what content to consume. However, we know that audience behaviour is much more complex than this. For example, we know that many TV viewers are non-selective in their viewing behaviour. We sit down and zap along till we find something that interests us enough to stick with it. Rational thoughts may not have taken place at all. The predictive power of the model (predicting media choice based on the gratifications it offers) is therefore weak (McQuail, 2005).

Furthermore, we would like to draw attention to the utilisation of gender in these studies. Gender is proposed as an explaining factor in a rather essentialist way. First, gender cannot be isolated from other markers such as class, ethnicity or media competences. Often these studies are quantitative in nature and only operationalise gender as a male/female dichotomy. The analyses usually focus on differences between male and female participants, which are then explained in terms of attributes that supposedly belong to male or females. For example, one of the explanations as to why men enjoy violent video games more than women do is that they score lower on the empathy trait (cf. Hartmann et al., 2014). Apparently, empathy is a female trait. Earlier studies (Zillmann, 1988) mostly attribute these kinds of differences to gender socialisation (or, in this particular study by Dolf Zillmann (1988) the place in the menstrual cycle!). Contemporary studies leave a nuanced explanation of gender differences behind. This is a kind of switching around the U&G approach that states that differences between audience members stem from content, experience and situation (and not because audience members are different by "nature"). By focusing the design and analysis solely on gender, these studies boil down to a group comparison, glossing over other aspects such as experiences and situation. The context of media use and how media are used in daily routines are absent (Bilfereyst, 1997). For example, in Chapter 6 we discussed the access to new media by girls. White, affluent girls have more access than any other group of girls, allowing these girls to develop certain skills that others cannot. Hence, they will have different media experiences than girls with less access, which is of crucial importance when studying U&G.

The difference in media experiences and their relation to U&G can be extended to a global level. Access to media technologies, literacy and social class are all part of the set of skills developed and experiences. On a global level, women have less access (see Chapter 6) and therefore develop less skills and less familiarity with media. Arguing from a U&G perspective, it can be expected that both uses and gratifications differ tremendously regionally. As Ali Salman and Samsudin Rahim (2012) show in their study on the differences between natives and migrants in Malaysia, for the latter group literacy is of crucial importance to getting any gratification from the internet.

U&G approach positions the audiences as more active than media effects studies and cultivation theory. However, it does not answer any questions about what happens in between, between the need that instigated a use and the gratification derived. Context and experience seem to have disappeared from the model altogether. Another approach that puts the activity of the audiences central in its study is the encoding/decoding model.

Encoding/Decoding

An even deeper approach into the activities of audiences is the encoding/decoding model, launched by Stuart Hall in 1973 in a paper called *Encoding And Decoding in Television Discourses*. Referring to Umberto Eco, Hall argues for a semiotic approach to what he calls "televisual language" that does not halt with the formalistic analysis of television discourse, but that 'must also include a concern with the "social relations" of the communicative process, and especially with the various kinds of "competences" (at the production and the receiving end) in the use of that language' (Hall, 1973: 2).

What is really innovative about this approach is that it views production, content and reception of television as interrelated to each other and as embedded in society, including its social and economic structures. At the heart of the encoding/decoding model we find the concept of sense making. Embedded in social and economic structures, but also in organisational routines, producers (encoders) construct (encode) a message, a sign vehicle using codes (that in turn are regulated by language – see Chapter 1 for an explanation of this semiotic understanding). Important here is that Hall (1973) notes that audiences' responses, images of the audiences, and expectations about the audiences are a vital part of the production process.

Once the product is accomplished, the message is distributed among the audiences, after which it must once more be translated into societal structures (decoded). Similar to encoders, the audiences are also embedded in social structures. The meanings they derive from the message are embedded in the audiences' frameworks of knowledge, the structures of production, and the technical infrastructure (as different technologies have different affordances).

The media message (the TV programme, the magazine ad, the newspaper article and so on) functions as a meaningful discourse.

There are a few important elements in the model that we would like to draw attention to: its circular character, the (a)symmetry between encoding and decoding, and the event of interpretation. First, as audiences are a part of the encoding process and the production context is part of decoding (as the audiences use this knowledge to construct meanings), the model is circular; encoding feeds into decoding, which in turn feeds into encoding again. Hence, it does not only visualise the relations between production, content and reception, it also discards of a linear idea of media transmission.

Second, the processes of encoding and decoding are not necessarily symmetric. This is due to the semiotic nature of codes. These codes are thought of as polysemic, though their polysemic potential is structured by both encoder's and decoder's environments (Hall, 1973). As encoder and decoder are not equivalent, their frameworks of knowledge (might) differ, something we will explore in Chapter 8. However, Hall (1973) argues that polysemic does not mean the same thing as plural:

> Indeed, the way it is structured in its combination with other elements serves to delimit its meanings within that specified field, and effects a "closure", so that a preferred meaning is suggested. There can never be only one, single, univocal and determined meaning for such a lexical item, but [...] its possible meanings will be organized within a scale which runs from *dominant* to *subordinate*. [emphasis in original]
>
> (Hall, 1973: 9)

Hall (1973) develops three possible readings: the dominant, the negotiated and the oppositional reading. The dominant reading is when an audience member decodes a message in terms of the reference code (the code used by the encoder) full and straight, as the producers hoped it would. This is, according to Hall, an ideal typical idea of "perfectly transparent communication". The negotiated reading refers to the negotiation of audiences with codes they, for example, object to. So, while there is acknowledgement of the dominant code, due to situational context some codes are adapted. The audience is trying to work around problems in the text (Staiger, 2005). The last reading, the oppositional one, refers to an audience member's reading of the codes as in opposition of the dominant code, fitting them into a different frame of knowledge. We have already visited many such interpretations when we discussed representations in Chapters 1 through 3.

Third, we would like to stand still at the moment of interpretation, as this shows a significant difference to previous models. The model presents to us the understanding of audiences as actively interpreting media texts they read. In a sense, this makes us understand audience activity taking place before anything else happens. As Hall (1973: 3) argues, '[b]efore this message can have an "effect" (however defined), or satisfy a "need" or be put to a "use", it must first be perceived as a meaningful discourse and meaningfully de-coded'.

Innovative as it might be, the encoding/decoding model is also subject to criticism. Some argue that not all texts do reproduce a dominant ideology (as we have seen in Chapter 4 regarding *South Park*), therefore determining the preferred reading is difficult. Others argue that most readings are negotiated and therefore the model does not really explain anything (Staiger, 2005). In this regard, James Curran (1990) stresses that television texts are not totally open and the dominant preferred reading of the text steers possible readings even more. Another point of critique is the celebratory account of the activities of the audience. The active audience is often positioned as "reading against the grain," and resisting the dominant reading. We need to be careful to not entangle the notion of active audiences with that of resistance (cf. Kellner, 1995). Additionally, reading against the grain, or negotiated meanings are deemed as pleasurable. Meaning that audiences who construct an oppositional reading do so to derive pleasure from a media text that contains a preferred meaning they do not wish to engage with (cf. Fiske, 1987). This might not always be the case. Some audiences do not derive any pleasure from certain media texts, because they do not understand it, misinterpret it or simply because they feel there is nothing to like (cf. Kuipers, 2006). Morley (1980) called this a rejected reading. Also, Hermes (2005) argues that some audiences are just not that active at all. Despite these criticisms, the model has generated a diversity of research on media audiences and has firm grounding in cultural studies.

Many groundbreaking studies have been conducted from this perspective. Examples are David Morley's (1980) *Nationwide*, Tamar Liebes and Elihu Katz's (1990) *Exporting Meanings*, and Ien Ang's (1985) *Watching Dallas*. None of these studies use gender as an essential feature explaining certain readings (be they subversive or not). The emphasis lies with questions of pleasure; how do certain audiences enjoy certain media types. Sometimes, this type of work results in ideas on gendered viewing. An example is the gendered genres, such as soap operas and the daily talk show. There is, however, a lot of room left for such research. Livingstone (1998), for example, questions why there is little to no research on male audiences of these genres.

Conclusion

The four strands of academic inquiry into media audiences are each useful to answer certain research questions. However, most (effect studies, cultivation theory and U&G approach) give us some insight into gendered patterns of media use but do not delve deeper into why this might be. The last approach, encoding/decoding, suits our purposes the best as it allows a fluid and dynamic conception of gender, gives room to the polysemic character of media texts and has embedded the idea that the production, content and reception of media are tightly related. In the following chapters we will further investigate audiences from this perspective. The frames of knowledge, the context of media audiences, will be a point of scrutiny in Chapter 8. What exactly are these frameworks made of and how can we understand them in relation to gender? In Chapter 9 we dig deeper into current debates on audiences and gender. Surely, almost 40 years after McRobbie and Garber (1976), times have changed and so have conceptions of audiences and gender.

Further Reading

The theories discussed in this chapter are discussed in most introductions to media studies. However, we recommend to your attention:

- Staiger, J. (2005). *Media Reception Studies*. New York/London: New York University Press.

Staiger presents us a detailed and critical account of research in media consumption touching upon various genres. Hence, the book offers a nuanced view on media audiences and intersections with gender, ethnicity and sexuality.

Chapter 8

The Consumer Situated

Media products can mean different things to different people. For example, about the videogame *Journey* (Sony) one player remarks: 'But playing it with another person was unbelievable. Mind-blowing. Thinking about it now as I'm writing this is still giving me chills. [...] And it's a truly unique and beautiful and amazing experience because of it' (Cundy, 2012). However, opinions differ and another player expresses an oppositional interpretation: 'After all the hype, when it's all said and done this is a terrible game. [...] The game itself is pretty but oh so simple and boring. As for the co-op all you do is watch other people doing their own thing. What a joke. and *[sic]* the game is so short it's not even funny' (Vagrant009, 2012). While the first player experienced a mind-blowing game, the second thought it was really boring. Clearly, these two people had contradictory experiences with the same game, or they have constructed different, even clashing, readings of the same media product. As it is impossible to find out who these two people are, we cannot interview them about their experiences. Therefore it is impossible to find out why they had such opposing experiences. In the previous chapter, we discovered that the social-historical context of the reader is at play here; different frameworks of knowledge can result in different interpretations. In this chapter we will explore this perspective further. How exactly does social-historical context contribute to the construction of different readings? How is gender of importance for your social-historical context? How is gender related to audiences' experiences of pleasure when they consume media? To answer these questions, we delve into the relationship between social context and one's identity and gender. As suggested in Chapter 2, our identities are discursive constructs that are partly informed by media texts. Media texts function as technologies of gender (De Lauretis, 1987). Media produce understandings of gender. However, one's identity (of which gender is part) is also quintessential in the development of discursive resources necessary to read any media text. This dialogic process of how identity and readings of media texts mutually inform each other forms the core of this chapter. At the end of the chapter we will still not be able to pinpoint why Cundy and Vagrant009 had such different experiences, but we will be able to envision it.

Identity and Frameworks of Knowledge

Our interpretation of any media product takes place within our personal, and therefore unique, framework of knowledge (Hall, 1973). In a metaphysical sense, our framework is dependent on the entirety of our existence, on "who we are". More concrete, frameworks of knowledge are tightly related to our identities. Our bodily, social and cultural features play a role in the construction of our identity, the reflexive "narrative about the self" (Giddens, 1991). Additionally, some features are pivotal for the development of cultural competences, or rather cultural capital. Both the reflexive narrative and the cultural capital relate to gender and both are pivotal for our frameworks of knowledge, also called discursive resources, in which decoding of media content takes place.

The reflexive narrative about the self (Giddens, 1991) is constructed by the individual. However, these narratives are discursive projects, meaning that the individual is not totally free to construct whatever narrative she or he wants to. For example, when you are someone's sister or brother, this is a part of your identity that you cannot change. Yet, it is up to you to decide what kind of sister or brother you are. Will you be the older sister who functions as a role model for a younger sibling to look up to? Or would you rather be the older sister who indulges in playing with the younger sibling, taking the opportunity to be "a child again"? This decision is not arbitrary, it impacts your identity and it is structured by the composition of your family, class, cultural norms and values, and so on (cf. Johnson, 1993). It does matter, for example, whether you and your sibling live together in a privately owned home with two parents who are together as opposed to being divorced. The way your parents interact with each other and with you and your sibling is of relevance. The years between you and your brother or sister are significant. Many years, say ten, offers different opportunities for relationships than between siblings of, say, two years apart.

Indubitably, gender is also a structuring factor, both in an embodied and disembodied way. Embodied experiences are related to physical features. For example, during adolescence, boys' voices break and girls get their period. Both experiences can lead to embarrassing moments and both are gender specific. If you experienced such an embarrassing moment during adolescence you might forever understand mediated stories about similar experiences differently than someone who did not live through such a moment. However, more often these gendered experiences are disembodied, or not directly related to the body. Social structures, then, play a more important role. US-based research in schools shows how teachers (male and female) tend to interact more often with male students than with female students. In general, male students receive more (positive and negative) comments on their academic endeavours and their conduct (Duffy, Warren and Walsh, 2001). Men therefore get a sense of being taken seriously on an academic level (even when they get negative comments), while women experience a lack of academic acknowledgment. It is easy to understand how this shapes your experiences as a student, and consequently also your narrative about yourself.

Media experiences are also important for the construction of our identities. Gendered representations inform us both on behaviour and looks. For example, in the *WikiHow* on 'how to be good brother', statements such as 'be respectful' (not big mouthing parents or teachers), 'be responsible' (do not use drugs or alcohol) and 'avoid violence' are top of the list (WikiHow, 2014a). While for being a sister, *WikiHow* lists advice such as 'be thoughtful' (remember birthdays and special occasions), 'help your sibling with homework or work' and 'attend any extracurricular activities with your sibling' (WikiHow, 2014b). The differences in advice are telling of how gender is expected to be part of siblinghood. If you are a boy, you are prone to get into fights (and you should show your sibling you know better) and as a girl you should be thoughtful towards your sibling's feelings (and care for them). As these are wiki-entries, they are the work of a group of people and therefore show a consensual understanding of sister- and brotherhood that are clearly gendered. In other words, they are part of the discourse on gender. The accompanying pictures also give an idea of what girls and boys are supposed to look like (cf. Barker, 2012). Media discourses on gender structure the reflexive narrative of our selves. This does not mean that gender determines the narrative – we are not only men or women – nor is gender a continuous aspect of our everyday lives.

We would now like to draw attention to the suggestion of "structuredness of the roles available". You can choose your role, though some positions will be more easily available and attractive than others. Partly, this is dependent on societal discourses and dominant notions on what it means to be a girl or a boy, a man or a woman. For another part, this is more specifically tied to your habitus and your cultural capital.

The habitus and cultural capital are concepts developed by French sociologist Pierre Bourdieu (2010 [1979]) in his theory of taste and class. Based on a large survey among over 1,200 people on their cultural preferences, Bourdieu (2010 [1979]) formulates his ideas on the habitus, cultural capital and distinction. The three notions are interrelated as follows: cultural taste (the division between highbrow and lowbrow taste) functions as a tool to maintain the status quo, to maintain the cultural boundaries between the elite and lower classes. For example, in the Western world visiting museums and enjoying classical music are highly valued and viewed as more legitimate forms of cultural consumption than reading comics and watching TV. According to Bourdieu, this is in the interest of the elite as it gives them a means to distinguish themselves from the lower classes in terms of "good taste". This "good taste" for the right cultural products is defined by cultural capital: the cultural competences one has developed either by schooling or by inheriting them from one's family. According to Paul DiMaggio (1991), cultural competences can be divided into cultural capital and cultural resources. DiMaggio formulates (1991: 134) cultural capital as referring 'to proficiency in the consumption of and discourse about generally prestigious – that is, institutionally screened and validated – cultural goods'. Cultural resources, which indicate 'any form of symbolic mastery that is useful in specific relational context', are different in that they do not engage with valorised symbolic goods.

Crucial here is the notion of the habitus: a kind of mental structure, a way of thinking, one develops from infancy to adulthood onwards that is dependent on one's environment. Through inculcation, Bourdieu (2010 [1979]) argues, certain dispositions are created, ways of feeling and doing things, among which is our cultural taste. Cultural taste hence feels natural, even though it is a construct. The elite uses cultural taste as a strategy to distinguish themselves from other social groups, and because you inherit cultural capital partly from your family, it is also a way to sustain this distinction over generations.

Bourdieu's (2010 [1979]) development of cultural capital is important in two ways, it makes us understand the difference in cultural competences in quite a direct way, and it makes us understand the gender differences in cultural taste, like gendered genre preferences. First, the direct way: cultural capital impacts your framework of knowledge directly. The education you received, the museums you did or did not visit, and many other practices all contribute to our framework. Second, and more indirectly, our habitus also impacts our perceptions of gender and what options with regard to our gender identity are available to us. A simple example from Bourdieu (2010 [1979]: 188) is his explanation of why fish is not considered a manly food in the lower classes. The reason for this, he describes, is the fact that fish has to be eaten 'with restraint, in small mouthfuls, chewed gently, with the front of the mouth, on the tips of the teeth (because of the bones). The whole masculine identity – what is called virility – is involved [...]'. Lower class men, in other words, need to be able to "dig in" and chew their food in an unrestrained way. Later he states that the higher up one goes in class, the less distinguished the differences between gender rules become. Higher class men experience their masculinity differently as lower class men, as they can eat their fish (and other things) in a restrained way as described by Bourdieu. As such, cultural capital informs us about gender. Some even take it one step further. For example, Charlotte Brunsdon (1982) argues, we can speak of female cultural competencies. The habitus in that sense is also responsible for the 'feminine competencies associated with the responsibility for "managing" the sphere of personal life' (Brunsdon, 1982: 36). Not, as Brunsdon (1982) emphasises, that these are natural, innate competences of females, rather they are culturally constructed skills.

The intersection with class is inevitable when discussing Bourdieu's (2010 [1979]) work. Rather, it was one of the main critiques of his work; Bourdieu focuses his work exclusively on class relations and positions these relations above other social divisions (Moores, 1993). Additionally, Bourdieu's work is rather functionalist. The elites reproduce their own cultural taste to maintain the status quo, allowing little room for radical social change (Moores, 1993). Nevertheless, Bourdieu's field theory is still today an important notion in the understanding of media consumption. Recently, the distinction between low- and high-class cultural consumption has been enriched and nuanced with the notion of the "cultural omnivore" (e.g. Van Eijck and Lievens, 2008). Many people do not only visit museums and classical music, but also enjoy watching TV and going to rock festivals: they consume "everything" and can therefore be called omnivores. The distinction between high- and low-brow culture is less distinct than it was in Bourdieu's day (though Koen Van Eijck and John Lievens (2008) argue, we can still distinguish different kinds of omnivores).

We have now an understanding of how gender (and numerous other features) structures parts of our identity. As stated earlier, we adopt a dialogic point of view and believe that our identity also structures our gender, or rather the possibilities of how we experience gender. A similar reasoning is valid for the relationship between identity and media consumptions. Identity, and our perceptions of gender as a discursive project is partly informed by our experiences with media. For example, the representations on gender in the media tell us how to behave and what we should look like. Our identity (and perceptions of gender) also inform our media consumption. For example, if we perceive masculinity as active, heroic and muscled, we might enjoy watching action movies such as *Die Hard* (FOX) or *The Expendables* (Lionsgate).

However, we are treading on dangerous ground here. It is all too easy to turn this into a determinist notion: because you are a man, you enjoy watching current affairs and sports; or because you are a woman, you enjoy watching soap operas and daytime talk shows. This is simply not the case. Many women enjoy watching football and rugby games, while many men enjoy watching daytime talk shows (cf. Ang, 1996; Livingstone, 1998; Van Zoonen, 1994).

Furthermore, gender is not a ubiquitous element of our everyday lives. As Ang (1996: 124) states eloquently:

> [I]n everyday life gender is not always relevant to what one experiences, how one feels, chooses to act or not to act. Since a subject is always multiply positioned in relation to a whole range of discourses, many of which do not concern gender, women do not always live in the prison house of gender.

A term to indicate this anti-essentialist notion on gender is derived from Donna Haraway (1988), "situatedness". Situatedness indicates reflection on the social-historical context of an individual. This context implicates that we never gain an objective, overarching knowledge, but only a partial, situated knowledge. More concrete, it means that we depart from a deterministic view on an individual's characteristics as determining the pleasures she or he can experience, but simultaneously take them seriously as the context that informs media practices (Ang, 1996). Situatedness does not refer to a 'site or place' but to a 'point of reference' (Murphy, 2005: 14).

Our frameworks of knowledge, our discursive resources, form the tools used for decoding media. As individuals have a unique composition of experiences, their discursive resources are also unique. We can now begin to understand why people might develop such contradictory readings of the same media product as the two users of the game *Journey* quoted above. We would like to emphasise once more the limitation of our interpretations with regard to our frameworks of knowledge in relation to decoding media content. It is not the case that because we are all unique individuals, all our readings are unique (suggesting that there are as many interpretations of any given media products as there are people). Meanings are constructed out of the conjuncture of the text with the socially situated reader.

> It would be ridiculous to suggest that all members of the working class or all women would construct identical meanings that were determined directly by their social situation. However, it would be equally ridiculous to suggest that there is no such thing as a working-class reading or a feminine reading.
>
> (Fiske, 1987: 80–81)

Keeping this last notion in mind, we will now turn to the question of what kind of pleasures audiences actually experience when consuming media and how gender is of relevance for these experiences.

Media Pleasures

Since the 1980s media scholars have focused on answering the question of why so many people enjoy (popular) media products and the notion of pleasure derived from media texts by the audiences became a focal point in audience studies. However, "pleasure" is a difficult term to define, and, as Barbara O'Connor and Elisabeth Klaus (2000: 370) argue, 'one of the most striking observations is the absence of a systematic approach to the concept'. So, while the notion of pleasure is now commonplace, in reception analyses we still have difficulty pinning it down. For example, O'Connor and Klaus (2000: 371) quote Simon Frith, who in 1982 writes,

> the concept refers to too disparate a set of events, individual and collective, active and passive, defined against different situations of displeasure/pain/ reality. Pleasure, in turn, is not just a psychological effect but refers to a set of experiences rooted in the social relations of production.

In short, Frith argues that pleasure itself is too complex to catch it in one definition. Around the same time, Fiske (1987: 224) states that pleasure should be understood as multidiscursive: '[I]t means differently in different discourses.' Nevertheless, Ang (1985) argues that pleasure comes into existence somewhere in the process of an audience interacting with the media text. While interacting, the audience members need to be able 'to identify with it [the media text] in some way or other, to integrate it into everyday life. In other words, popular pleasure is first and foremost a pleasure of recognition' (Ang, 1985: 20).

Fiske (1987) distinguishes three categories of the use of pleasure by academics and the different meanings these uses connote: psycho-analytic, physical and social. First, there is the psycho-analytic use. Feminist work on the gaze, for example, attaches the meaning of pleasure to desire (for example scopophilia and voyeurism). Second, there is the use of pleasure as what Barthes (1972 [1957]) calls *Plaisir* – pleasure which is of cultural origin – and *jouissance* – pleasure that is related to physical pleasure. Third, Fiske (1987) argues, there is the use of pleasure in relation to social structures and the social practices that individuals engage in. These three categories, or meanings of pleasure, are deeply interrelated and hence turn the notion of pleasure in a multidiscursive construct.

As pleasure is situated in the process of audience members' interactions with the text, the text is pivotal in the experience of pleasure. What do media texts offer the reader that induces pleasure? (cf. Ang, 1985; Fiske, 1987). Following Barthes (1977), Fiske (1987) proposes that a text opens up for different interpretations, and that pleasure can be derived from playing with these possibilities. For example, in Chapter 6 we studied how the text opens up multiple subject positions. The subject positions an audience member engages in or recognises is dependent on the unique characteristics of the particular audience member. In other words, the play, as indicated by Fiske (1987), is dependent on the social-historical situat-edness of the individual. For example, female participants of ethnographic studies, like Ang's (1985) famous study on viewers of *Dallas* (CBS) and Dorothy Hobson's (1982) study on *Crossroads* (ATV/Central), repeatedly report that part of the pleasure of watching soap opera is located in the play with the representation and questions of power related to these representations.

The notion of pleasure has been developed around the notion of popular culture. Popular culture, as a form of mass media, was (and often still is) identified as "low art" and "low brow". However, when researchers engaged seriously with popular culture, they soon discovered the complexities of these low brow media contents and the many competences audiences have to have to interpret these texts, give meaning to them and ultimately derive pleasure from them. Paul Willis (1998) distinguishes "symbolic work", "symbolic creativity" and "symbolic extension". First, Willis (1998) argues, media consumption takes a lot of (symbolic) work. Think about the tremendous investment of time and energy in selecting what music we want to listen to, or which movie we want to see. Second, audiences use media products in a (symbolically) creative way. Think of the times you have discussed with your friends how well or not well a TV show was made, or when we use pop songs to explain our experiences. Third, Willis (1998) discusses symbolic extension, a concept that refers to the use of media products to engage in other activities. For example, to discuss issues we have encountered in our everyday lives.

Figure 8.1 Rapunzel cartoon (Wildvlees in *Lover* magazine)

Figure 8.1 is illustrative of these notions. First it takes quite a few moments to discover what is going on. Immediately, we recognise the picture as a cartoon, next we identify the girl as a princess. Subsequently, we might identify the fairy tale princess Rapunzel, who was locked up in a tower without a door, her hair grown so long that people could climb into the tower using her hair. Last but not least, we see the pun: it is not the hair on her head, but her pubic hair that she's grown so long (this is already a fair amount of symbolic work). This latter aspect refers to feminist debates on the shaving of legs, arm pits and pubic areas as a way of disciplining the body. The identification of the princess as Rapunzel and the use of her pubic hair as referring to feminist debate both require specific cultural capital. Combined, they offer for an interpretation of this seemingly simple cartoon as a critique on the objectification of the female body in fairy tales. This might bring pleasure to those with that specific cultural capital. The picture might also be read as a critique on fairy tales and the role of women in them (women are always pretty but simultaneously always the victim of some evil stepmother or wicked witch, in need to be rescued by the manly prince to live happily ever after). This interpretation of the cartoon might bring pleasure in a more confrontational way: confronting us with the relatively uncritical representations of gender roles in fairy tales we had not noticed before. The cartoon is also tongue-in-cheek provocative, as armpit hair would be less "shocking" than the pubic hair. Bringing pleasure in terms of a more emotional experience: the picture shows us something incongruent, namely a princess with lots of pubic hair while, most often, the view of pretty princesses certainly does not contain lots of hair. Last but not least, even when one is not aware of the princess being Rapunzel or the feminist debates, one is still able to interpret the cartoon and derive pleasure from it. All of the interpretations/ pleasures are forms of symbolic creativity.

There are three important points here. First, even a simple cartoon like this enables multiple pleasures for the audiences to experience. Second, each of these pleasures is informed by the audience members' social-historical situatedness. In the past decades, especially feminist scholars have dedicated time and energy to studying how gender matters when we discuss pleasure and media. Third, as Willis (1998) also emphasises, we should not forget how the meanings produced are still enabled by the provided form (in this case a cartoon).

Gendered Pleasures

Gendered pleasures are, as a matter of course, multiple, varied and diverse. For example, visual pleasures, the pleasure of gossip, the pleasure of turning oneself into an aficionado, identity play, and the pleasure found in resistance. However, we would like to argue with Ang (1985) that each of these pleasures encapsulates the recognition of something in the text. Before exploring these different notions and their gendered aspects we would like to emphasise that these notions should not be understood as mutually exclusive. Rather they are overlapping, complementary explanations of audiences' pleasures in reading and making sense of media texts. For the sake of clarity we will discuss them separately.

We can distinguish two research disciplines that address pleasure and media, the psycho-analytic tradition, also called *Screen Theory* (after the name of the journal *Screen* that a lot of this work is published in) and cultural studies referred to as the CCCS tradition (referring to the Birmingham Centre for Contemporary Cultural Studies that instigated this line of work). Often *Screen* theorists and CCCS scholars are positioned in opposition to one another (Hermes and Reesink, 2003). While *Screen* theorists are thought to be too heavy on in-text constructions of subject positions, CCCS scholars are thought to focus too much on the popular. Ang and Hermes (1996: 112) draw on the terminology developed by Annette Kuhn to explicate these positions: '[T]he analysis of *spectatorship*, conceived as a set of subject positions constructed in and through texts, and the analysis of *social audiences*, understood as the empirical social subjects actually engaged in watching television, film going, reading novels and magazines, and so on' [italics in original]. The psycho-analytical tradition focuses on spectatorship, while cultural studies focuses on social audiences. In feminist media studies we sometimes find approaches that use or discuss insights from both disciplines (e.g. Pisters, 2011; Van Zoonen, 1994).

Box 8.1 Exercise: Music Discourses

Pick a song of your liking. This can be a song in any music genre. Download (or transcribe) the lyrics of this song. The lyrics form the basis for your analysis.

1. Explore the social, cultural, political or historical contexts of the song (for example by answering the questions: Who produced it originally? Who is the original artist? In which country does the song originate?).
2. Now construct three possible audience readings: dominant, negotiated and oppositional.
3. Try to explain how the three readings are informed by cultural resources.

However, most often they are discussed separately. We find this regretful, as we believe that text and audience (together with production) depend strongly on each other and therefore insights about the audience and the text should be thought of as complementary and mutually inform each other.

The clearest notion of pleasure in psycho-analytic studies is visual pleasure. Mulvey (2009) identified scopophilia (the pleasure one can experience by looking at another person as an erotic object) and the gaze (with women often functioning as passive objects to "be-looked-at" and men as the active subjects that "look-at" them) as visual pleasures of cinema audiences (see Chapter 1 for a more elaborate explanation). Mulvey's concepts were further theorised into the notion of (female) *spectatorship*. Countering the rather dichotomous idea of passive females and active males in Mulvey's theory, feminist scholars like Van Zoonen (1994) explore the male and female spectatorship, arguing that women enjoy and derive as much pleasure from looking at male actors such as Robert Pattinson, Antonio Banderas, George Clooney, Christian Bale and Keanu Reeves (cf. Van Zoonen, 1994). However, most studies on spectatorship focus on how the text induces subject positions and not on the studying of actual audiences.

Some of these subject positions are directly related to pleasure. For example, some subject positions challenge heteronormative displays of men and women and are therefore pleasurable to identify with (they can empower us, for example). Soap operas are indicated as providers of such pleasures: in soap opera we find more businesswomen, more sexually aggressive women and more single, childless women taking care of themselves than in other popular genres. In this genre, women are primordial and are displayed as 'perceiving of themselves as strong and active subjects' (Seiter, Borchers, Kreutzner and Warth, 1991: 244). These characters challenge the traditional heteronormative narrative, common in Western society, and therefore identification with them might bring pleasure.

This kind of pleasure is also proffered sometimes in what we might call masculine genres. For example, Tania Modleski (2009) convincingly argued the case of male weepies. Taking some Clint Eastwood movies as examples, she shows how they are of great melodramatic quality, presenting us with alternative views on masculinity (though at the end Modleski maintains the view that these alternative views do not undermine, let alone subvert, the patriarchal order of society). Another genre in which traditional heteronormative displays are challenged is the horror genre. For example, most horror movies feature a "final girl". The final girl refers to the female character who is the last living victim and has to face the serial killer or monster in the movies. These final girls are usually the least feminine of all female characters in the movies: they have "masculine names" such as Laurie, Teddy or Billy, are usually a bit of a tomboy, and by no means a damsel in distress (Clover, 1992). This final girl allows for cross-sex identification: most audience members of horror movies are male but the main protagonist they can identify with is female.

Another way in which the text creates a pleasurable position for identification is the so-called "good mother". Drawing on Nancy Chodorow's psycho-analytical theories, Modleski (1984) argues that some texts (especially melodramatic ones), position the viewer as an all-knowing good mother. As a viewer, you know all that has happened as you see the events in all characters' lives. Because women are thought to identify with their mother during their childhood, women are thought to take comfort (and hence derive pleasure) from taking this position.

Focusing more on the audiences than on the text, in cultural studies identification in general is considered pleasurable. On the one hand this can be the pleasure of recognition of 'the familiar and its adequacy' (Fiske, 1987: 12). Fiske uses the derogative term "easy pleasures" for this kind of pleasure, even though it is, in our view, a type of pleasure we often derive from the media. Oftentimes we enjoy media simply because they are there and our experiences are not always profound (cf. Hermes, 1995). On the other hand, though, this pleasure can also be subversive (Fiske, 1987). There are multiple ways in which identification might be subversive. Identification might mean a sense of control; you choose who to identify with. Additionally, identification can symbolise empowerment for the subordinated individual. Identifying with a strong female character can offer the opportunity to create one's own meanings around issues addressed by the strong female. As Ellen Seiter *et al.* (1991: 240) show in their reception analysis of soap operas, '[w]omen openly and enthusiastically admitted their delight in following soap operas as stories of female transgressions which destroy the ideological nucleus of the text: the priority and sacredness of the family'. Identification with the subject positions created by soap opera offers the opportunity to subvert the traditional patriarchal order.

Also grounded in cultural studies is the conception of pleasure that (television) audiences derive from gossip. Sharing protagonists' secrets that only a few are privy to (Buckingham, 1987), while simultaneously engaging in the renegotiation of moral boundaries is an important way to experience pleasure. Gossip is one way to establish and explore the moral rules of everyday life (Krijnen, 2007). Sharing interpretations of media content hence sometimes re-establishes, sometimes critiques social norms and values.

Taking the renegotiation of social boundaries one step further, we could argue that mediated narratives offer audiences possibilities to reflect on their own everyday lives, problems and events. Mediated narratives are thought to have a reflexive function. Especially popular genres, like soap opera, are thought to be of value: their narratives usually do not have clear cut endings; they offer many insights on who did what and why; and they closely resemble audiences' everyday lives (Coolen, 1997; Geraghty, 1998; Krijnen, 2011). As these popular genres are more often watched by women than men, women engage in this pleasure a bit more often (Krijnen and Verboord, 2011).

In opposition to this pleasure of the reflexive function is another pleasure that is directly linked to the fantastic potential of these popular genres. This fantastic potential creates opportunities (for characters) and is detached from the audiences' own situation. Pleasure is not so much derived from identification and reflection, but from transgression, surpassing one's own situation (Kaplan, 1986). Entering an "unreal" situation where, for example, female characters are strong, have agency and break out of their ordinary everyday lives. It offers a dream world and a fantasy.

All the pleasures discussed (sometimes implicitly) encompass a potential for subversiveness or resistance. For example, renegotiation of social norms can sometimes lead to the resistance of dominant ideological concerns. Some scholars, of whom John Fiske (1987) is the most prominent, even argue that all of the pleasures discussed in this paragraph are forms of resistance. This view postulates the audiences as extremely active during their media consumption (and we have already briefly addressed this "over activity" as a point of critique (Hermes, 1995) earlier in this chapter), resistance of dominant ideology does deserve our attention. It is here that many of the gendered pleasures are articulated.

Resistance

Similar to ideas on the active audience and studies in audiences' perception of popular culture, the notion of resistance has been developed around a Marxist conception of media content. The line of argument is then as follows: the context of production, which in many countries is a capitalist system, turns media products into commodities, goods that are supposed to earn as much money as possible for the producers. This dynamic has an effect on the content of the product; they are of bad quality and represent the ideology of the producers (cf. Ang, 1985; Downey, 2006). Not only is such a view deterministic of how media production works, it is also deterministic with regard to the audiences. This view also implies that audiences take over the preferred reading (which is ideologically laden in the interest of the producers) and therefore the agency of the audiences is denied. Investigating media audiences themselves, cultural studies scholars have developed the notion of resistance – emphasising that many of the pleasures derived from the media are actually born out of resisting a preferred reading. As such, resistance is a core concept in the cultural studies paradigm.

Within cultural studies, there are two understandings of resistance. One understanding formulates resistance as a means of challenging the determinacy of hegemonic power (Murphy, 2005) and is mostly elaborated upon by Fiske. The other understanding formulates resistance as less centred on countering hegemonic ideologies and more on the Foucaultian notion of micro-relations power in everyday life. According to Foucault (1980), there is not one source of power that is centralised in society, rather power is dispersed and operates in many ways, such as through education, medicine, social reform, et cetera (Barker, 2012). De Lauretis' (1987) conceptualisation of technologies of gender relates to this operationalisation of power. Both understandings are important for us in terms of gender.

Counter-Hegemonic Resistance

Counter-hegemonic resistance is by far the best known formulation of resistance in cultural studies, due to the work of Fiske (1987). Fiske critiqued approaches that took the media text as a starting point of investigation and argued about its possible effects on the audiences, stating that a media text is something other than a media product, the text is not the same as the product (Fiske calls media products commodities), as the text only becomes by its readers. In other words, if no one consumes the product, the text does not receive meaning and therefore does not exist and neither do its effects. 'So a program becomes a text at the moment of reading, that is, when its interaction with one of its many audiences activates some of the meanings/pleasures that it is capable of provoking.' (Fiske, 1987: 14). As the production of the product and the text are both discursive, the text can be seen as a site of conflict between what the producers want (the forces of production) and what the audiences do with them (modes of reception). Media then can be seen as site for ideological struggle (Hall, 2013).

Important within this notion is that the audiences are not just active but productive, they create meanings (this is indeed very similar to what Willis (1998) calls symbolic creativity, though Willis does not relate his notion to resistance per se). It is here that Fiske (1987) locates resistance. In his seminal work *Television Culture* Fiske proposed lots of examples of such ideological, counter-hegemonic resistance, emphasising the pleasure that comes with resistances. Audiences rarely adopt the preferred reading but always negotiate with it. In these negotiations pleasure is multifarious.

This is, of course, a rather radical position to take as (almost) every encounter with media is an act of resistance. Indeed, critics direct their

Figure 8.2 Harajuku-style (Photo credit: Jeroen de Kloet)

attention to this celebratory notion of the overly active audiences that engage in resisting dominant ideologies at all times and that often our experiences are not so profound (Hermes, 1995). Nevertheless, next to resistance, the notion of the productive audiences also resulted in studies on fan productivity. Often, fan productivity combines certain activities of the audiences with resistance. As discussed in Chapter 6, fans have always existed and were always productive, creating fan-art, fan-fiction, fan-videos, fan comics and many more things (cf. Jenkins, 1992). Though we do not always know who exactly produces these fan works (in terms of gender, age, ethnicity and so on) we do know something about the reasons why they produce these fan works; part of the activity is instigated by resisting the preferred reading in the original media product. For example, interviewing fans who produce so-called slash videos (in which two same-sex characters from a certain media product are presented in a romantic relationship that does not exist in the original text) Adriaan Bakker

(2013) shows how fans are discontent with parts of the story and hence create others with different interpretations. One *Twilight* slash producer, for example, states that the relationship between the two main protagonists Bella and Edward is just not that realistic, but that the two males competing for Bella's affection, Edward and Jacob, have a 'lovely hate dynamic' (Bakker, 2013). Hence resisting the dominant storyline that presents a traditional heterosexual relationship, this fan engages in a certain type of activity (producing something), creating a homosexual storyline in a video anyone can access on YouTube.

So far, we have discussed the notion of resistance as it was originally formulated by the CCCS. Resistance is then grounded in resisting capitalist ideology, media as commodities "selling" traditional notions of femininity and masculinity. What we would like to draw attention to now is the Western origin of the notion of resistance. Notions such as resisting the patriarchal order or heteronormative discourses in media products have been developed in the West and are grounded in Western-based empirical work. An increasingly global media environment changes the context of consumption in multiple ways: audiences view more than just these Western media products; audiences can be located anywhere; social and cultural norms vary across the globe and therefore resistance might also. We will now investigate the pleasures derived by audiences consuming transnational media content in a global context.

Transnational Pleasures

Globalisation is not only a phenomenon of importance when we discuss the production of media but also when we think of media reception.

As we saw in Chapter 3, an increasing concentration of the media industries, with a strong centre in the West (specifically the US) has the side effect of Western gender discourses being broadcasted globally (see Kuipers, 2012). The question remains what audiences actually do with this kind of transnational content. In other words, just because media production is increasingly concentrated in the West, resulting in a transnational broadcasting of Western gender conventions, does not mean that audiences on a global level simply adopt these ideological representations. A good illustration is the style of young Japanese women in the Harajuku region of Tokyo. Rejecting the stream of often Western images (on TV, in ads, et cetera) that increasingly show more of the naked body, young women developed a clothing style to counter this. By now, there are many Harajuku-styles and the region is well known for its impact on fashion. Harajuku-style is just one example of audiences resisting Western media content. Obviously, many more interesting things happen as we look into global media consumption, and the consumption of gendered ideologies in specific.

There are multiple ways in which audiences consume transnational media content. First, through migration, we can now find many diaspora audiences that sometimes consume a large, multinational palette of media content. On the other hand, through the international trade in media, transnational media travel the globe and are consumed by a wide palette of audiences in a multitude of countries. Diaspora audiences are usually discussed in terms of holding on to their "own countries' values" in studies, and their identities are positioned within the problematic frame of the multicultural society. This is peculiar; framing diaspora audiences like this invokes an out-dated hypodermic needle theory to assess these audiences' reception (Aksoy and Robins, 2000). Secondly, these diaspora audiences that are studied are usually audiences that relocated themselves to the West (and not Westerners who relocated to Latin America for example), employing an essentialist frame based on audiences' countries of origin. The viewing of transnational media products is usually framed with a much more positive sounding word "appropriation". Appropriation refers to negotiation with media content that involves audiences adopting (parts of) this content in existing frameworks of knowledge. Though this latter frame seems to contradict the essentialist frame, studies employing either frame usually conclude something similar: transnational media can be used to negotiate identities or to renegotiate cultural values. The moment of recognition is again pivotal to experience pleasure (Ang, 1985). With regard to transnational media consumption, the notion of cultural proximity is usually employed to indicate such recognition. Cultural proximity refers to the closeness of cultural values and features displayed in media to the cultural values of the viewers. Hence, cultural 'proximity is based in language, dress, based in cultural elements per se: dress, ethnic types, gestures, body language, definitions of humour, ideas about story pacing, music traditions, religious elements, et cetera' (La Pastina and Straubhaar, 2003: 274).

The well-travelling format of the telenovela, for example, has been studied extensively for its attraction in foreign countries. Telenovelas are melodramatic series that resemble soap opera, but have a distinct end to the narrative. They are produced in Latin-American countries and have been broadcasted virtually all over the world, with more or less success. As the telenovela is produced in Latin America, the spoken language is usually Spanish or Portuguese. Last but not least, they are mostly watched by women and children. Partly, of course, as they are broadcasted mostly during daytime hours. This timeslot, in many countries, is still reserved for women and children as in a traditional setting men work during the day (cf. Rector and Trinta, 1981). However, there are other reasons of why women (and men) would experience pleasure from telenovelas.

According to Jean-François Werner (2006), women can use these telenovelas to find their way in a rapidly changing world. Telenovelas, Werner (2006) argues, offer a whole gamut of issues revolving around gender in terms of love and family. Therefore, Senegalese women, part of the audience group Werner (2006) studied, are inspired to renegotiate some of the gendered dimensions in their own lives.

Another reason is cultural proximity. Antonio La Pastina and Joseph Straubhaar (2003) show how a Brazilian telenovela *Terra Nostra* (Rede Globo) is popular among an Italian community, as most people in the community had relatives in Brazil and perceived of the telenovela as a way to connect to their relatives' experiences. The Italian audience had a historical bond with the narrative of *Terra Nostra*.

Cultural proximity is not only relevant for telenovelas. Brian Larkin (1997) shows how Bollywood movies are popular amongst a particular ethnic group in Nigeria, the Hausa people. The reason for this, Larkin (1997) shows, is that the Bollywood movies display cultural values that address romance, which opens up a space to discuss and renegotiate the cultural practices in a changing Hausa society. Similarly, See Kam Tan (2011) shows how Chinese viewers of the sitcom *Friends* also use this sitcom to negotiate gendered norms on romance, while simultaneously circumventing messages about homosexuality.

First of all, then, we have to conclude that pleasures and resistances of transnational media content are multifarious. Above we have given you a few hints of what transnational media pleasures could entail. However, there is much more to explore. Secondly, an important conclusion is that the Western gender conventions that travel the globe, as a side effect of increasing media industry with a strong centre in the West, do have an impact transnationally. The few reception studies we have reviewed indicate that audiences do use popular media content to negotiate gender norms. However, we have also tried to show that not only Western media content can open up spaces for negotiation, but Bollywood movies and Latin-American telenovelas (and many other media products) also have this capacity.

New Pleasures?

Next to the context of media consumption changing due to globalisation, new technologies (and therefore new media) also have an impact on media consumption. In Chapters 3 and 6 we discussed the relation of new technologies on the content and the production of media. Aided by new technologies, media texts are now increasingly convergent and users produce part of the texts; each of these developments impacts media content (which is understood as highly intertextual, disrupting gender representations). New technologies have yet another relation to media and gender: the context of media consumption, especially in terms of time and space, is more dynamic than ever.

Let us first look into the space dimension. New media technologies have always had an impact on space in a very material way. For example, the invention of paper enabled the dispersion of knowledge over large geographical districts, as paper was easier to carry than stone tablets (cf. Appadurai, 1996). In Chapter 7 we discussed how TV impacted the organisation of the domestic space. Likewise, new media technologies have their own effects. One of them is the increase of the number of media devices in the household. For example, in the US the number of households that had a PC with internet access went up from 75% in 2009 to 80% in 2013 (Nielsen, 2014), while 19% of households had a smartphone in 2009, whereas 65% did in 2013. The kind of devices is of importance here; internet access and smartphones enable people to watch TV anywhere and anytime. However, this use of new media devices appears not to be gendered. A recent study in the Netherlands shows small differences between men and women in the amount of use of these devices (SKO, 2014). Hence, we cannot assume anything in terms of gendered pleasures of new media in this regard.

New media technologies also have an effect in terms of time. Due to the higher interactivity that is enabled in new media, we consume media in a different way than we used to. For example, if we want to watch a TV series, we are now able to watch multiple episodes in one sitting (either on DVD or by legal/illegal download), giving rise to the new term "binge watching". Also, we are able to watch TV shows we missed on the internet, to pre-listen to music we might want to buy, and engage in multiplayer games online.

Taking time and space together, Aphra Kerr, Julian Kücklich, and Pat Brereton (2006) argue that there are five dimensions that are relevant when looking at new media and the pleasures they offer: control, immersion, performance, inter-texuality and narrative. Control refers to the amount of control we actually have, be it via the remote control or mouse clicks. Immersion refers to binge watching, but also to losing oneself in a videogame. Performance refers to the concept of being able to play with one's identity. Games and chat rooms make this possible. Narrative and intertextuality refer both to content features that audiences might enjoy, but in our opinion these two features are not that different for traditional or new media. Performance especially encourages playing with one's identity. It is gendered, though this requires a very active audience (or rather, performer). In the next chapter we will revisit this idea of playing with one's gender identity, and we will discuss how this play is structured.

Conclusion

In this chapter we have investigated why people consume certain media products and not others. Starting from the viewpoint of an individual's social-historical context we understood how people develop different tastes, and enjoy the different pleasures proffered to them by media texts. We also have seen how globalisation and new media technologies impact these pleasures, or rather structure them. This brings us back to the basic balance of agency and structure that underlies many of the concepts we have discussed with regard to gender and the media. As Willis (1998: 168) argues, '[b]ut, it should be remembered, they were expressing these points in ways that would have been difficult without the form, the provided form'. The media industries shape our media products. Industries now consciously use concepts of pleasures to market their products (Kerr et al., 2006; Willis, 1998). Though we strongly believe in audiences' agency, in our view this does not mean we now live a reception democracy. In the next chapter, we delve into questions on the media industry and consumer culture and how much these might or might not structure our experiences. Especially in relation to gender (though often intersecting with age and ethnicity) this balance is heavily debated in terms of pornofication, sexualisation and so on. Therefore, in the next chapter we will outline the debate and arguments for both sides.

Further Reading

Curious about situatedness and how media relate to it? We recommend this seminal work:

- De Lauretis, T. (1987). *Technologies of Gender: Essays on Theory, Film, and Fiction*. Bloomington/Indianapolis: Indiana University Press.

De Lauretis slowly builds up her argument, starting with a Foucaultian notion of technologies of gender, critically connecting feminist theory to film theory. For a more current exploration of media audiences we suggest:

- Butsch, R. and Livingstone, S. (Eds.) (2014). *Meanings of Audiences: Comparative Discourses*. London/New York: Routledge.

This edited volume contains a diversity of essays truly addressing the international audiences. The chapters engage with a detailed examination of how audiences are related to discourses. By paying attention to social-historical contexts of these audiences, the volume shows the differences and similarities in international audiences.

Chapter 9

Empowered Audiences

In class, while watching parts of the movie *Sex And The City 2* (SATC 2 – 2010) in which the four characters, Carrie, Miranda, Samantha and Charlotte make a trip to Abu Dhabi, the discussion among students focused on the essentialist notions of ethnicity prevalent in the movie. Students were critical towards the representation of Muslim women wearing burkas and the behaviour of the four characters (one student commenting: 'It's like they're at the zoo.') and of how Arab men were portrayed. Many students thought of this misrepresentation as offensive to Muslim and Arab people. Though the students were right in this regard, more striking to us was the fact that the discussion focused on the ethnic imagery and not on the question whether the display of four women whose romantic and sexual escapades that form the centre of the narrative is a feminist and/or empowering portrayal or not. A discussion on gender, sexuality and feminism instigated by SATC has been part of our classrooms since the start of the TV series (1998). Apparently, things have changed.

Two major changes in the media landscape have been discussed throughout this book, increasing globalisation and the dynamic of new media technologies. Similar to the representation of gender and production of media, audiences' reception is also shaped by these developments. While reception in relation to globalisation has been discussed in the previous chapter, new media have only been touched upon briefly. We distinguished Kerr *et al.*'s (2006) five dimensions, control, immersion, performance, intertexuality and narrative, to look into what pleasures new media proffer. However, we have neglected to discuss the relation of these dimensions to audiences in detail, leaving out questions such as 'What is the significance of control for audiences and how they experience themselves?'. A broader discussion of media technologies and audiences' reception is in place. As argued in the introduction and Chapter 6, new media technologies have an impact on time and space. The material impacts of media technologies on time and space are discussed in previous chapters. For example, domestic space was altered when the TV entered the living room (Spigel, 1992) and binge watching is extremely popular and enabled by companies such as Netflix and HBO (that offer streaming of their series as a standalone product).

However, the impact of new technologies and audiences' reception runs deeper than the material.

The convergence of time and space (cf. Giddens, 1984) with regard to new media also means audiences consume images from places they have never visited, are in contact with people they never met, know about events that happen in faraway places, and so on (Appadurai, 1996; Morley, 2001; Silverstone, 2007). This development has been cause for hopes and concerns. Hopes, as knowing of events that happen in faraway places is thought to enhance a capacity to empathise with people in those places (Silverstone, 2007). Worries, because the increased access has impact on one's sense of location and, connected, sense of identity (Morley, 2001).

Another boundary transgressed is what Joshua Meyrowitz (1986) calls situational geography of everyday life. Not only the location based changes are significant, but also the mental locations. New media, according to Meyrowitz (1986), enable one to come into contact with aspects of social life that previously were less easy to access. For example, reality programmes such as *Wife Swap* (ABC) give us a glimpse of other people's private family life. Meyrowitz (1986) emphasised the blurring boundaries between childhood and adulthood as children now have access to content that was previously reserved for adults. For example TV, movies and a part of the internet offer information on adult topics such as sexuality. This kind of information formerly was contained in books. The difference between TV, internet and movies and books is that the former do not require eloquent reading skills. Though we are uncertain the media is the sole motor of the changes in situational geography, we do believe media have had an impact on it.

As Meyrowitz (1986) focused his arguments on television, we think his ideas are further complicated by the blurring boundaries between producing and consuming media. The notion of the prosumer discussed in Chapter 6, for example, confuses the actors in Meyrowitz's theory. Not only do adolescents consume adult media content, they create it as well. This active approach on media and the changing situational geographies causes a lot of heated debates. With regard to gender, new media, and changing situational geographies, the major concern lies with sexualisation. There have been many heated debates in both academia and the public sphere. The debate, we will argue, forms an example per excellence of how complicated the relations between media, gender and reception actually are and why our students do not discuss SATC anymore in terms of girl power.

What Is Sexualisation?

Sexualisation has become a buzz-word. Pornofication accompanies sexualisation but is slightly less trendy. Sexualisation refers to a societal trend that tends to connect everything – from clothing and music to driving a car and eating dinner – with sex and sexuality. Though the current use of the word came into vogue during the 1990s, sexualisation existed before then. As Shayla Thiel-Stern (2014) convincingly shows in an historical analysis of American popular culture, gender and moral norms on sexuality have often been the cause of heated debate. For example, Elvis Presley was a major cause of concern. As Thiel-Stern (2014: 109) argues, '[p]eople who were wary of Elvis's gyrations in concert and on television worried primarily that teen girls who felt comfortable enough to scream and carry on hysterically in public would also be more apt to stray morally in their private lives'. Several definitions of sexualisation circulate. Gill (2007a: 256) for example defines sexualisation as, 'the extraordinary proliferation of discourses about sex and sexuality across all media forms, as well as [...] the increasingly frequent erotic presentation of girls', women's and (to a lesser extent) men's bodies in public spaces'. Gill (2007a) thus defines sexualisation as a concept referring to two developments: the increase of discourses about sex and an increasingly erotic representation of people in public spaces (including the media). Examples are aplenty: teen magazines discussing how to be sexy, thongs for seven-year-olds, child pageant queens in bikinis, the promotion of pole dancing as a workout in sports centres, et cetera. Responding to this trend the American Psychological Association (APA) turned out the *Report of the APA Task Force on the Sexualisation of Girls* in 2010 that defined sexualisation in a narrower sense. According to the APA (2010: 1), sexualisation exists out of several components that set sexualisation apart from healthy sexuality. The components are:

- a person's value comes only from his or her sexual appeal or behaviour, to the exclusion of other characteristics;
- [a] person is held to a standard that equates physical attractiveness (narrowly defined) with being sexy;
- [a] person is sexually objectified – that is, made into a thing for others' sexual use, rather than seen as a person with the capacity for independent action and decision making; and/or
- sexuality is inappropriately imposed upon a person.

Components one to three are similar to Gill's formulation on the representation of individuals in the public sphere and component four comes close to the proliferation of discourses on sex and sexuality noted by Gill (2007a). Both definitions postulate sexualisation as a negative trend in society. Additionally, though the definitions include "everyone", sexualisation is mostly related to girls (the title of the APA report is telling, for example).

This sexualisation and the promotion of a sexualised lifestyle, is considered a threat and especially young girls are thought to suffer the consequences. Interestingly, most studies and reports on sexualisation are rather elusive about the effects. At best they mention the APA Report's discussion of low self-esteem, depression and eating disorders (APA, 2010: 20–23). Be careful to note that the APA uses very tentative phrasings such as 'sexualized messages and products may be', 'the drop in self-esteem may be related', 'that sex-ualisation practices may function'. In other words, the harmful effects of sexualisation in terms of eating disorders and depression are not grounded in empirical research but suggested and insinuated. Danielle Egan and Gail Hawkes (2008) argue in their deconstruction of the sexualisation debate that, indeed, reports like the APA's construct a rhetorical link instead of empirical link between sexual content and sexualisation and its supposed effects. Sometimes the effects are defined in a more general way (beyond the eating disorders, let's say). Amy Dobson (2014) quotes a report from the Australian Parliament on the consequences of sexualised media content: '[it] may "awaken" the sexuality of girls "before they are mentally able to be responsible for their actions or have a morally formed conscience only to be deeply hurt leading to an increase in teenage pregnancy, sexual diseases and mental breakdown"' (Dobson, 2014: 99).

This last formulation of the effects of sexualisation, together with reports like the one from APA, caused, and still causes, a lot of debate in the public as well as in the academic sphere. This might be surprising, as no one in their right mind would approve of 'inappropriately imposing sexuality on someone' or to 'judge people by their sex appeal'. We only have to switch on the TV to see that many programmes, from soap opera to talk show, are about sex. However, sexualisation is immensely more complex and, according to some, less a threat to society than is often suggested. In that sense, sexualisation can also be viewed as a media panic. A media panic is a moral panic in which the media themselves are the subject and location of the debate. In other words media are considered as one of the primary perpetrators of sexualisation, but they also form the arena in which the debate takes place (Drotner, 1999).

The background of the debate is a changing political and social climate that has been identified in Western countries. McRobbie (2009) proposes the con-cept of the double entanglement to understand the position individuals in the West find themselves in and the debate on sexualisation. The double entan-glement, she argues, 'comprises the co-existence of neo-conservative values in relation to gender, sexuality and family life [...], with processes of liberalisation in regard to choice and diversity in domestic, sexual and kinship relations [...]' (McRobbie, 2009: 12). While individuals are confronted with the promotion of relatively traditional (and heteronormative) social values such as the promotion of marriage and "no sex before marriage", they are simultaneously encouraged to exercise their agency in the organisation of their private life (as in many Western countries marriage is not necessary to obtain full legal rights as a couple, for example).

This double entanglement is part and parcel of the sexualisation debate which we will now explore more in-depth. We will pay specific attention to history of sexualisation, commercialisation, the productive power of the discourse and the agency of girls themselves.

The History of Sexualisation

Sexualisation is nothing new. Cas Wouters (2010), Shayla Thiel-Stern (2014), Linda Duits and Liesbet Van Zoonen (2009), Sara Bragg, David Buckingham, Rachel Russell and Rebekah Willet (2011), and Danielle Egan and Gail Hawkes (2008), among others, argue that sexualisation as a concept and the debate that revolves around it should both be (re)viewed in a historical context. Wouters (2010) takes a macro perspective and positions sexualisation as a long-term social process that follows after a long period of desexualisation accumulating with the sexual restrictiveness of the Victorian time, for example, in terms of dress and behaviour (manners). From the late nineteenth century Wouters (2010) identifies a trend towards sexualisation in full swing. Wouters (2010) argues that the contemporary notions of sexualisation are part of a much larger social process of integration and emancipation of sexuality. In this process, media have played their part much more as an accelerator than as the driver of sexualisation.

In her historical investigation of moral panics surrounding media, girls and sexuality in the United States Thiel-Stern (2014) starts with a vivid description of the dance halls in 1905. She shows how ragtime, the precursor of jazz music, attracted many young people, especially young, working-class women who earned their own wages. The popularity of these dance halls and the concerns about the young women who visited them became known, in American press coverage, as the Dance Hall Evil. The concerns were about gender and sexuality and the space that these dance halls offered to negotiate both. Thiel-Stern (2014) concludes this case with the remark that the moral panic may have died down, but the narrative that poses 'women social reformers at one end of the moral spectrum and the working-class girls who went to dance halls at the other end' is still evident (Thiel-Stern, 2014: 53). Class intersects with gender in this case and, we would like to argue, it still does. We will discuss this intersection later.

What is particularly interesting in Thiel-Stern's (2014) analyses is the tripartite of media, moral entrepreneurs and moral panics. Though the media might be able to reinforce, sustain and maybe even create moral panics, the media are not solely responsible. First of all, because 'the dialectical process directly and indirectly involves audiences. Furthermore, media is [sic] not a one-way flow but rather a complicated process of meaning making between message and receiver […]' (Thiel-Stern, 2014: 15). Additionally, Thiel-Stern (2014) argues, moral panics need moral entrepreneurs. Citing Howard Becker's work, she explains that moral entrepreneurs are people who are in the position, have the power and/or have the authority to make rules or reinforce them. The moral entrepreneur that creates rules, is, what Becker calls, a crusading reformer. This reformer then sees an evil cause, a threat to society that needs to be corrected. A contemporary example is the activist Jean Kilbourne, discussed in Chapter 1, who travels the US with a documentary *Killing Us Softly*

(Kilbourne, 2013), in which the relationship between advertising and, among other things, sexualisation is explored. Her main argument is that the representation of women in advertising should be considered a public health problem (Kilbourne, 2013), as it causes eating disorders, depression and low self-esteem (as mentioned by the APA report). Moral entrepreneurs thus make a contribution to the formulation of normative dimensions on sexuality (i.e. heterosexual, within a romantic relationship, et cetera) (Charles, 2012).

We would like to draw attention to one important element in Kilbourne's account: the commercial aspect. She, and many scholars with her, focuses on the advertising industry responsible for the commercial marketing of commodities that carry sexualised content. This commercial aspect forms an important ingredient for the debate on sexualisation.

Commercialisation of Sexuality

Sexualisation seems intimately tied to commercialisation. Though (almost) no one is arguing that a monolithic power block formed by the media industry is responsible for sexualisation, the commercial aspect of sexualisation is emphasised by many. To formulate it somewhat crudely, what has happened is that feminist ideals such as the freedom and right to exercise choice (in clothing, career, appearance, et cetera) have been taken up by advertisers and the media industry and are repackaged and sold back to women. Hence, they re-articulate ideals into a new regime of truth of what women are supposed to look like and how they should behave (cf. McRobbie, 2009). Consumer culture – the notion that the creation of a lifestyle and the building of one's identity is intimately connected with consumption of aesthetic signs (Featherstone, 2007) – is crucial. For example, the Diesel Campaign 'Be Stupid' celebrates a lifestyle that is the opposite of sensible and smart. As Diesel's stupid philosophy tells us: 'Well, we're with stupid. Stupid is the relentless pursuit of a regret free life' (Diesel. com, 2010). The campaign involved many print ads featuring women in bikinis or their underwear involved in "stupid" situations. One of the ads contains a woman in a red bikini busy photographing inside her bikini shorts. In the background we see a hungry looking lion coming out of the forest. Arguably this image (and other images) contains sexualised elements. Not only is the model wearing a bikini with a push up top that emphasises her breasts, she is also photographing her genitals. The accompanying slogan says it might be stupid to do this, but it is ballsy. So, while on the one hand the ad breaths neoliberal ideal of the freedom of choice, to be stupid instead of smart (and suggesting you will have more fun that way), it also dictates appearance (a push up bikini) and behaviour (photographing what is inside your pants as something normal to do).

This tension, between a liberating slogan and a continuation and reinforcement of a gendered discourse on appearance and behaviour, is the core of much debate on sexualisation. While on the one hand the possibilities for young girls (and boys) have multiplied, on the other hand a strong gendered discourse is re-articulated (McRobbie, 2009). According to Gill (2007a, 2007b), a new regime on women as desiring sexual subjects has been formulated. It is not so much a choice any more, but a societal demand for (young) women to position themselves as sex-savvy. After all, thanks to feminists in the '60s, '70s and '80s, they are now liberated from the restrains of patriarchy and should celebrate their sexuality. The tricky part is that demanding one's celebration of sexuality is as restricting as forbidding one to be an active sexual subject. Complicating things even further, as we can see in the Diesel ad, this message is often embedded in ironic context (the ad is so over the top it might be funny). This rhetoric makes it difficult to object to the sexual objectification of women in this ad. All too easily one is accused of not having a sense of humour, misunderstanding ironic context, et cetera (cf. Gill, 2007b; McRobbie, 2009).

Media products then are thought to contribute to a context in which individuals' choices are structured towards a sexual agency while letting them think they are all individuals. The idea of a "false consciousness" is revived and very rarely the voices of young women are present. Over and over we have now seen how interpretations of any message are manifold, how each media message has a polysemic potential. Additionally, we have argued (in Chapters 7 and 8) that the content by no means should be taken as a predictor of what people actually do with this content in everyday life. Indeed, all our knowledge on how symbolic goods get meaning seems discarded (cf. Attwood and Smith, 2011; Bragg et al., 2011; Lemish, 2011). The major question that forces itself upon us is of course what do (young) women do with media content like this? As Duits and Van Zoonen (2006, 2007) justly point out, the voices of the young women who allegedly suffer from sexualisation are absent in the debates. We now turn our attention to these young women and questions of agency.

Girls' Agency

The one crucial voice missing in the debate on sexualisation is the voice of the ones at risk of it, young girls (and boys). Even though the perspective of the media as a hypodermic needle has been outdated, it appears to make its return once more in the debate on sexualisation (Egan and Hawkes, 2008). Expressions such as 'normative requirement' (of wearing a G-string) (Gill, 2007b: 72) and 'compulsory sexual agency' (Gill, 2008: 40), imply that the structure of post-feminist consumer culture is so strong that it is inescapable. Though these authors do emphasise that they, like advocates of agency, do not believe in a monolithic power block brainwashing young girls into sexualisation, they do emphasise the power structures. Indeed, as Emma Renold and Jessica Ringrose (2013: 247) argue, we can speak of 'binary formations of celebratory postfeminist "girl power" vs. crisis discourses of "girls at risk"'. As was said before, we strongly believe in an understanding of the media that combines industry, content and audience. Therefore we also think it is crucial to investigate the voice of these young girls that apparently fall victim to sexualisation so easily. The few studies that explicitly focus on this topic, give us some interesting insights into the debate.

First, research shows us the shortcoming of analysing media content to draw conclusions about its possible impact. Melanie Lowe (2003), for example, studied girls' reception of Britney Spears. Britney Spears is one of the icons of sexualised culture. Her transgression from innocent young female pop singer to a mature sexual one, while maintaining a young audience, has been just one example of the worries expressed in the sexualisation debate.

Box 9.1 Resisting Sexualisation: FEMEN

Not only academics are aware of sexualisation, young women themselves are too. As (Duschinsky, 2013) argues, next to a lot of worries, sexualisation also gave rise to feminist activism. A good example is formed by the action group FEMEN. This action group acts against sexism, homophobia and general suppression of women by "sextremism": 'female sexuality rebelling against patriarchy and embodied in the extremal political direct action events' (FEMEN, n.d.). Therefore, during their protests the women are topless.

However, in her investigation of what girls particularly like and dislike about Britney Spears, Lowe (2003) shows how the girls she interviewed seemed to not negotiate the sexuality of Britney at all. Their interest is in Britney's ability to empower. For example, Lowe (2003) shows how the girls interpret one of Britney's songs *Sometimes*. According to these girls, the song is about how you can be many things at the same time. The song's lyrics however seem to tell a story of a young woman who is being pressured by her boyfriend to have sex. In the song, the girl asks him to be more patient. The theme/story of the song, then, is quite a common theme and not about having multiple personality traits. What is important to note here, is that the interpretation of the song is far removed from the manifest meaning proffered by the lyrics. Though Lowe's (2003) study is small scale, it does once more prove the point of content analyses' inability to predict meanings that audiences derive from media content.

Second, studies also show how girls are not only media-savvy, but very aware of their position in society and its structures. Girls often show an ability to reflect on their own position therein, contradicting and challenging the structuring powers of consumer culture. For example, in their attempt to give girls a voice, Linda Duits and Pauline Van Romondt Vis (2009) discussed celebrities with girls. In the debate on girls and the risks they run, celebrities are often used as a vehicle to emphasise the false consciousness of girls.

Celebrities produce a sense of individual autonomy that suits the neo-liberal individualist project and ignores the many relations of power in which the subject is immersed. In those perspectives, the reflexive audience practices invited by the celebrity text must be seen as successful, but basically mistaken, absorptions of neo-liberal discourse.

(Duits and Van Romondt Vis, 2009: 43)

Their analysis of the focus groups conducted, like Lowe's (2003) study, shows not only that girls construct media content within their own terms, but that they struggle within this entanglement of the structure as laid out before, and their own agency. In our opinion, their most important contribution to the debate is the fact that girls are aware of the structuring forces, aware of having some sense of agency, but that they have to constantly navigate them.

The contradiction that emulates from the struggle of girls with their agency and autonomy within the context structured for them by societal forces is characteristic of the debate on sexualisation. Indeed, girls engage with sexualisation in an active way. Not only by discussing it, but by embracing clothing devices such as the G-string, loving Christina Aguilera's song *Dirrty* (2002), posting sexy selfies and belfies on SNS sites and so on. In other words, girls are not only media-savvy (knowing that media content is trying to persuade them), not only aware of their agency (even though they might be overestimating their autonomy to choose), they are contributing to sexualisation by sexualising themselves (cf. Ringrose, Harvey, Gill and Livingstone, 2013). In a way, girls are thought to be complicit to sexualisation, although, as we have seen, some would argue that they cannot help this, as they are more or less forced to adopt this normative requirement to femininity. However, mostly these studies base themselves on content analyses. Talking to girls themselves complicates matters. As Dana Edell, Lyn Brown and Deborah Tolman (2013: 276) argue, '[i]t is much easier to theorise the intent, meaning, and implications of girls' choices to self-sexualise *without* girls than to develop a theoretically informed practice *with* girls' [italics in original]. Talking with girls presents feminist authors with a problem, an intergenerational gap (Edell *et al.*, 2013). Feminist authors who have studied media content for years and formulated theory on sexualisation should grapple with the contradictions of girls' agency and resistance (Edell *et al.*, 2013). This becomes apparent in the few studies that do tackle these issues. For example Cilia Willem, Núria Araüna, Lucrezia Crescenzi and Iolanda Tortajada (2012) and Sander De Ridder and Sofie Van Bauwel (2013) show how adolescents also experience a lot of pleasure and play when engaging with SNS. Nicknames are often directly related to sex such as 'fuck me wildly' or 'it doesn't fit in your hand' (Willem *et al.*, 2012) or more indirectly such as a girl using the nickname 'menstruation cycle' (De Ridder and Van Bauwel, 2013). The pleasure and play point towards the complexities of self-sexualisation.

Therefore, we would like to emphasise once more, we cannot understand sexualisation if we do not investigate the industry, the media content produced by that industry, and the negotiation and appropriation thereof by its audiences. Taking all three into account, we can now deconstruct the discourse on sexualisation produced by industry, academia, audiences and the general public.

Productive Power of the Sexualisation Debate

So far we have viewed multiple sites of argumentation in the sexualisation debate. The media industry has managed to repackage feminists' hard won rights to women's autonomy over the body and their sexuality. Turning both into a commodity and selling it back to their audiences. Feminist scholars and other academics have debated this trend. On the one hand condemning sexualisation and the hypersexualised portrayal of (mainly) women in mainstream culture (though men are more and more sexualised as well), arguing possible harmful effects. On the other hand, voices have also called to view the sexualisation in media content as part of a larger, historical, social development and urged us to listen to young women themselves.

Though we have visited several definitions of sexualisation in the beginning of this chapter, we now see that these definitions do not cover the full meaning of sexualisation.

Box 9.2 Exercise: Sexualisation in Music Videos

Watch the music videos that accompany the songs listed in this month's music charts. Which videos feature content that is explicitly related to sex and sexuality? Which videos do not? Try to categorise videos in terms of genre and answer the following questions:

- Which genres can you distinguish?
- How do they relate to gender (see chapter 2 for an explanation of genre and gender)?
- What does this tell us about sexualisation and media content?

So, let's try to deconstruct the discourse on sexualisation and start with a major component so far undiscussed: sex. The sexualisation debate does produce a certain meaning of sex and sexuality; there is good sexuality and bad sexuality (cf. Attwood and Smith, 2011; Bale, 2011). It is as if, Feona Attwood (2014) argues, there is some kind of natural sexuality (the APA called this healthy sexuality) that is stolen away by sexualisation. This "bad sexuality", as we have seen, is assumed to be harmful for young people. A normative framework on sexuality is hence articulated and reinforced (Bale, 2011). Furthermore, the harm that is assumed from bad sex might not always occur. There is very little empirical evidence about the impact of media on sexuality (Bale, 2011). The rare studies that do ask youngsters for their opinion show that 'while a small number of young people are clearly offended by porn that they encounter, there is no evidence to suggest that they are harmed by it' (Tsaliki, 2011: 299). Similarly, the EU Kids Online Project, investigating multiple risks to young children (9 to 16 years of age) encountered online in 25 European countries with a survey, shows that what is termed as risk does often not translate into harm when encountered (Livingstone, Haddon, Görzig and Ólafsson, 2011). In fact, they report that only 12% of the children that encountered sexual content online reported to be bothered by it.

Furthermore, sex is also produced as the focal point in teenagers' lives (Van Zoonen, 2014) and also, we would like to add, as the focal point of the media industry. All the rumours about sexting, selfies and belfies, G-strings (i.e. bad sex and sexuality), suggest that sex is what makes the world of teenagers and the media industry go round. In other words, wrong sex and sexuality have taken over the globe. This, we feel, is at least doubtful. Teenagers have other pastimes, such as sports, music and arts. Media industries are extremely diverse as are the products they produce.

This brings us to the next part of what the discourse produces. Next to situating the media industry as one of the main perpetrators, it also produces girls as victims. Girls have neither the knowledge nor the power to resist the heteronormative ideals of female sexuality imposed upon them by the media industry (Bale, 2011; Egan and Hawkes, 2008; Lumby and Albury, 2010). Moral entrepreneurs exacerbate the positioning of girls as docile bodies that are in need of protection (cf. Charles, 2012).

As the discourse is productive, it also obscures certain elements. By centralising on sex and sexuality as the core to media industries and teenagers' everyday lives, the discourse obscures diversity in the media industry and diversity among teenagers. As we have seen, many teenagers struggle with the double entanglement demanded from them. Adding to that, not all girls run similar risks. Girls who already have fewer opportunities in life because they are, for example, from a poor background or a dysfunctional family, run much more the risk of falling victim to internet predators (Van Zoonen, 2014). Situating all girls as victims is a rather essentialist approach to girls themselves.

Additionally, the discourse also obscures the diversity found in media themselves. All the examples used by media scholars to show how sexualisation is apparent in media content shows that there is indeed something important going on in terms of the representation of women and men in media. However, we argue, these instances of convincing examples need to be placed in the context of the media diet. We need a more holistic view of the media, since the (cultural) content of TV is interpreted within the whole of what audiences view (Signorielli, 2009).

Somehow, you might get a feeling the debate on sexualisation sounds somewhat familiar. You might have thought 'we already knew that'. Women have been misrepresented since the early rise of the media industry (see Chapters 1 to 3). Sexualisation in itself has been defined much earlier by feminist scholars.

Dan Edell, Lyn Brown and Deborah Tolman (2013) quote Teresa De Lauretis (1984) and Laura Mulvey (1975) when they state that sexualisation is defined as, 'the commodification of a specific glorified and objectified female body for the consumption of what is presumed to be a heterosexual male gaze'. There are, however, two major differences between sexualisation that has always been part of the media, and the surge of scholarly and public debate about it as it marks contemporary debates, formulating sexualisation as a health problem (as we have discussed earlier in this chapter) and the rise of new media.

An important part of the sexualisation debate is taken up recently by new media such as the smartphone and SNS. These media proffer affordances that "older media" do not have, posing new risks. As we have seen in Chapter 6, mass media and digital media in particular blur the boundaries between childhood and adulthood. New media, i.e. the internet, gives adolescents access to sexually explicit content such as porn that was previously less easily accessed by them. Viewing porn at an early age is deemed harmful. However, talking to (Greek) youngsters themselves, Liza Tsaliki (2011) shows how adolescent boys and girls indeed encountered pornographic content online, but that most of them do not feel they have been harmed. While some felt disgusted, others were not interested at all, and only a very small minority felt harmed. Of course, one study does not prove there is nothing to worry about (and neither is this Tsaliki's point), but it does show that: 1) it is important to engage young people themselves in the debate to empirically ground assumptions and thoughts; and 2) that the general line of recent research that shows that the consequences of internet use for youngsters are beneficial (Valkenburg and Peter, 2009) might be extrapolated to the risks of sexualisation and the internet.

However, there are some other points to be made when discussing digital media and sexualisation. Digital media, and specifically SNS and online messaging, have some properties that other media and face-to-face communication do not have. According to danah boyd (2008) we can distinguish four such properties: persistence, searchability, replicability and invisible audience. Each of these properties is of interest for the debate on sexualisation. The risks posed by sexting and posting sexy pictures of oneself on one's profile page are high because the internet "never forgets". In other words, what is posted online is always there (persistent), it can be found (searchable), it can be reproduced without (or with) one's consent (replicability), and we do not control who is viewing our posts (invisible audience). These affordances do change the game with respect to "misrepresentation" of women in general and earlier formulations of sexualisation.

Conclusion

The debate on sexualisation serves as an illustration of the complexities of gendered media consumption in an age of globalisation and new media technologies. It is undeniable that something is going on in terms of sexualisation and media. It is also undeniable that many people worry about this development and that there are many reasons to do so. However, we have also drawn attention to the voices of girls that are not part of this debate. Girls and young women are excluded from the debate and are thus silenced. They are only talked about, and very rarely talked with. Together with the authors that informed this chapter like Feona Attwood, Liesbet van Zoonen, Melanie Lowe, Danielle Egan and Gail Hawkes, we would like to argue that the only step forwards for media studies is to start this conversation with girls and boys. Questions such as 'How do media impact their social geographies?', 'How do they navigate double standards on sexuality?', 'How do they experience encounters with porn?', and many more, are in need of an answer. Maybe then we find out why our class discussion on *SATC* has changed and what this development means.

Further Reading

Recently many media research is geared to young people and new media. For a comprehensive overview we refer to:

- Buckingham, D. (Ed.) (2008). *Youth, Identity, and Digital Media.* Cambridge MA: MIT Press.

The essays in this edited volume investigate the relations between youth and online practices on various levels addressing topics such as SNS, identity and consumer culture.

For a detailed overview and account on the sexualisation debate we recommend two books:

- McRobbie, A. (2009). *The Aftermath of Feminism: Gender, Culture and Social Change.* Los Angeles/London/New Delhi/Singapore/Washington DC: Sage.
- Thiel-Stern, S. (2014). *From The Dance Hall to Facebook: Teen Girls, Mass Media, and Moral Panic in the United States, 1905–2010.* Amherst/Boston: University of Massachusetts Press.

While McRobbie offers us a very detailed, nuanced and critical analysis of contemporary media and the status of feminism in the UK, Thiel-Stern offers us a historical analysis of moral panics revolving around girls and mass media. We view the books as complementary. McRobbie's valuable insights are based on developments in the UK, but might be viewed as valid in a broader context (though we feel some reflection on the context of McRobbie's arguments is useful). Thiel-Stern's analysis is located on US debates, but, similar to McRobbie, has use and value in a broader context. Thiel-Stern's historical account is valuable to reflect on the contemporary developments discussed by McRobbie.

Afterthoughts for the Future

The aim of this book is to provide the reader with the tools to critically assess contemporary debates on the intersections of media and gender. In order to do so, we have (artificially) split up the tripartite representation, production and consumption in relation to these issues in separate sections. For each section we started with very basic questions that gave rise to more complicated and theoretical questions of why and how gender is related to the media the way it is. At the end of this journey, we feel it is appropriate to reconnect these sections in the context of globalisation and advancing media technology. Throughout this book we have argued that the production, content and consumption of media are always interrelated and cannot be understood as singular concepts or entities. Indeed, we have seen that much of the research devoted to each of these themes is instigated by questions about another theme. For example, the vast amount of time and energy devoted to investigating the number of women and men present in the media industries is done with the firm belief that this number has an impact on media content. In turn, media content is often studied because researchers believe that the consumption of media content is related to identity construction. Media are then considered as technologies of gender (De Lauretis, 1987).

As of yet we cannot answer the question whether or not these assumptions or beliefs are true. Research that investigates the number of women in TV production and the representation of gender in TV, for example, is very scarce (cf. Lauzen, Dozier and Cleveland, 2006). Likewise, a lot of current research on the representation of gender assumes an effect but more often than not neglects to investigate whether these assumptions are relevant. This lack of answers and clarity on important issues within the study of gender and media might feel like a disappointment. Rather, though, we would like to take them as future opportunities for studying gender and media.

The prominence of the themes mentioned above in the fields encompassed by "gender and media" indicates their importance. However, we sometimes feel that, on a theoretical level, the themes have somewhat stagnated in their development (cf. Krijnen, Van Bauwel and Alvares, 2012). All too often, we hear concluding remarks at conference presentations stating that nothing has really changed in the last 40 years with regard to the number of female journalists in news production, representation of gender in advertising, or the popularity of soap operas with female audiences. Media, however, are in a constant state of flux. The increasing speed of media technology developments and globalisation especially contribute to this status of media. As the relationship between media and society is a dialectic one, we would like to emphasise that society and gender are also continuously changing. Within this framework we would like to suggest five possible routes of research to advance the fields of gender and media. These five orientations focus on gender, taking seriously social-historical contexts of gender and media, transnational research, intersectionality and, what we could call, yoking research.

The first new route focuses on the conceptualisation of gender itself. We have seen throughout this book that most studies on gender and media take either women and femininities or men and masculinities as their starting point. Recently, we have seen an increase in the conflation of "sex" and "gender". In the introduction we argued that both sex and gender should be understood as continuums instead of dichotomies. In current research (with the exception of research in the field of queer studies) on gender and media, sex and gender are still usually presented as dichotomies. Moreover, more and more studies present a number on biological sex (a body-count) and call it gender. Of course research informing us about the numbers of who plays what videogame, or what the ratio of female and male news producers actually is, is interesting in itself, as we strongly believe that it is useful to know what we are talking about before we engage with more theoretical questions. However, research that claims to engage with gender, and thus inform us about the social constructs attached to biological sex, and then gives us a body count, is not informative, as it usually does not present the state of affairs on the research topic nor engage with more theoretical issues related to them. Gender is then disconnected from its articulation as a social construct embedded in the power structures in society, and its value as a concept of meaning is diminished.

Additionally, in Chapter 2 we have discussed both conceptualisations of femininity and masculinity as objects of study. While studies in masculinity have always formulated masculinity in diversity (cf. Craig, 1992; Moss, 2011), studies in femininity have often articulated femininity as contrasting to masculinity (though recently, some studies in femininities have taken multiple femininities as a starting point of investigation (cf. Holland and Harpin, 2013)). Taking either femininity or masculinity as a starting point of investigation carries with it this epistemological context. The result is that we know quite a lot about a certain kind of femininity (white, Western, middle-class femininity) and how it is represented in advertising, but we do not know that much about masculinity and how femininity and masculinity relate to a more fluid conception of gender. Therefore, we would like to propose another starting point for such research that would be more explorative and less burdened by epistemological differences. Possible research questions would focus more on the articulation of gender in advertising. Not simply by looking at how men and women are represented, but by first scrutinising how perfume ads, for example, are constituted and how gender relates to this.

Taking this different approach to gender also gives rise to the second new research orientation: taking social-historical contexts of whatever topic is under investigation seriously. Most (recent) research we encountered is meticulous in situating the gendered subject, be it girls, boys, men, women, masculinity or femininity. Most articles mention something similar as we did ourselves in our introduction, that is, we realise gender intersects with many other, sometimes more important, aspects of our identities such as ethnicity, class and age and will try as best as we can to generate insights within this understanding of social-historical contexts. However, we would like to argue that this should not only be a matter of course for gender but also for the topic of investigation. Many of the mechanisms laid bare by the studies discussed in this volume, such as the old-boys'-network, social role theory and gender displays, were developed more than 30 years ago. Societal changes and academic transgressions have taken place everywhere with repercussions for the discussed mechanisms (cf. Krijnen et al., 2012). For example, the gender displays developed by Goffman (1979) very often form the backbone of studies on the gender representations in advertising. However, as Goffman argues, the displays should be read within their cultural contexts. More than thirty years later, cultural contexts have changed. Taking the gendered displays Goffman articulates as a starting point of investigation should therefore be done within a critical reflective perspective on their history.

In general, we argue that within an environment of ever-converging media, mediatisation and globalisation, we should be critical towards notions of gender and media and their validity in contemporary times. We explicitly do not mean to discard "old theories", as they are extremely valuable as starting points and form the building blocks of our understandings. However, we do argue to take "old theories" seriously within their context. The concept of gendered genres, for example, is still a valid tool to assess media products and it still explains (at least partly) vertical and horizontal segregation in media production. The concept, however, was developed with explicit references to the social-historical context of genres studied. For example, Gledhill and Ball (2013) show how soap opera became a feminine genre as its roots lie in advertising household detergents to female audiences. Taking up the concept for study in contemporary times, we should also realise that genres are increasingly complex. Firstly, there are more and more genres in a singular medium like TV. Glen Creeber (2008), in his book on TV genres, distinguishes nine primary genres each with subgenres, while arguing in the preface, '[t]he book still does not touch upon all the genres and programmes that I would have liked' (Creeber, 2008: n.p.). Second, genres are increasingly hybrid; we have action-oriented reality TV shows like *Survivor* (CBS) but also the romantically inclined reality shows like *Temptation Island* (FOX). Studying gendered genres then becomes a very complex affair if we take the concept seriously within its social-historical context. Research that would seriously engage with the context of both gender and media context would still be able to take developed notions such as gender displays, the old-boys'-network or gendered genres as a starting point, but would critically assess the developments within the media and society so that the existing theories form the foundations to formulate new insights.

Taking both of the above into consideration, a third route for gender and media studies opens up. As seen, the meanings of gender diverge on a global level. The meaning of the words themselves is ambiguous at best on a global level. As argued in Chapter 2, the sex/gender dichotomy loses value in a Chinese context where the notion of sex already provides space for more than one gender performance (De Kloet, 2008). Subsequently, we see differences in research results on gender and media on a global level. The ratio of women and men in news production and the positions they hold is largely divergent per region. In the East and Nordic European countries women more often hold managerial positions compared to women in other countries (IWMF, 2011). Likewise, though men outnumber women in advertising representations on a global level, representations of masculinity or femininity are regionally diverse. For example, Luyt (2012) shows how hegemonic masculinity is related to race in South African advertising. With regard to media consumption we stumbled upon similar results. In Chapter 6, for example, we described how the use of social media diverges on a regional level with 50% of US adults using a social network site, while only 3% of Pakistani adults do (Pew Research Center, 2012). In many studies, a general comment about cultural differences is offered that explains carefully why in this or that region the relation between gender and media is the way the results of that particular study describe it. However, we feel that the field of gender and media is in need of internationally comparative research in order to advance the understanding of gender in multiple ways.

This research orientation would not only focus on articulations of gender in different cultural contexts but also take the transnational media industries into account. Media industries form a transnational field with multiple centres of production that compete with one another (Kuipers, 2011). Gender representation in advertising from such a perspective would engage with production processes in a transnational field. Most advertising these days is not meant to sell a product to a local, but to a global audience. Gender representations are therefore assumed to be constructed in ways that interpolate on a global level. Whether this is true, how this is done by the advertising industries and what this means for the cultural meanings of these representations are all questions that are in need of an answer.

Connected to the issue above, the fourth new route is a serious take on the concept of intersectionality. Though many white feminists' work now engages with intersectionality, especially in relation to ethnicity, often this work suffers from the same weakness as our own. In the introduction we write that it is impossible to discuss all important issues (meaning ethnicity, sexuality, (dis) ability, age, et cetera) and that we will therefore concentrate on gender. As Terese Jonsson (2014) argues, this kind of text often functions as a disclaimer for white feminists to not engage with black feminists' work. Often, Ien Ang (2003 [1995]) argues, this way of "inclusion" is not so self-reflective. To truly engage with, and not only acknowledge, black feminists' work, experiences and critiques Ang (2003 [1995]: 193) proposes 'a focus on how the gulf between mainstream feminism and "other" women is constructed and reproduced, and paying attention to, rather [than] turning our gaze away from, those painful moments at which communication seems unavoidably to *fail*' [italics in original]. In other words, this research orientation moves beyond formulating "multiple femininities" by engaging with questions of whiteness. The approach should be like the one proposed for gender: not taking gender and ethnicity as a starting point of investigation, but absorbing oneself reflectively with the articulations of intersectionality in media content, production and consumption.

Lastly, we would like to suggest "yoking research" in media and gender. Though present in all chapters in this book, the results of isolating media content from production and consumption became especially apparent in Chapter 9. Much of the research that takes issue with sexualisation focuses on media content, with an implicit effects framework underlying the research approach. This becomes obvious in the phrasing of research results that "may" have some effect on the sexual behaviour of adolescents. More often than not, the ones in danger of sexualisation, i.e. young girls, are not engaged in the conversation. The APA report, for example, states that '[m]uch of the research reviewed in this report concerns the sexualization of women (college age and older) rather than girls' (APA, 2010: 3). Yet, even though the research itself is on mature women, effects on young girls are suggested. More advanced studies on sexualisation, like Gill's (2007a, 2007b) explorations of the normative discourse on the sexually liberated young women in media content, often do not engage with these young women themselves, denying them agency. Over and over, we have emphasised that media texts in general are polysemic and intertextual, and therefore often offer multiple subject positions. Moreover, media content does not predict audiences' meaning constructions. Studies concentrating on media consumption mostly show that audiences construct a welter of meanings. Some of them match the preferred meaning embedded in the media text, others negotiate, reject or resist such meanings. Sometimes, we argue, the *Playboy* bunny is just a cute bunny. However, studies that engage with young women's experiences of media content often neglect to reflect on the organisation of media content and (in this case) sexualisation thereof. Celebrating girls' agency, the power of discourses, and the regimes of truth on gender identities articulated are glossed over. In other words, while one line of research emphasises discursive structures and ignores audiences' agency, the other line of research emphasises audiences' agency but ignores discursive structures. The sexualisation debate therefore finds itself in a deadlock. To undo this impasse, we propose "yoking research" in which the triangle of content, production and consumption is the centre of attention and investigated as such. In other words, we propose to set up studies that engage in both content and consumption analyses, in both production and content analyses, or in both production and consumption analyses. Hence, to not only investigate the contents of girls' magazines, but to discuss the results of such analysis with girls themselves and/or with its producers; to not only scrutinise news reports for the women and men present in them, but to also discuss these results with the producers of exactly these reports and/or with their audiences.

These new routes in research would, in our view, advance the field of study in gender and media. Research orientations that centralise on fluid conceptualisation of gender, taking social-historical contexts of gender and media into account, seriously engage with intersectionality, and yokes media production, consumption and representation also enable the reformulation and furthering of political agendas of many researchers in the field of gender and media. Perhaps in the future we will be able to answer the big questions raised in our introduction.

Glossary

Above-the-line the media professionals who are in creative profession and are situated on a standard production budget sheet above the bold horizontal line between creative and technical costs.

Agency the capacity and willingness of an individual to act in the world.

Below-the-line the media professionals who are in craft professions and are situated on a standard production budget sheet below the bold horizontal line between creative and technical costs.

Biological determinism the view that biological differences determine one's gender.

Camp a form of parody and a kind of intertextuality which transgresses the boundaries between high and low culture or presents a combination of things that actually do not fit together.

Connotation the second order of signification or the full interpretation of a message.

Content analysis research methodology in social science analysing media texts in a quantitative and/or qualitative way.

Convergence culture the confluence of media production technologies for both media industries and audiences.

Critical mass the idea that once enough women take part in media production (with an emphasis on managerial positions), media content will become unbiased with regard to gender representations.

Cultivation theory (aka cultivation hypothesis, cultivation thesis) perceiving media, specifically television, as a symbolic world that sustains values and norms upon which humans act and base their behaviour.

Cultural capital the cultural competences one has developed in relation to taste and cultural products.

Cultural imperialism the dominance of one nation or culture imposing their norms and values leading ultimately to the homogenisation of a global culture; also referred to as media imperialism.

Cultural proximity the closeness of cultural values and features displayed in media to the cultural values of the viewers.

Denotation first order of signification or the more literal meaning of a message.

Digital native   person who has been interacting with media technologies from the day he or she was born.

Discourse analysis   a research method that concentrates on how meanings are produced, by whom and how power intersects, focusing on the ideological meaning of patterns.

Discourse   a group of statements which provide a language for talking about – a way of representing the knowledge about – a particular topic at a particular historical moment.

Distinction   the activity of distancing of one social class from another embedded in differences in tastes.

Dominant reading   when an audience member decodes a message in terms of the reference code (the code used by the encoder) full and straight, as the producers hoped it would.

Economic drivers   point to the decreased costs in internet access and availability of tools for the creation and an increased commercial interest in UGC.

Effect theories   can be understood as different studies which look into a causal relation between media content and individuals' behaviour or perspectives on the world.

Encoding/decoding model   embedded in social and economic structures, but also in organisational routines, producers (encoders) construct (encode) a message, a sign vehicle using codes, which is deconstructed (decoding) by its audiences. Where the encoding and decoding overlap, we find a meaningful discourse.

Essentialism   a theory or believe that specific characteristics such as sex, race or sexuality are an essence (by nature) of an identity.

Framing analysis   a research methodology in social science were the communication source is seen as constructing frames.

Gaze theory   the way in which movies construct characters as objects for pleasure, enabling a particular way of 'looking at' people, exercising the gaze. The gaze has the psychological effect that the subject of this gaze loses some sense of autonomy upon realising that he or she is a visible object.

Gender   socially constructed meanings of one's physical sex whereby femininity and masculinity are viewed as socially constructed conventions and norms with regard to behaviour and appearance of women and men.

Gender role   people are expected to perform a gender that fits their sex. Because she is of the female sex, she is expected to perform according to the norms on feminine behaviour and because he is of the male sex, he is expected to perform according to the norms on masculine behaviour.

Genre   an organising principle by generic codes that is used by both the audiences and the media industry.

Glass ceiling   gender inequality that is hierarchically organised, as the inequality increases towards the top, that cannot be explained by any other characteristics of the employee.

Global Media Monitoring Project (GMMP) a longitudinal project monitoring the representation and portrayal of women and men in world's news media and creating media awareness.

Goffmanian analysis a research method that focuses on the analysis of gender representations in advertisements using 'gender displays' (expressions of gender) that are socially learned. Gender displays function as a ritualistic affirmation of the social hierarchy.

Habitus a kind of mental structure, a way of thinking, one develops from infancy to adulthood onwards that is dependent on one's environment.

Hard media media content (especially types and genres of news production) that are considered as being of high status and characterised as masculine.

Hegemonic masculinity the dominant understanding of what "normal" masculinity is in a certain society.

Hegemony process whereby the dominant group in society maintains their power in the form of spontaneous consent with their views and value systems.

Heteronormativity the norm is represented in such a way that heterosexuality is the only or "good" sexual orientation in society.

Horizontal intertextuality the relations between primary texts which are explicitly linked to one another focusing on the similarities between different media texts.

Horizontal segregation the relation of specialisations within a certain field, for example like journalism, with gender; indicating that women are likely to specialise in different topics than men.

Hyperfemininity the exaggeration of female stereotypical behaviour.

Hypermasculinity the exaggeration of male stereotypical behaviour.

Hypersexuality increased referencing to sexuality in behaviour or in the way that sexuality is represented in media content.

Hypodermic needle/magic bullet theory the notion that media inject content into audiences.

Identification the process by which individuals or groups to recognise certain features in a representation.

Identity a group of features which construct the notion of how we describe ourselves to each other, including a self-identity and a social identity.

Institutional and legal drivers the legislation on copyrights and licensing and the way they have become more flexible, hence allowing for more UGC.

Intermediality the way communication takes place in an increasing number of media channels and communication technologies which are all inherently linked to each other.

Intersectionality the understanding that the meaning of the concept of gender should be understood in relation to concepts such as class, age, sexuality and ethnicity. Like gender, these concepts are also viewed as social constructs of which the meanings change over time.

Intertextuality meaning that the construction of any given text does take place within a wider context. A text is not a fully autonomous entity but its meanings are produced by other texts. In the interaction of the reader and the text a network of other texts is evoked that take part in the meaning-making process.

Liberal perspective on media beliefs that the media industry is profit driven and that they sell what audiences want.

Male gaze male characters in movies are more often bearers of the gaze, while female characters are more often subjected to it.

Mass media paradigm conception of the audiences as a mass with a centralised source and a multitude of dispersed viewers.

Media panic a moral panic in which the media themselves are the subject and location of the debate.

Mediatisation a theory stressing the role of media in shaping discourses in the context of modernisation.

Moral entrepreneurs people who are in the position, have the power and/or authority to make rules or reinforce them.

Moral panic process in which there is discrepancy between what a society, or part of a society, perceives as a threat of the social order that is not sustained by the actual state of affairs; a gap between threat and reaction.

Multicasting differentiation as the key element in a business plan of the media industry today. Offering different identity representations to provide attractive content for different audiences in order to accumulate a larger audience.

Narrowcasting practice of the media industry to aim their products on a particular segment of the audience.

Negotiated reading the negotiation of audiences with codes they, for example, object to. While there is acknowledgement of the dominant code, due to situational context some codes are adapted.

Network society the way societies are organised in networks with various centres.

New-girls'-network professional organisations founded by and for women to enhance women's professional lives.

Objectification the way a person is treated as a thing, an object.

Old-boys'-network an informal system of friendship and mutual assistance through which men who are acquainted with each other exchange favours and connections.

Oppositional reading an audience member's reading of the codes in opposition of the dominant code, and fitting these codes into a different frame of knowledge.

Parody a form of intertextuality where an imitation of an existing media text intends to mock, comment or trivialise the original (sometimes also labelled as camp).

Participatory culture concept which celebrates the activity of the consumer as taking part in the production of media content.

Pastiche form of intertextuality where a media text is solely constructed out of a variety of other, identifiable texts.

Patriarchy the structural domination of women by men reflected in the social organisation and institutions of society.

Performativity speech, gestures and behaviour constructing identities by performative actions.

Pleasure a notion which refers mostly to the activity of an audience of media content and comes with the process of interacting with media content. This interactivity is mostly on the level of giving meaning to the media content as a signifying practice.

Political economy A perspective within the field of media studies focusing on ownership and structures of media companies stating that media products reflect and serve the interests of the owners.

Politics of representation the practice of representing seen as articulations of power and identity.

Polysemy the potential of a media text to carry different reading and meanings within it.

Pornofication the use of aesthetic elements of the porn industry for non-porn media products.

Post-feminism a development in society in which women are thought to enjoy the benefits of feminist activists' hard-won freedoms, but are not willing to carry the burdens of positioning oneself as a feminist.

Primary texts media products.

Prosumer a contraction of producer and consumer, referring to the fact that a media consumer is becoming a producer in a convergent media sphere. Also referred to as produser.

Queer theory an academic field which critically evaluates all categorisations of gender and sexuality and concentrates on non-normative representations of sexuality and gender.

Queer functions as an umbrella term for those who articulate sexual and gender identity positions as not-categorised and not fixed.

Reception the study of interpretations or the way an audience member or a group give meaning to a media text.

Representation the portrayal and imagining in media and the meanings attached to these portrayals. The result of a production process in which many decisions and selections are made.

Resistance developed in cultural studies emphasising that many of the pleasures derived from the media are actually born out of resisting a preferred reading and creating a counter-hegemonic discourse.

Science and Technology Studies (STS) a field of study focusing on the content of technology and the processes of innovation.

Scopophilia the pleasure of looking at another person as an erotic object.

Screen theory the psycho-analytic tradition in film studies focusing on in-text constructions of subject positions.

Semiotics a structuralist approach that concerns how signs work starts with an understanding of the sign as "dyadic" or a two-part model of the sign.

Sex role analysis referring to a method based on Sex Role Theory. This perspective stresses that gender behaviour is regulated by social norms that are applicable to the social roles people occupy. One is socialised into this behaviour, for which several institutes are deemed relevant: family, peers, education and media.

Sex/gender dichotomy essentialists' approach were gender is formulated as inherent to sex and both genders are considered to be essentially different, articulating gender and the assumed differences as natural and unchangeable.

Sex/gender system refers to the link between gender, sexuality and reproduction, where gender is defined as an imposed social distinction between the two sexes and is conceptualised as a product of social sexual relationships.

Sex physical sex viewed as out of chromosomal, anatomical and hormonal features. Usually understood as a biological fact referring to the biological differences between women and men.

Sexualisation turning everything – behaviour, representations, clothes, et cetera – into something related to sexuality.

Sign composed by a signifier (the form that the sign takes) and the signified (the concept it represents). The sign is the whole that results from the association of the signifier with the signified.

Situatedness the social-historical context of an individual. Reflection on this context implicates that we never gain an objective, overarching knowledge, but only a partial, a situated knowledge.

Slash videos a form of fan work where, in an audio-visual media content, two same-sex characters from a certain media product are presented in a romantic relationship.

Social constructivism postulates that meanings are dynamic and prone to changes.

Social drivers an increased willingness of media consumers to share content and an increased desire to express oneself online.

Social role theory behaviour is regulated by social norms that are applicable to the social roles people occupy. One is socialised into this behaviour, for which several institutes are deemed relevant: family, peers, education and the media.

Social shaping of technology (SST) focusing on human choices and actions in technological change beside the technological, political and ethical dimension.

Social-liberal perspective on media a combination of political economy perspective and liberal perspective advocating a dual system of private and public media in a context of governmental regulations on public media granting media access to everyone, while also maintaining space for private media with a more profit driven profile.

Soft media   media types like human interest – with a lower status than hard media – in which commonly more women are at work and are characterised as feminine.

Stereotyping   a signifying practice which reduces people to few characteristics that are presented as essential and natural. As a signifying practice it produces knowledge on the deviant, but also on the normal. As products of discourse, stereotypes change over time and are geographically situated.

Subject position   a poststructuralist understanding of subjectivity which opens up the possibility for change and for multiple subject positions relating to our identities.

Subjectivity   the place for the subject created by the text.

Symbolic annihilation   refers to the under-representation or absence of representations of groups in in certain spaces.

Symbolic creativity   audiences use media products in a (symbolically) creative way.

Symbolic extension   the use of media products to engage in other activities.

Symbolic work   media consumption takes work in terms of the investment (in time and energy) when one engages with media.

Technological determinism   technology is considered as the cause for social change.

Technological drivers   the development of technologies which increase UGC.

Technologies of gender   the operationalisation of power in relation to the effects of technology in terms of gender.

Tertiary texts   texts on the level of the audience and their interpretation (for example, a letter to a celebrity, fan fiction or an interpretation of a song).

Textual determinism   a position where research only focuses on the meaning of the media text without studying the production or audiences of the media text.

Textual poaching   a fan activity of media consumers who take bits and pieces from existing media texts and re-appropriate them.

User generated content (UGC)   new media content produced by a media consumer.

Uses and Gratifications theory (U&G)   a theory approach where the focus is on 'what do people do with media' and stress that media content is offering certain options to the audience. The audience is active and acts on a certain need, seeking to gratify it with media content.

Vertical intertextuality   the relations of the primary texts with secondary and tertiary texts that refer specifically to it.

Vertical segregation   the idea that women in the media industry are found less in managerial positions than men.

Web 2.0 paradigm   refers to audiences who match with the prosumer (audiences producing and consuming media content).

References

Adams, D. (2005 [1999]). *The Salmon of Doubt: Hitchhiking the Galaxy One Last Time*. New York: Ballantine Books.

Adriaens, F., Van Damme, E. and Courtois, C. (2011). The Spatial and Social Contexts of Television-viewing Adolescents. *Poetics, 39*(3), 205–27.

Aksoy, A. and Robins, K. (2000). Thinking Across Spaces: Transnational Television From Turkey. *European Journal of Cultural Studies, 3*(3), 343–65.

AL.com. (2013, 15 March 2013). *Loathing Lena Dunham: Which Celeb Do You Love to Hate?* (poll). Retrieved 24 May, 2013, from www.al.com/entertainment/index.ssf/2013/03/loathing_lena_dunham_which_cel.html.

American Psychological Association (2010). *Report of the APA Task Force on the Sexualization of Girls*. Retrieved 1 October, 2014, from www.apa.org/pi/women/programs/girls/report-full.pdf.

Anderson, B. (1983). *Imagined Communities: Reflections on the Origins and Spread of Nationalism*. London: Verso.

Ang, I. (1985). *Watching Dallas: Soap Opera and the Melodramatic Imagination*. London: Methuen.

——(1996). *Living Room Wars: Rethinking Media Audiences for a Postmodern World*. London/New York: Routledge.

——(2003 [1995]). I'm a Feminist but … 'Other' Women and Postnational Feminism. In R. Lewis and S. Mills (Eds.), *Feminist Postcolonial Theory: A Reader* (pp. 190–206). Edinburgh: Edinburgh University Press.

Ang, I. and Hermes, J. (1996). Gender and/in Media Consumption. In J. Curran and M. Gurevitch (Eds.), *Mass Media and Society* (pp. 325–47). London: Routledge.

Appadurai, A. (1996). *Modernity at Large: Cultural Dimensions of Globalization*. Minneapolis: University of Minnesota Press.

ArtsReformation.com (2006). *The Motion Picture Production Code of 1930 (Hays Code)*. Retrieved 3 July, 2013, from www.artsreformation.com/a001/hays-code.html.

Arulampalan, W., Booth, A.L. and Bryan, M.L. (2007). Is There a Glass Ceiling over Europe? Exploring the Gender Pay Gap across the Wage Distribution. *Industrial and Labor Relations Review, 60*(2), 163–86.

Attwood, F. (2005). What Do People Do with Porn? Qualitative Research into the Consumption, Use, and Experience of Pornography and Other Sexually Explicit Media. *Sexuality and Culture, 9*(2), 65–86.

——(2014). *Foucault 2.0. Moral Panics and The Question of Sexual Liberties.* Paper presented at the Opening Event Amsterdam Research Center for Gender and Sexuality, Amsterdam.

Attwood, F. and Smith, C. (2011). Investigating Young People's Sexual Cultures: An Introduction. *Sex Education: Sexuality, Society and Learning, 11*(3), 235–42.

Bakker, A. (2013). *Men to be Together. Motives for the Production of Slash Videos on YouTube.* BA Thesis Erasmus University Rotterdam.

Bakker, P. and Scholten, O. (2005). *Communicatiekaart van Nederland. Overzicht van media en communicatie.* Amsterdam: Kluwer.

Balaji, M. (2010). Vixen Resistin':. Redefining Black Womanhood in Hip-Hop Music Videos. *Journal of Black Studies, 41*(1), 5–20.

Bale, C. (2011). Raunch or Romance? Framing and Interpreting The Relationship Between Sexualized Culture and Young People's Sexual Health. *Sex Education: Sexuality, Society and Learning, 11*(3), 303–13.

Banks, M.J. (2009). Gender Below-the-Line. Defining Feminist Production Studies. In V. Mayer, M.J. Banks and J.T. Caldwell (Eds.), *Production Studies. Cultural Studies of Media Industries* (pp. 87–98). New York/London: Routledge.

Barker, C. (2012). *Cultural Studies: Theory and Practice* (4th edition). London/Thousand Oaks: Sage.

Barret, G. (1984). Job Satisfaction Among Newspaper Women. *Journalism Quarterly, 61*(3), 593–99.

Barthes, R. (1972). *Mythologies.* London: Cape.

——(1977). *Image-Music-Text* (S. Heath, trans.). New York: Hill and Wang.

——(1994). The Advertising Message. In *The Semiotic Challenge* (R. Howard, trans.) (pp. 173–78). Berkeley/Los Angeles: University of California Press.

Basnet, S. (2010). Bridging Gaping Inequalities in Community Radio. *Women in Action,* (1), 94. Retrieved 23 April, 2012, from www.isiswomen.org/index.php?option=com_ content&view-article&id=1473%3Awia-2010-1-converging-communications-empow ering-women-transforming-communities&Itemid=206.

Battles, K. and Hilton-Morrow, W. (2002). Gay Characters in Conventional Spaces: Will and Grace and the Situation Comedy Genre. *Critical Studies in Mass Communication, 1*(3), 87–105.

BBC. (2011). *Annual Report 2010/2011 – Part 2 – The BBC Executive's Review and Assessment.* Retrieved 28 April, 2012, from http://downloads.bbc.co.uk/annualreport/ pdf/bbc_executive_2010_11.pdf.

Beasley, C. (2008). Rethinking Hegemonic Masculinity in a Globalizing World. *Men and Masculinities, 11*(1), 86–103.

Beasley, M.H. (1993). Newspapers: Is There a New Majority Defining the News? In P.M. Creedon (Ed.), *Women in Mass Communication* (2nd edition, pp. 118–33). London/Newbury Park: Sage.

Beck, B. (2011). Fearless Vampire Kissers: Bloodsuckers We Love in *Twilight, True Blood* and Others. *Multicultural Perspectives, 13*(2), 90–92.

Bell, P. and Milic, M. (2002). Goffman's Gender Advertisements Revisited: Combining Content Analysis with Semiotic Analysis. *Visual Communication, 1*(2), 203–22.

Bem, S. (1974). The Measurement of Psychological Androgyny. *Journal of Counseling and Clinical Psychology, 42*(1), 155–62.

——(2013). *Bem Sex Role Inventory: A Measure of Androgyny andRender role.* Retrieved 15 August, 2013, from www.mindgarden.com/products/bemss.htm.

Berggren, K. (2014). Hip Hop Feminism in Sweden: Intersectionality, Feminist Critique and Female Masculinity. *European Journal of Women's Studies, 21*(3), 233–50.

Bielby, D.D. (2009). Gender Inequality in Culture Industries: Women and Men Writers in Film and Television. *Sociologie du Travail, 51*(2), 237–52.

Bielby, D.D. and Bielby, W.T. (1996). Women and Men in Film: Gender Inequality Among Writers in a Culture Industry. *Gender and Society, 10*(3), 248–70.

Bielby, D.D. and Harrington, C.L. (2008). *Global TV. Exporting Television and Culture in the World Market.* New York/London: New York University Press.

Biltereyst, D. (1997). Theoretische en methodologische fundering van receptie-onderzoek. In J. Servaes and V. Frissen (Eds.), *De interpretatieve benadering in de communicatiewetenschap. Theorie, methodologie en case-studie* (pp. 67–85). Leuven/Amersfoort: Acco.

Biltereyst, D., Meers, Ph. and Van Bauwel, S. (2000). *Realiteit en Fictie: Tweemaal hetzelfde?* Brussel: Koning Boudewijn Stichting.

Bird, S.E. (2011). Are We All Produsers Now? Convergence and Media Audience Practices. *Cultural Studies, 25*(4–5), 502–16.

Blank, G. and Reisdorf, B.C. (2012). The Participatory Web: A User Perspective on Web 2.0. *Information, Communication and Society, 15*(4), 537–54.

Bobo, J. (1995). *Black Women as Cultural Readers.* New York: Columbia University Press.

Booth, A.L., Francesconia, M. and Frank, J. (2003). A Sticky Floors Model of Promotion, pay, and gender. *European Economic Review, 47*(2), 295–322.

Bourdieu, P. (2010 [1979]). *Distinction. A Social Critique of the Judgement of Taste* (R. Nice, Trans.). London/New York: Routledge.

boyd, d. (2008). Why Youth [heart] Social Network Sites: The Role of Networked Publics in Teenage Social Life. In D. Buckingham (Ed.), *Youth, Identity, and Digital Media* (pp. 119–42). Cambridge MA: MIT Press.

Brace, P. and Arp, R. (2010). Coming Out of the Coffin and Coming Out of the Closet. In G.A. Dunn and R. Housel (Eds.), *True Blood and Philosophy: We Wanna Think Bad Things with You* (pp. 93–108). Hoboken: Wiley.

Bragg, S., Buckingham, D., Russell, R. and Willett, R. (2011). Too Much, too Soon? Children, 'Sexualization' and Consumer Culture. *Sex Education: Sexuality, Society and Learning, 11*(3), 279–92.

Bresnahan, M.J., Inoue, Y., Liu, W.Y. and Nishida, T. (2001). Changing Gender Roles in Prime-Time Commercials in Malaysia, Japan, Taiwan, and the United States. *Sex Roles, 45*(1/2), 117–31.

Britannica Editors. (2010). Is Lady Gaga a Feminist? 5 Questions for Philosopher Nancy Bauer, *Britannica Blog*. Retrieved 19 May, 2011, from www.britannica.com/blogs/2010/07/is-lady-gaga-a-feminist-5-questions-for-philosopher-nancy-bauer/.

Broadband Commission – Working Group on Broadband and Gender (2013). *Doubling Digital Opportunities. Enhancing the Inclusion of Women and Girls In the Information Society.* Paris: UNESCO.

Brouns, M. (1995). Theoretische kaders. In M. Brouns, M. Verloo and M. Grünell (Eds.), *Vrouwenstudies in de jaren, 90* (pp. 53–76). Bussum: Dick Coutinho.

Bruns, A. (2006). Towards Produsage: Futures for User-Led Content Production. *Proceedings Cultural Attitudes towards Communication and Technology*, 1–10. Retrieved 20 February, 2014, from http://eprints.qut.edu.au/4863/1/4863_1.pdf.

Brunsdon, C. (1982). *Crossroads:* Notes on Soap Opera. *Screen, 22*(4), 32–37.

Buckingham, D. (1987). *Public Secrets: 'Eastenders' and its Audience*. London: British Film Institute.

Butler, J. (1993). *Bodies That Matter. On the Discursive Limits of 'Sex'*. London/New York: Routledge.

Butler, J. (1990). *Gender Trouble: Feminism and the Subversion of Identity*. London/ New York: Routledge.

Butsch, R. and Livingstone, S. (2014). Introduction: 'Translating' Audiences, Provincializing Europe. In R. Butsch and S. Livingstone (Eds.), *Meanings of Audiences: Comparative Discourses* (pp. 1–19). London/New York: Routledge.

Byerly, C.M. (2004). Feminist Interventions in Newsrooms. In K. Ross and C.M. Byerly (Eds.), *Women and Media: International Perspectives* (pp. 109–31). Oxford/Malden/ Carlton: Blackwell.

Byerly, C.M. and Ross, K. (2004). Part II – Women's Agency in Media Production. In K. Ross and C.M. Byerly (Eds.), *Women and Media: International Perspectives* (pp. 105–8). Oxford/Malden/Carlton: Blackwell.

Caldwell, J.T. (2008). *Production Culture: Industrial Reflexivity and Critical Practice in Film and Television*. Durham/London: Duke University Press.

Cantril, H. (1954). The Invasion from Mars. In W. Schramm (Ed.), *The Process and Effects of Mass Communication* (pp. 411–23). Urbana: University of Illinois Press.

Carr, N. (2008). *Is Google Making Us Stupid? What the Internet is Doing to our Brains* Retrieved 23 November, 2014, from www.theatlantic.com/magazine/archive/2008/07/ is-google-making-us-stupid/306868/.

Carter, C., Branston, G. and Allan, S. (1998). Introduction. In C. Carter, G. Branston and S. Allan (Eds.), *News, Gender and Power* (pp. 141–44). London/New York: Routledge.

Castells, M. (1996). *The Rise of the Network Society*. Oxford/Malden: Blackwell.

Ceulemans, M. and Fauconnier, G. (1979). *Mass Media: The Image, Role, and Social Conditions of Women. A Collection and Analysis of Research Materials*. Paris: UNESCO.

Charles, C.E. (2012). New Girl Heroes: The Rise of Popular Feminist Commentators in an Era of Sexualisation. *Gender and Education, 24*(3), 317–23.

Chow, Y.F. (2008). Martial Arts Films and Dutch-Chinese Masculinities. *China Information, 22*(2), 331–59.

Claringbould, I., Knoppers, A. and Elling, A. (2004). Exclusionary Practices in Sport Journalism. *Sex Roles, 51*(11/12), 709–18.

Clover, C.J. (1992). *Men, Women, and Chain Saws: Gender in the Modern Horror Film*. Princeton: Princeton University Press.

CNNMoney. (2011). *Fortune 500 2014*. Retrieved 8 November, 2014, from http://fortune. com/fortune500/viacom-inc-210/.

Cochrane, K. (2010). Is Lady Gaga a Feminist Icon? *The Guardian* (Vol. 17 September 2010).

Connell, R. W. and Messerschmidt, J.W. (2005). Hegemonic Masculinity: Rethinking the Concept. *Gender and Society, 19*(6), 829–59.

Cook, G. (2001). *The Discourse of Advertising* (2nd edition). London/New York: Routledge.

Cook, P. (1983). Melodrama and the Woman's Picture. In S. Aspinall and R. Murphy (Eds.), *Gainsborough Melodrama* (pp. 14–28). London: British Film Institute.

Coolen, M. (1997). De reflexieve functie van soap. In G.A.M. Widdershoven and A.W.M. Mooij (Eds.), *Hermeneutiek & politiek* (pp. 123–39). Delft: Uitgeverij Eburon.

Cotter, D.A., Hermsen, J.M., Ovadia, S. and Vanneman, R. (2001). The Glass Ceiling Effect. *Social Forces*, *80*(2), 655–81.

Couldry, N. and Hepp, A. (2013). Conceptualizing Mediatization: Contexts, Traditions, Arguments. *Communication Theory*, *23*(3), 191–202.

Cover, R. (2000). First Contact, Queer Theory, Sexual Identity, and 'Mainstream' Film. *International Journal of Sexuality and Gender Studies*, *5*(1): 71–89.

Craig, S. (1992). Introduction: Considering Men and the Media. In S. Craig (Ed.), *Men, Masculinity, and the Media* (pp. 1–7). Newbury Park/London/New Delhi: Sage.

Cragin, B. (2010). Beyond the Feminine: Intersectionality and Hybridity in Talk Shows. *Women's Studies in Communication*, *33*, 154–72.

Cramer, J. (2007). Radio: The More Things Change … The More They Stay the Same. In P.J. Creedon and J. Cramer (Eds.), *Women in Mass Communication* (3rd edition, pp. 59–72). Thousand Oaks/London/New Delhi: Sage.

Crane, D. (2002). Culture and Globalization: Theoretical Models and Emerging Trends. In D. Crane, N. Kawashima and K. Kawasaki (Eds.), *Global Culture: Media, Arts, Policy and Globalization* (pp. 150–80). London/New York: Routledge.

Creeber, G. (Ed.) (2008). *The Television Genre Book* (2nd edition). St. Edmundsbury: St. Edmundsbury Press.

Creekmur, C.K. and Doty, A. (Eds.) (1995). *Out in Culture: Gay, Lesbian and Queer Essays on Popular Culture*. Durham, NC and London: Duke University Press.

Crenshaw, K. (1989). Demarginalizing the Intersection of Race and Sex: A Black Feminist Critique of Antidiscrimination Doctrine, Feminist Theory and Antiracist Politics. *The University of Chicago Legal Forum, 1989: Feminism in the Law: Theory, Practice and Criticism*, 139–67.

Croteau, D.R. and Hoynes, W.D. (2014). *Media/Society: Industry, Images and Audiences* (5th edition). Thousand Oaks/London/New Delhi: Sage.

Cundy, M. (2012). *So last night I had one of the most amazing gaming experiences of my life. This is what happened …* Retrieved 27 June, 2014, from www.gamesradar.com/so-last-night-i-had-one-most-amazing-gaming-experiences-my-life-what-happened/.

Curran, J. (1990). The Crisis of Opposition: A Reappraisal. In B. Pimlott and A. Wright (Eds.), *The Alternative*. London: W.H. Allen.

——(2002). *Media and Power*. London/New York: Routledge.

Curran, J. and Park, M.J. (2000). Beyond Globalization Theory. In J. Curran and M.J. Park (Eds.), *De-Westernizing Media Studies* (pp. 3–18). London/New York: Routledge.

Curran, J., Fenton, N. and Freedman, D. (2012). *Misunderstanding the Internet*. London/New York: Routledge.

D'Haenens, L., Klokhuis, M. and Van Summeren, C. (2001). *Kijken of surfen? Mediagebruik van kinderen en adolescenten*. Leuven/Amersfoort: Acco.

De Beauvoir, S. (1949) (translation 1989). *The Second Sex* (H.M. Parshley, trans.). London: Vintage Books, Random House.

De Bruin, M. (2000). Gender, Organizational and Professional Identities in Journalism. *Journalism*, *1*(2), 217–38.

De Bruin, M. and Ross, K. (2004). *Gender and Newsroom Cultures: Identities at Work*. Cresskill, NJ: Hampton Press.

De Clercq, M. (2003). Nieuws, democratie en burgerschap. Onderzoek over hedendaagse nieuwsmedia. In D. Biltereyst and Y. Peeren (Eds.), *Nieuws, democratie en burgerschap: Onderzoek over hedendaagse nieuwsmedia* (pp. 79–110). Ghent: Academia Press.

De Kloet, J. (2008). Gendering China Studies. *China Information, 22*(2), 195–219.

Delano, A. (2003). Women Journalists: What's the Difference? *Journalism Studies, 4*(2), 273–86.

De Lauretis, T. (1987). *Technologies of Gender. Essays on Theory, Film, and Fiction.* Bloomington/Indianapolis: Indiana University Press.

——(1984). *Alice Doesn't: Feminism. Semiotics. Cinema.* Bloomington/Indianapolis: Indiana University Press.

De Ridder, S. and Van Bauwel, S. (2013). Commenting on Pictures: Teens Negotiating Gender and Sexualities on Social Networking Sites. *Sexualities, 16*(5/6), 565–86.

De Ridder, S. (2013). Are Digital Media Institutions Shaping Youth's Intimate Stories? Strategies and Tactics in the Social Networking Site Netlog. *New Media and Society,* online first doi: 10.1177/1461444813504273.

De Saussure, F. (1983 [1972]). *Course in General Linguistics* (Roy Harris, trans.). London: Duckworth.

Deuze, M. (2007). Convergence Culture in the Creative Industries. *International Journal of Cultural Studies, 10*(2), 243–63.

De Valck, M. and Teurlings, J. (2013). After the Break. Television Theory Today. In M. De Valck and J. Teurlings (Eds.), *After the Break: Television Theory Today* (pp. 7–17). Amsterdam: Amsterdam University Press.

Dhaenens, F., Van Bauwel, S. and Biltereyst, D. (2008). Slashing the Fiction of Queer Theory: Slash Fiction, Queer Reading, and Transgressing the Boundaries of Screen Studies, Representations, and Audiences. *Journal of Communication Inquiry, 32*(4): 335–47.

Dhaenens, F. (2013). The Fantastic Queer: Reading Gay Representations in *Torchwood* and *True Blood* as Articulations of Queer Resistance. *Critical Studies in Media Communication, 30*(2): 102–16.

Diaz Soloaga, P. and Muñiz, P. (2008). Women Stereotypes Portrayed in Print Ads by Luxury Fashion Brands: A Content Analysis from 2002–5. *Observatorio, 4*: 291–305.

Diaz Soloaga, P. and Carlos Muñiz, C. (2013). Women's Portraits Present in Print Fashion Advertisements: A Content Analysis of Spanish Fashion Magazines from 2002 to 2009. In A.N. Valdivia and S.R. Mazzarella (Eds.), *The International Encyclopedia of Media Studies, Volume III: Content and Representation.* (pp. 74–94). London: Blackwell.

Diesel.com. (2010). *Diesel Stupid Philosophy.* Retrieved 21 October, 2014, from www.creativeadawards.com/diesel-be-stupid-advertising-campaign/.

Dill, K.E. and Thill, K.P. (2007). Video Game Characters and The Socialization of Gender Roles: Young People's Perception Mirror Sexist Media Depictions. *Sex Roles, 57*(11/12), 851–64.

DiMaggio, P. (1991). Social Structure, Institutions, and Cultural Goods: The Case of the United States. In P. Bourdieu and J.S. Coleman (Eds.), *Social Theory For a Changing Society* (pp. 133–55). Boulder, CO: Westview Press.

Dimova, S. (2012). English in Macedonian Television Commercials. *World Englishes, 31*(1), 15–29.

Djerf-Pierre, M. (2007). The Gender of Journalism: The Structure and Logic of the Field in the Twentieth Century. *Nordicom Review, Jubilee Issue 2007*, 81–104.

Dobson, A.S. (2014). Performative Shamelessness on Young Women's Social Network Sites: Shielding the Self and Resisting Gender Melancholia. *Feminism and Psychology, 24*(1), 97–114.

Doty, A. (2000). *Flaming Classics: Queering the Film Canon.* New York: Routledge.

Dowd, T.J. and Janssen, S. (2011). Globalization and Diversity in Cultural Fields: Comparative Perspectives on Television, Music and Literature. *American Behavioral Scientist, 55*(5), 519–24.

Downey, J. (2006). The Media Industries: Do Ownership, Size and Internationalisation Matter? In D. Hesmondhalgh (Ed.), *Media Production* (pp. 7–47). Maidenhead: Open University Press.

Driscoll, C. and Gregg, M. (2011). Convergence Culture and the Legacy of Feminist Cultural Studies. *Cultural Studies, 25*(4/5), 566–84.

Drotner, K. (1999). Dangerous Media? Panic Discourses and Dilemmas of Modernity. *Paedagogica Historica: International Journal of the History of Education, 35*(3), 593–619.

Duffy, J., Warren, K. and Walsh, M. (2001). Classroom Interactions: Gender of Teacher, Gender of Student, and Classroom Subject. *Sex Roles, 45*(9/10), 579–93.

Duits, L. and Van Romondt Vis, P. (2009). Girls Make Sense. Girls, Celebrities and Identities. *European Journal of Cultural Studies, 12*(1), 41–58.

Duits, L. and Van Zoonen, L. (2006). Headscarves and Porno-Chic. Disciplining Girls' Bodies in the European Multicultural Society. *European Journal of Women's Studies, 133*(2), 103–17.

——(2007). Who's Afraid of Female Agency? A Rejoinder to Gill. *European Journal of Women's Studies, 14*(2), 161–70.

——(2009). Against Amensia: 30+ Years of Girls' Studies. *Feminist Media Studies, 9*(1), 111–15.

——(2011). Coming to Terms With Sexualization. *European Journal of Cultural Studies, 14*(5), 491–506.

Dunphy, R. (2000). *Sexual Politics. An Introduction*. Edinburgh: Edinburgh University Press.

Duschinsky, R. (2013). What Does Sexualisation Mean? *Feminist Theory, 14*(3), 255–64.

Dworkin, A. and MacKinnon, C.A. (1988). *Pornography and Civil Rights. A New Day for Women's Equality*. Minneapolis: Organizing Against Pornography.

Dyer, R. (1990). *Now You See It: Historical Studies on Lesbian and Gay Film*. London: Routledge.

Eagly, A.H. (1987). *Sex Differences in Social Behavior: A Social Role Interpretation*. Hillsdale NJ: Erlbaum.

Eagly, A.H. and Carli, L.L. (2007). *Through the Labyrinth: The Truth About How Women Become Leaders*. Boston, MA: Harvard Business School Press.

Edell, D., Brown, L.M. and Tolman, D. (2013). Embodying Sexualisation: When Theory Meets Practice in Intergenerational Feminist Activism. *Feminist Theory, 14*(3), 275–84.

Edgar, A. and Sedgwick, P. (1999). *Key Concepts in Cultural Theory*. London: Routledge.

Edwards, L.H. (2012). Transmedia Storytelling, Corporate Synergy, and Audience Expression. *Global Media Journal, 12*(20), 1–12.

Edwards, T. (1998). Queer Fears: Against the Cultural Turn. *Sexualities, 1*(4), 471–84.

Egan, R.D. and Hawkes, G.L. (2008). Endangered Girls and Incendiary Objects: Unpacking the Discourse on Sexualisation. *Sexuality and Culture, 12*(4), 291–311.

Eie, B. (1998). *Who Speaks in Television? An International Comparative Study on Female Participation in Television Programmes*. Oslo: NRK.

Engstrom, E. (2010). Alternative Feminist Media on the Airwaves: Radio and Women's Music. *Journal of Radio and Audio Media*, 17(1), 18–32.

Essed, P. (1982). Racisme en feminisme. *Socialisties feministiese teksten*, 7, 9–40.

Evans, C. and Gramman, L. (1995). The Gaze Revisited, or Reviewing Queer Viewing. In P. Burston and C. Richardson (Eds.), *A Queer Romance: Lesbians, Gay Men and Popular Culture* (pp. 13–56). London: Routledge.

Fausto-Sterling, A. (2000). *Sexing the Body: Gender Politics and the Construction of Sexuality*. New York: Basic Books.

Featherstone, M. (2007). *Consumer Culture and Postmodernism* (2nd edition). London/Thousasd Oaks/New Delhi: Sage.

Federal Glass Ceiling Commission (1995). *Good for Business: Making Full Use of the Nation's Human Capital: The Environmental Scan*. Washington DC.

Fejes, F.J. (1992). Masculinity as Fact: A Review of Empirical Mass Communication Research on Masculinity. In S. Craig (Ed.), *Men, Masculinity, and the Media* (pp. 9–22). London: Sage.

FEMEN. (n.d.). *Femen Is a Death For Patriarchy*. Retrieved 24 October, 2014, from http://femen.org/about.

Fiske, J. (1987). *Television Culture*. London/New York: Routledge.

Flitterman-Lewis, S. (1992). Psychoanalysis, Film, and Television. In R.C. Allen (Ed.), *Channels of Discourse, Reassembled: Television and Contemporary Criticism* (2nd edition, pp. 203–46). London/New York: Routledge.

Foucault, M. (1980). *Power/Knowledge*. New York: Pantheon.

——(1982). Technologies of The Self. In P. Rabinow (Ed.), *Ethics – Subjectivity and Truth* (pp. 223–51). London: Penguin Books.

——(1989). *The Order of Things*. London/New York: Routledge.

Frankenberg, R. (1993). *White Women, Race Matters: The Social Construction of Whiteness*. London/New York: Routledge.

Fröhlich, R. (2004). *The 'Friendliness Trap': Feminine and Feminist Values as Obstacles for Women's Future and Career in Journalism*. Paper presented at the UNESCO JourNet Conference, Newcastle.

Furnham, A., Mak, T. and Tanidjojo, L. (2000). An Asian Perspective on the Portrayal of Men and Women in Television Advertisements: Studies From Hong Kong and Indonesian Television. *Journal of Applied Social Psychology*, 30(11), 2341–64.

Furnham, A. and Paltzer, S. (2010). The Portrayal of Men and Women in Television Advertisements: An Updated Review of 30 Studies Published Since 2000. *Scandinavian Journal of Psychology*, 51, 216–36.

Gallagher, M. (1995). *An Unfinished Story: Gender Patterns in Media Employment*. Paris: UNESCO.

——(2001). *Gender Setting*. London: WACC.

Gamba, M. and Kleiner, B.H. (2001). The Old Boys' Network Today. *International Journal of Sociology and Social Policy*, 21(8), 101–7.

Gauntlett, D. (1998). Ten Things Wrong with the 'Effects Model'. In R. Dickinson, R. Harindranath and O. Linné (Eds.), *Approaches to Audiences: A Reader* (pp. 120–30). London: Arnold.

Geraghty, C. (1998). Soap Opera and Utopia. In J. Storey (Ed.), *Cultural Theory and Popular Culture: A Reader* (2nd edition, pp. 319–27). London: Harvester Wheatsheaf.

Gerbner, G. and Gross, L. (1979). Living with Television: The Violence Profile. *Journal of Communication*, 26(2), 172–99.

——(1976). The Scary World of TV's Heavy Viewer. *Psychology Today*, 9(11), 41–5, 89. Reprinted in D.M. White and J. Pendleton (Eds.), *Popular Culture: Mirror of American Life* (pp. 123–7). Del Mar, CA: Publishers, Inc.

Gerritsen, M., Verdonk, T. and Visser, A. (2013). *De monitor vrouwelijke hoogleraren 2012*. Retrieved 24 November 2014, from www.stichtingdebeauvoir.nl/wp-content/uploads/Monitor_Vrouwelijke_Hoogleraren_2012.pdf.

Giddens, A. (1984). *The Constitution of Sociey: Outline of the Theory of of Structuration*. Cambridge/Malden: Polity Press.

——(1991). *Modernity and Self-Identity. Self and Society in the Late Modern Age*. Cambridge/Malden: Polity Press.

Gill, R. (2007a). *Gender and the Media*. Cambridge/Malden: Polity Press.

——(2007b). Critical Respect: The Difficulties and Dilemmas of Agency and 'Choice' for Feminism. A Reply to Duits and Van Zoonen. *European Journal of Women's Studies*, 14(1), 69–80.

——(2008). Empowerment/Sexism: Figuring Female Sexual Agency in Contemporary Advertising. *Feminism and Psychology*, 18(1), 35–60.

Gitlin, T. (2000). *Inside Prime Time*. (1994 revised edition). Berkeley/Los Angeles/London: University of California Press.

Gittings, C. (2001). Zero Patience, Genre, Difference, and Ideology: Singing and Dancing Queer Nation. *Cinema Journal*, 41(1): 28–39.

Glascock, J. (2001). Gender Roles on Prime-Time Network Television: Demographics and Behaviors. *Journal of Broadcasting and Electronic Media*, 45(4), 656–69.

Gledhill, C. (1997). Genre and Gender: The Case of Soap Opera. In S. Hall (Ed.), *Representation* (pp. 337–86). London: Sage.

Gledhill, C. and Ball, V. (2013). Genre and Gender: The Case of Soap Opera. In S. Hall, J. Evans and S. Nixon (Eds.), *Representation* (pp. 335–84). London/Thousasd Oaks/New Delhi: Sage.

Global Brands Magazine (2013). *Most Desired Clothing Brands Across the Globe*. Retrieved 1 November, 2014, from www.globalbrandsmagazine.com/most-desired-clothing-brands-across-the-globe/.

Glyn, D. and Needham, G. (Eds.) (2009). *Queer Television: Theories, Histories, Politics*. London/New York: Routledge.

GMMP. (2010). *Who Makes The News?* London/Toronto: World Association for Christian Communication.

Goffman, E. (1979). *Gender Advertisements*. New York: Harper and Row Publishers, Inc.

Goldstein, J. (1998). Immortal Kombat: War Toys and Violent Video Games. In J. Goldstein (Ed.), *Why We Watch: The Attractions of Violent Entertainment* (pp. 53–67). Oxford: Oxford University Press.

Gray, A. (1992). *Video Playtime: The Gendering of a Leisure Technology*. London: Routledge.

Gray, J. (2005). *Watching with The Simpsons: Television, Parody, and Intertextuality*. London: Routledge.

Greenfield, R. (2013). Gamers Can't Handle the New Female Head at Xbox. *The Atlantic Wire* Retrieved 23 August, 2013, from http://m.theatlanticwire.com/technology/2013/07/gamers-cant-handle-new-female-head-xbox/67073/.

Gross, L. (1998). Minorities, Majorities and the Media. In T. Liebes and J. Curran (Eds.), *Media, Ritual and Identity* (pp. 87–102). London: Routledge.

Hall, S. (1973). Encoding and Decoding in the Television Discourse. *Paper for the Council of Europe Colloquy on 'Training in the Critical Reading of Televisual Language'*. Leicester: Council and the Centre for Mass Communication Research.

——(1986). Media Power and Class Power. In J. Curran, J., Ecclestone, G. Oakley and A. Richardson (Eds.) *Bending Reality: The State of the Media* (pp. 5–14). London: Pluto Press.

——(1996). Introduction. Who needs identity? In S. Hall and P. Du Gay (Eds.), *Questions of Cultural Identity* (pp. 1–17). London: Sage.

——(2013). The Work of Representation. In S. Hall, J. Evans and S. Nixon (Eds.), *Representation* (2nd edition, pp. 1–59). London/Thousand Oaks/New Delhi: Sage.

Hall, S., Evans, J. and Nixon, S. (Eds.) (2013). *Representation* (2nd edition). London/Thousand Oaks/New Delhi: Sage.

Hallin, D.C. and Mancini, P. (2004). *Comparing Media Systems. Three Models of Media and Politics*. New York/Cambridge: Cambridge University Press.

Hamilton, J.F. (2014). Historical Forms of User Production. *Media, Culture and Society, 36*(4), 491–507.

Haraway, D. (1988). Situated Knowledge: The Science Question in Feminism and the Privilege of Partial Perspective. *Feminist Studies, 14*(3), 575–99.

Hardin, M. and Whiteside, E. (2009). Token Responses to Gendered Newsrooms: Factors in the Career-related Decisions of Female Newspaper Sports Journalists. *Journalism, 10*(5), 627–46.

Hardy, J. (2014). *Critical Political Economy of the Media: An Introduction*. London/New York: Routledge.

Hartmann, T., Möller, I. and Krause, C. (2014). Factors Underlying Male and Female Use of Violent Video Games. *New Media and Society, online first doi: 10.1177/1461444814533067.*

Hay, J. and Couldry, N. (2011). Rethinking Convergence/Culture. *Cultural Studies, 25*(4/5), 473–86.

Hayward, S. (2000). *Cinema Studies: The Key Concepts*. London: Routledge.

Hedge, R.S. (2011). Introduction. In R.S. Hedge (Ed.), *Circuits of Visibility: Gender and Transnational Media Cultures* (pp. 1–17). New York/London: New York University Press.

Heilman, E.H. (2001). Description and Prescription: How Gender Stereotypes Prevent Women's Ascent Up to the Organizational Ladder. *Journal of Social Issues, 57*(4), 657–74.

Hennesse, J.A. and Nicholson, J. (1972). Now Says: TV Commercials Insult Women. *New York Times Magazine*, 12/13: 48–51.

Herkman, J. (2012). Convergence or Intermediality? Finnish Political Communication in the New Media Age. *Convergence: The International Journal of Research into New Media Technologies, 18*(4), 369–84.

Hermes, J. (1995). *Reading Women's Magazines: An Analysis of Everyday Media Use*. Cambridge/Malden: Polity Press.

——(2005). *Re-Reading Popular Culture*. Malden/Oxford/Carlton: Blackwell.

——(2014). Caught. Critical Versus Everyday Perspectives on Television. In M. De Valck and J. Teurlings (Eds.), *After the Break: Television Theory Today* (pp. 35–49). Amsterdam: Amsterdam University Press.

Hermes, J. and Reesink, M. (2003). *Inleiding televisiestudies*. Amsterdam: Boom.

Herzog, H. (1944). What Do We Really Know about Day-time Serial Listeners? In P. Lazarsfeld and F. Stanton (Eds.), *Radio Research* (pp. 3–33). New York: Duell, Sloan and Pearce.

Hesmondhalgh, D. (2006a). The Media as Symbol Makers. In D. Hesmondhalgh (Ed.), *Media Production* (pp. 1–6). Maidenhead: Open University Press.

——(2006b). Media Organisations and Media Texts: Production, Autonomy and Power. In D. Hesmondhalgh (Ed.), *Media Production* (pp. 49–89). Maidenhead: Open University Press.

——(2007). *The Cultural Industries* (2nd edition). Los Angeles/London/New Delhi/ Singapore: Sage.

Hesmondhalgh, D. and Baker, S. (2011). *Creative Labour: Media work in Three Cultural Industries*. London/New York: Routledge.

Himberg, J. (2014). Multicasting: Lesbian Programming and the Changing Landscape of Cable TV. *Television and New Media, 15*(4), 289–304.

Hobson, D. (1982). *Crossroads: The Drama of Soap Opera*. London: Methuen.

Holland, S. and Harpin, J. (2013). Who is the 'Girly' Girl? Tomboys, Hyper-femininity and Gender. *Journal of Gender Studies, online first*, 1–17.

hoogland, r.c. (2007). Seksualiteit als strijdtoneel: de *tomboy* en *queer* studies. In R. Buikema and I. Van der Tuin (Eds.), *Gender in media, kunst en cultuur* (pp. 109–22). Bussum: Uitgeverij Coutinho.

hooks, bell (1992). *Representing Whiteness in the Black Imagination*. London: Routledge.

Humphreys, S. and Vered, K. (2014). Reflecting on Gender and Digital Networked Media. *Television and New Media, 15*(1), 3–13.

Hutcheon, L. (1989). *The Politics of Postmodernism*. London/New York: Routledge.

——(2000). *A Theory of Parody: The Teachings from Twentieth-century Art Forms*. Urbana/Chicago: University of Illinois Press.

Information is Beautiful (2009). *More Truth About Twitter*. Retrieved 28 February, 2014, from http://www.informationisbeautiful.net/2009/more-truth-about-twitter/.

——(2012). *Chicks Rule? Gender Balance and Social Network Sites*. Retrieved 28 February, 2014, from www.informationisbeautiful.net/visualizations/chicks-rule/.

ITU (2014). *Measuring the Information Society. Executive Summary*. Geneva: International Telecommunication Union.

IWMF. (2011). *Global Report on the Status of Women in the News Media*. Washington: International Women's Media Foundation.

Jackson, L.A., Ervin, K.S., Gardner, P.D. and Schmitt, N. (2001). Gender and the Internet: Women Communicating and Men Searching. *Sex Roles, 44*(5/6), 363–79.

Jackson, L.A., Zhao, Y., Kolenic III, A., Fitzgerald, H.E., Harold, R. and Von Eye, A. (2008). Race, Gender, and Information Technology Use: The New Digital Divide. *CyberPsychology and Behavior, 11*(4), 437–42.

Jenkins, H. (1992). *Textual Poachers: Television Fans and Participatory Culture*. New York/London: Routledge.

——(2004). The Cultural Logic of Media Convergence. *International Journal of Cultural Studies, 7*(1), 33–43.

——(2006). *Convergence Culture: Where Old and New Media Collide*. New York/ London: New York University Press.

Jenkins, H. and Deuze, M. (2008). Editiorial. Convergence Culture. *Convergence: The International Journal of Research into New Media Technologies, 14*(1), 5–12.

Ji, P. and Skoric, M. (2013). Gender and Social Resources: Digital Divides of Social Network Sites and Mobile Phone Use in Singapore. *Chinese Journal of Communication*, 6(2), 221–39.

Johnson, M. (1993). *Moral Imagination: Implications of Cognitive Science for Ethics.* Chicago/London: The University of Chicago Press.

Johnson, S. (1995). The Gentleman and Lady's Town and Country Magazine. In K.L. Endres and T.L. Lueck (Eds.), *Women's Periodicals in the United States: Consumer Magazines* (pp. 96–107). Westport: Greenwood Press.

——(2007). Women's Salary and Status in the Magazine Industry. In P.J. Creedon and J. Cramer (Eds.), *Women in Mass Communication* (3rd edition, pp. 47–57). Thousand Oaks/London/New Delhi: Sage.

Jonsson, T. (2014). White Feminist Stories: Locating Race in Representations of Feminism in The Guardian. *Feminist Media Studies*, online first doi: 10.1080/14680777.2014.903287.

Joseph, A. (2004). Working, Watching, and Waiting: Women and Issues of Access, Employment, and Decision-Making in the Media in India. In K. Ross and C.M. Byerly (Eds.), *Women and Media: International Perspectives* (pp. 132–55). Malden/Oxford/Carlton: Blackwell.

Joyrich, L. (1996). *Re-Viewing Reception. Television, Gender, and Postmodern Culture.* Bloomington/Indianapolis: Indiana University Press.

——(2014). Queer Television Studies: Currents, Flows, and (Main)streams. *Cinema Journal, 53*(2), 133–9.

Kang, M.E. (1997). The Portrayal of Women's Images in Magazine Advertisements: Goffman's Gender Analysis Revisited. *Sex Roles, 37*(11/12), 979–96.

Kaplan, C. (1986). *Sea Changes: Culture and Feminism.* London: Verso.

Katz, E. (1959). Mass Communications Research and the Study of Popular Culture: An Editorial Note on a Possible Future for this Journal. *Annenberg School for Communication Departmental Papers*, 1–6. Retrieved 5 June, 2014, from http://repository.upenn.edu/ascpapers/165.

Kearney, M.C. (2006). *Girls Make Media.* New York/London: Routledge.

Kellner, D. (1995). *Media Culture: Cultural studies, Identity and Politics Between the Modern and the Postmodern.* London/New York: Routledge.

Kendall, L. (2011). "White and Nerdy": Computers, Race, and the Nerd Stereotype. *Journal of Popular Culture, 44*(3), 505–24.

Kerr, A., Kücklich, J. and Brereton, P. (2006). New Media – New Pleasures? *International Journal of Cultural Studies, 9*(1), 63–82.

Kilbourne, J. (2013). *JeanKilbourne.* Retrieved 15 August, 2013, from http://www.jeankilbourne.com/.

Kimmel, M.S. (1994). Masculinities as Homophobia: Fear, Shame, and Silence in the Construction of Gender Identity. In H. Brod and M. Kaufman (Eds.), *Theorizing Masculinities* (pp. 199–141). Thousand Oaks/London/New Delhi: Sage.

Knauss, C., Paxton, S.J. and Alsaker, F.D. (2007). Relationships Amongst Body Dissatisfaction, Internalization of the Media Body Ideal and Perceived Pressure from Media Adolescent Girls and Boys. *Body Image, 4*(4), 353–60.

Knobloch-Westerwick, S. and Romero, J.P. (2011). Body Ideals in the Media: Perceived Attainability and Social Comparison Choices. *Media Psychology, 14*(1), 27–48.

Krijnen, T. (2007). *There Is More(s) In Television. Studying the Relationship Between Television and Moral Imagination.* Dissertation. University of Amsterdam: Amsterdam.

——(2011). Engaging the Moral Imagination by Watching Television: Different Modes of Moral Reflection. *Participations. International Journal of Audience Research, 8*(2), 52–73.

Krijnen, T. and Verboord, M. (2011). De televisie als morele oefenruimte. Een kwantitatieve exploratie van morele reflectie naar aanleiding van televisieverhalen. *Tijdschrift voor Communicatiewetenschap, 39*(2), 57–76.

Krijnen, T., Van Bauwel, S. and Alvares, C. (2012). New Questions and Themes in Studying Gender and Communication. *Interactions: Studies in Communication and Culture, 2*(3), 171–77.

Kristeva, J. (1986). Word, Dialogue and Novel. In T. Moi (Ed.), *The Kristeva Reader* (pp. 34–61). Oxford: Blackwell.

Kuipers, G. (2006). Television and Taste Hierarchy: The Case of Dutch Television Comedy. *Media Culture and Society, 28*(3), 359–78.

——(2011). Cultural Globalization as the Emergence of a Transnational Cultural Field: Transnational Television and National Media Landscapes in Four European Countries. *American Behavioral Scientist, 55*(5), 541–57.

——(2012). *South Park* Boys and *Sex and the City* Women: Television Trade, Narrowcasting and the Export of Gender Categories. *Interactions: Studies in Communication and Culture, 2*(3), 179–96.

Kuppens, A. (2009). Authenticating subcultural identities: African-American and Jamaican English in niche media. *Journal of Communication Inquiry, 33*(1): 43–57.

Lafrance, M., Worcester, L. and Burns, L. (2011). Gender and the *Billboard* Top 40 Charts between 1997 and 2007. *Popular Music and Society, 34*(5), 557–70.

La Pastina, A.C. and Straubhaar, J.D. (2003). Multiple Proximities Between Television Genres and Audiences. The Schisms between Telenovelas' Global Distribution and Local Consumption. *Gazette: The International Journal for Communication Studies, 67*(3), 271–88.

Larkin, B. (1997). Indian Films and Nigerian Lovers: Media and the Creation of Parallel Modernities. *Africa, 67*(3), 406–39.

Lauzen, M.M. and Deiss Jr., D.M. (2009). Breaking the Fourth Wall and Sex Role Stereotypes: An Examination of the 2006–7 Prime-Time Season. *Sex Roles, 60*(5), 379–86.

Lauzen, M.M., Dozier, D.M. and Cleveland, E. (2006). Genre Matters: An Examination of Women Working Behind the Scenes and On-screen Portrayals in Reality and Scripted Prime-Time Programming. *Sex Roles, 55*(7), 445–55.

Lazar, M.M. (Ed.) (2005) Feminist Critical Discourse Analysis: Gender, Power and Ideology in Discourse. London: Palgrave.

Lemish, D. (2011). 'Can't Talk About Sex': Producers of Children's Television Around the World Speak Out. *Sex Education: Sexuality, Society and Learning, 11*(3), 267–77.

Lewis, J. (1991). *Ideological Octopus: An Exploration of TV and Its Audience.* London/ New York: Routledge.

Liebes, T. and Katz, E. (1990). *The Export of Meaning. Cross-cultural Readings of Dallas.* Oxford: Oxford University Press.

Lievrouw, L.A. (2006). New Media Design and Development: Diffusion of Innnovations v Social Shaping of Technology. In L.A. Lievrouw and S. Livingstone (Eds.), *The Handbook of New Media: Updated Student Edition* (pp. 246–65). London/Thousand Oaks/New Delhi/Singapore: Sage.

Lievrouw, L.A. and Livingstone, S. (2006). Introduction to the Updated Student Edition. In L.A. Lievrouw and S. Livingstone (Eds.), *Handbook of New Media: Social*

Shaping and Social Consequences of ICTs: Updated Student Edition (pp. 1–14). London/Thousand Oaks/New Delhi/Singapore: Sage.

Lindner, K. (2004). Images of Women in General Interest and Fashion Magazine Advertisements from 1955 to 2002. *Sex Roles, 51*(7/8), 409–21.

Livingstone, S. (1998). Relationships Between Media and Audiences: Prospects for Audience Reception Studies. In T. Liebes and J. Curran (Eds.), *Media, Ritual and Identity: Essays in Honor of Elihu Katz* (pp. 237–55). London/New York: Routledge.

Livingstone, S., Haddon, L., Görzig, A. and Ólafsson, K. (2011). *Risks and Safety on the Internet: The Perspective of European Children*. London: EU Kids Online Network.

Longworth, J.L. (2002). *TV Creators: Conversations with Amercia's Top Producers of Television Drama* (Vol. 2). New York: Syracuse University Press.

Lont, C. (1995). *Women and Media: Content, Careers and Criticism*. California: Wadsworth.

Lotz, A. (2006). *Redesigning Women: Television after the Network Era*. Urbana/Chicago: University of Illinois Press.

——(2007). *The Television Will Be Revolutionized*. New York/London: New York University Press.

Lowe, M. (2003). Colliding Feminisms: Britney Spears, 'Tweens', and the Politics of Reception. *Popular Music and Society, 26*(2), 123–40.

Luenenborg, M., Roeser, J., Maier, T. and Mueller, K.F. (2011). Gender Analysis of Mediated Politics in Germany. In T. Krijnen, S. Van Bauwel and C. Alvares (Eds.), *Gendered Transformations: Theory and Practices on Gender and Media* (pp. 57–75). Bristol: Intellect.

Lumby, C. and Albury, K. (2010). Too much? Too young? The Sexualisation of Children Debate in Australia. *Media Interational Australia, 135*, 141–52.

Luyt, R. (2011). Representation of Gender in South African Television Advertising: A Content Analysis. *Sex Roles, 65*(5), 356–70.

——(2012). Representation of Masculinities and Race in South African Television Advertising: A Content Analysis. *Journal of Gender Studies, 21*(1), 35–60.

MacDonald, M. (1995). *Representing Women: Myths of Femininity in the Popular Media*. London: Arnold.

McIntosh, I. (1997). *Classical Sociological Theory*. Edinburgh: Edinburgh University Press.

MacKenzie, D. and Wajcman, J. (Eds.) (1999). *The Social Shaping of Technology* (2nd edition). Philadelphia/London: Open University Press/Taylor & Francis.

McLuhan, M. (1962). *The Gutenberg Galaxy: The Making of Typographic Man*. Toronto: University of Toronto Press.

McQuail, D. (2005). *McQuail's Mass Communication Theory* (5th edition). London/Thousand Oaks/New Delhi: Sage.

McRobbie, A. and Garber, J. (1976). Girls and Subcultures. In S. Hall and T. Jefferson (Eds.), *Resistance Through Rituals: Youth Subcultures in Post-war Britain* (pp. 209–22). London: Hutchinson.

McRobbie, A. (1984). *Postmodernism and Popular Culture*. London New York: Routledge.

——(2009). *The Aftermath of Feminism: Gender, Culture and Social Change*. Los Angeles/London/New Delhi/Singapore/Washington DC: Sage.

——(2011). Beyond Post-feminism. *Public Policy Research 18*(3):179–84.

Meyrowitz, J. (1986). *No Sense of Place*. Oxford: Oxford University Press.

Michelle, C. (2012). Co-Constructions of Gender and Ethnicity in New Zealand Television Advertising. *Sex Roles,* 66(1/2), 21–37.

Migrioletto, B. (2010). Towards Gender Equality – the Journey of AMARC-WIN Asia Pacific. *Women in Action,* (1). Retrieved 4 April, 2010, from Isis International website: www.isiswomen.org/index.php?option=com_content&view-article&id=1473%3Awia-2010-1-converging-communications-empowering-women-transforming-communities& Itemid=206.

Milestone, K. and Meyer, A. (2012). *Gender and Popular Culture.* Cambridge/Malden: Polity Press.

Mitchell, C. (2004). 'Dangerously Feminine?' Theory and Praxis of Women's Alternative Radio. In K. Ross and C.M. Byerly (Eds.), *Women and Media: International Perspectives* (pp. 157–85). Malden/Oxford/Carlton: Blackwell.

Modleski, T. (1984). *Loving With a Vengeance. Mass Produced Fantasies for Women.* London: Methuen.

——(2009). Clint Eastwood and Male Weepies. *American Literary History,* 22(1), 136–58.

Moores, S. (1993). *Interpreting Audiences: The Ethnography of Media Consumption.* London/Thousand Oaks/New Delhi: Sage.

Morgan, R. (1977). *Theory and Practice: Pornography and Rape Going Too Far. The Personal Chronicle of a Feminist* (pp. 163–69). New York: Random House.

Morley, D. (1980). *The Nationwide Audience: Structure and Decoding.* London: British Film Institute.

——(1986). *Family Television: Cultural Power and Domestic Leisure.* London: Comedia.

——(2001). Belongings: Place, Space and Identity in a Mediated World. *European Journal of Cultural Studies,* 4(4), 425–48.

——(2006). Unanswered Questions in Audience Research. *The Communication Review,* 9(2), 101–21.

Moss, M. (2011). *The Media and the Models of Masculinity.* Lanham/Boulder/New York/Toronto/Plymouth: Lexington Books.

Mulvey, L. (1975). Visual Pleasure and Narrative Cinema. *Screen,* 16(3), 6–18.

——(2009). *Visual and Other Pleasures* (2nd edition). Basingstoke: Palgrave Macmillan.

Murphy, P.D. (2005). Fielding the Study of Reception: Notes on 'Negotiation' for Global Media Studies. *Popular Communication,* 3(3), 167–80.

Nassif, A. and Gunter, B. (2008). Gender Representation in Television Advertisements in Britain and Saudi Arabia. *Sex Roles,* 58(11/12), 752–60.

Ndlovu, T. (2013). Fixing Families Through Television? *Cultural Studies,* 27(3), 379–403.

Nielsen Company (2014). *The Digital Consumer.* Retrieved 12 September, 2014, from www.nielsen.com/us/en/insights/reports/2014/the-us-digital-consumer-report.html.

Nonnecke, B. and Preece, J. (2000). *Lurker Demographics: Counting the Silent.* Paper presented at the CHI'2000, The Hague.

Novak, D. and Krijnen, T. (2014). Exploring Visual Aspects of Audience Membership: Media Studies and Photovoice. In F. Darling-Wolf (Ed.), *Research Methods in Media studies, Volume 7* (The International Encyclopedia of Media Studies) (pp. 445–72). Malden/Oxford/Carlton: Wiley-Blackwell.

Novaseeker (2009). *The Myth of the 'Glass Ceiling'.* Retrieved 16 January, 2013, from www.the-spearhead.com/2009/10/05/the-myth-of-the-glass-ceiling/.

NPO (2014). *Jaarverslag 2013.* Retrieved 24 May, 2014, from http://assets.www.npo.nl/uploads/media_item/media_item/57/14/NPO_Jaarverslag_2013–1407849947.pdf.

Oakley, A. (1972). *Sex, Gender and Society: Towards a New Society.* London: Maurice Temple Smith Ltd.

O'Connor, B. and Klaus, E. (2000). Pleasure and Meaningful Discourse: An Overview of Research Issues. *International Journal of Cultural Studies, 3*(3), 369–87.

OECD (2007). *Participative Web and User-created Content: Web 2.0, Wikis and Social Networking.* Paris: Organisation for Economic Co-operation and Development.

Ofcom (2014). *The Communications Market 2014* Retrieved 23 November, 2014, from http://stakeholders.ofcom.org.uk/market-data-research/market-data/communications-market-reports/cmr14/.

Oliver, P., Marwell, G. and Teixeira, R. (1985). A Theory of the Critical Mass. I. Interdependence, Group Heterogeneity, and the Production of Collective Action. *American Journal of Sociology, 91*(3), 522–56.

Oudshoorn, N., Rommes, E. and Stienstra, M. (2004). Configuring the Use as Everybody: Gender and Design Cultures in Information and Communication Technologies. *Science, Technology and Human Value, 29*(1), 30–63.

Paasonen, S. (2009). Healthy Sex and Pop Porn: Pornography, Feminism and the Finnish Context. *Sexualities, 12*(5), 586–604.

Pandian, H. (1999). Engendering Communication Policy: Key Issues in the International Women-and-Media Arena and Obstacles to Forging and Enforcing Policy. *Media, Culture and Society, 21*(4), 459–80.

Panigrahi, D. and Chandra, N.D.R. (2013). Intertextuality in Advertising. *Language in India, 13*(9), 251–63.

Paoletti, J.B. (2012). *Pink and Blue: Telling the Boys from the Girls in America.* Bloomington: Indiana University Press.

Pew Research Center – Global Attitudes Project (2012). *Social Networking Popular Across Globe: Arab Publics Most Likely to Express Political Views Online.* Retrieved 20 November 2014, from www.pewglobal.org/files/2012/12/Pew-Global-Attitudes-Project-Technology-Report-.

Phoenix, A. and Pattynama, P. (2006). Intersectionality. *European Journal of Women's Studies, 13*(3), 187–92.

Pisters, P. (2011). *Lessen van Hitchcock: Een inleiding in mediatheorie.* Amsterdam: Amsterdam University Press.

Pooley, J.D. and Socolow, M.J. (2013). Checking Up on The Invasion from Mars: Hadley Cantril, Paul F. Lazarsfeld, and the Making of a Misremembered Classic. *International Journal of Communication, 7,* 1920–48.

Postman, N. (2000, 29 April 2014). *The Humanism of Media Ecology.* Paper presented at the Media Ecology Association Convention, New York.

Prensky, M. (2001). Digital Natives, Digital Immigrants. *On the Horizon, 9*(5), 1–6.

Press, A.L. (1991). *Women Watching Television: Gender, Class, and Generation in the American Television Experience.* Philadelphia: University of Pennsylvania Press.

——(2006). Audience Research in the Post-Audience Age: An Introduction to Barker and Morley. *The Communication Review, 9,* 93–100.

Radway, J. (1988). Reception Study: Ethnography and the Problems of Dispersed Audiences and Nomadic Subjects. *Cultural Studies, 2*(3), 359–76.

Rakow, L. F. (1986). Rethinking Gender Research in Communication. *Journal of Communication, 36*(4), 11–26.

Rector, M. and Trinta, A.R. (1981). The Telenovela. *Diogenes, 29*(113–14), 194–204.

Reinemann, C., Stanyer, J., Scherr, S. and Legnante, G. (2012). Hard and Soft News: A Review of Concepts, Operationalizations and Key Findings. *Journalism*, 13(2), 221–39.

Renold, E. and Ringrose, J. (2013). Feminisms Re-figuring 'Sexualisation', Sexuality and 'the Girl'. *Feminist Theory*, 14(3), 247–54.

Rich, R. (2004). New Queer Cinema. In M. Aaron (Ed.), *New Queer Cinema: A Critical Reader* (pp. 15–22). Edinburgh: Edinburgh University Press.

Ringrose, J., Harvey, L., Gill, R. and Livingstone, S. (2013). Teen Girls, Sexual Double Standards and 'Sexting': Gendered Value in Digital Image Exchange. *Feminist Theory*, 14(3), 305–23.

Rodero, E., Larrea, O. and Vázquez, M. (2013). Male and Female Voices in Commercials: Analysis of Effectiveness, Adequacy for the Product, Attention and Recall. *Sex Roles*, 68(5/6), 349–62.

Roe, K. (2000). Adolescents Media Use: A European View. *Journal of Adolescent Health*, 27(2), 15–21.

Rooney, B. (2011). *Women And Children First: Technology And Moral Panic*. Retrieved 6 June, 2014, from http://blogs.wsj.com/tech-europe/2011/07/11/women-and-children-first-technology-and-moral-panic/?mod=wsj_valettop_email.

Rosen, J. (2006). *The People Formerly Known as the Audience*. Retrieved 6 June, 2014, from http://archive.pressthink.org/2006/06/27/ppl_frmr.html.

Ross, K. (2004). Sex at Work: Gender Politics and Newsroom Culture. In M. De Bruin and K. Ross (Eds.), *Gender and Newsroom Cultures: Identities at Work*. (pp. 145–62). Cresskill, NJ: Hampton Press.

Ross, K. and Carter, C. (2011). Women and News: A Long and Winding Road. *Media, Culture and Society* 33(8), 1148–65.

Roy, W.G. and Dowd, T.J. (2010). What Is Sociological about Music? *Annual Review of Sociology*, 36, 183–203.

Rubin, G. (1975). The Traffic in Women: Notes on the 'Political Economy' of Sex. In R.R. Reiter (Ed.), *Towards an Anthropology of Women* (pp. 157–210). New York: Monthly Review Press.

Ruíz, C. (2004). Losing Fear: Video and Radio Productions of Native Aymara Women. In C. Carter and L. Steiner (Eds.), *Critical Readings: Media and Gender* (pp. 179–97). Maidenhead: Open University Press.

Salman, A. and Rahim, S.A. (2012). From Access to Gratification: Towards an Inclusive Digital Society. *Asian Social Science*, 8(5), 5–15.

Schein, V.E. (2007). Women in Management: Reflections and Projections. *Women in Management Review*, 22(1), 6–18.

Schilling, M. (2013). *Surprise! Women Are Still Under-Represented in Media*. Ms. *Magazine blog*. Retrieved 9 July, 2013, from http://msmagazine.com/blog/2013/02/25/surprise-women-are-still-under-represented-in-media/.

Seidman S. (1996). Introduction. In S. Seitman (Ed.), *Queer Theory/Sociology* (pp. 1–29). Cambridge: Blackwell.

Seiter, E., Borchers, H., Kreutzner, G. and Warth, E.M. (1991). 'Don't Treat Us Like We're so Stupid and Naïve': Toward an Ethnography of Soap Opera Viewers. In E. Seiter, H. Borchers, G. Kreutzner and E.M. Warth (Eds.), *Remote Control: Television, Audiences, and Cultural Power* (pp. 223–47). London/New York: Routledge.

Shattuc, J.M. (1997). *The Talking Cure, TV, Talk Shows and Women*. London: Routledge.

——(2008). The Confessional Talk Show. In G. Creeber (Ed.), *The Television Genre Book* (2nd edition). London: Palgrave Macmillan.

Shooler, D. and Trinh, S. (2011). Longitudinal Associations Between Television Viewing Patterns and Adolescent Body Satisfaction. *Body Image, 8*(1), 34–42.

Siapera, E. (2010). *Cultural Diversity and Global Media: The Mediation of Difference.* Oxford/Malden/Carlton: Wiley-Blackwell.

Signorielli, N. (1989). Television and Conceptions about Sex Roles: Maintaining Conventionality and the Status Quo. *Sex Roles, 21*(5/6), 341–60.

——(1997). *Reflections of Girls in the Media: A Content Analysis. A Study of Television Shows and Commercials, Movies, Music Videos, and Teen Magazine Articles and Ads. An Executive Summary.* Oakland: The Henry J. Kaiser Family Foundation.

——(2009). Race and Sex in Prime Time: A Look at Occupation and Occupational Appeal. *Mass Communication and Society, 12*, 332–52.

Signorielli, N. and Bacue, A. (1999). Recognition and Respect: A Content Analysis of Prime-time Television Characters Across Three Decades. *Sex Roles, 40*(7/8), 527–44.

Signorielli, N. and Morgan, M. (2001). Television and the Family: the Cultivation Perspective. In J. Bryant and J.A. Bryant (Eds.), *Television and the American Family* (pp. 333–51). Mahwah: Lawrence Erlbaum Associates, Inc.

Silverstone, R. (2007). *Media and Morality: On the Rise of the Mediapolis.* Cambridge/Malden: Polity Press.

SKO (2014). *TV in Nederland 2013. Ontwikkelingen in tv bezit en tv gebruik.* Amsterdam: Stichting Kijkonderzoek.

——(2014). *Jaarpersbericht Kijkcijfers 2013.* Amsterdam: Stichting Kijkonderzoek.

Smelik, A. (1999). *Effectief beeldvormen. Theorie, analyse en praktijk van beeldvormingsprocessen.* Assen: Van Gorcum.

Smith, E. R. and Mackie, D. M. (2007). *Social Psychology* (3rd edition). Hove/New York: Psychology Press.

Smith Maguire, J. and Matthews, J. (2012). Are We All Cultural Intermediaries Now? An Introduction to Cultural Intermediaries in Context. *European Journal of Cultural Studies, 15*(5), 551–62.

Social Bakers (2013). *Statistics.* Retrieved 22 March, 2014, from www.socialbakers.com.

Spears, G. and Seydegart, K. (2000). *Who Makes the News?* London: WACC.

Spielmann, Y. (2007). *Video: The Reflexive Medium.* Cambridge: MIT Press.

Spigel, L. (1992). *Make Room for TV: Television and the Family Ideal in Postwar America.* Chicago: The University of Chicago Press.

Staiger, J. (1983). 'Tame' Authors and the Corporate Laboratory: Stories, Writers, and Scenarios in Hollywood. *Quarterly Review of Film Studies, 8*(4), 33–45.

——(2005). *Media Reception Studies.* New York/London: New York University Press.

Stanfill, M. (2014). The Interface as Discourse: The Production of Norms Through Web Design. *New Media and Society, online first doi: 10.1177/1461444814520873.*

Stein, A. and Plummer, K. (1996). 'I Can't Think Straight': 'Queer' Theory and the Missing Sexual Revolution in Sociology. In S. Seitman (Ed.), *Queer Theory/Sociology* (pp. 129–44). Cambridge: Blackwell.

Steiner, L. (1992). The History and Structure of Women's Alternative Media. In L.F. Rakow (Ed.), *Participatory Communication for Social Change* (pp. 197–212). London/Thousand Oaks/New Delhi: Sage.

Strate, L. (1992). Beer Commecials: A Manual on Masculinity. In S. Craig (Ed.), *Men, Masculinity, and the Media* (pp. 78–92). London: Sage.

Straubhaar, J. (2007). *World Television: From Global to Local.* London/Thousand Oaks/New Delhi: Sage.

Sundar, S.S. and Limperos, A.M. (2013). Uses and Grats 2.0: New Gratifications for New Media. *Journal of Broadcasting and Electronic Media, 57*(4), 504–25.

Sundet, V.S. and Ytreberg, E. (2009). Working Notions of Active Audiences. Further Research on the Active Participant in Convergent Media Industries. *Convergence: The International Journal of Research into New Media Technologies, 15*(4), 383–90.

Tan, S.K. (2011). Global Hollywood, Narrative Transparency, and Chinese Media Poachers: Narrating Cross-Cultural Negotiations of *Friends* in South China. *Television and New Media, 12*(3), 207–27.

The Economist (2009, 17 June 2014). *Boxed in. Who Watches Most Television?*, from http://www.economist.com/node/14252309.

Thiel-Stern, S. (2014). *From The Dance Hall to Facebook: Teen Girls, Mass Media, and Moral Panic in the United States, 1905–2010.* Amherst/Boston: University of Massachusetts Press.

Tiggeman, M. and Miller, J. (2010). The Internet and Adolescent Girls' Weight Satisfaction and Drive for Thinness. *Sex Roles, 63*(1/2), 79–90.

Tiggeman, M. and Pickering, A.S. (1996). Role of Television in Adolescent Women's Body Dissatisfaction and Drive for Thinness. *International Journal of Eating Disorders, 20*(2), 199–203.

Time Warner (2012). *Our Content.* Retrieved 28 June, 2012, from www.timewarner.com/our-content/time-inc/.

Toffler, A. (1971). *Future Shock.* New York: Bantam Books Inc.

Torkkola, S. and Ruoho, I. (2011). Looking For Gender Equality In Journalism. In T. Krijnen, C. Alvares and S. Van Bauwel (Eds.), *Gendered Transformations: Theory and Practices on Gender and Media.* (pp. 203–20). Bristol: Intellect.

Trappe, J., Meier, W.A., D'Haenens, L., Steemers, J. and Thomass, B. (Eds.) (2011). *Media in Europe Today.* Bristol: Intellect.

Tsaliki, L. (2011). Playing with Porn: Greek Children's Explorations in Pornography. *Sex Education: Sexuality, Society and Learning, 11*(3), 293–302.

Tuchman, G. (1973). Making News by Doing Work: Routinizing the Unexpected. *American Journal of Sociology, 79*(1), 110–31.

——(1978). Introduction: The Symbolic Annihilation of Women by the Mass Media. In G. Tuchman, A. Kaplan Daniels and J. W. Benét (Eds.), *Hearth and Home: Images of Women in the Mass Media* (pp. 3–38). New York/Oxford: Oxford University Press.

Tunstall, J. (1993). *Television Producers.* London/New York: Routledge.

US Bureau of Labor Statistics (2011). *Women in the Labor Force: A Databook.* Retrieved 2 April, 2012, from http://www.bls.gov/cps/wlf-databook2011.htm.

——(2014). *American Time Use Survey Summary.* Retrieved 23 November, 2014, from http://www.bls.gov/news.release/atus.nr0.htm.

Vagrant009. (2012). *Metacritic.* Retrieved 27 June, 2014, from www.metacritic.com/game/playstation-3/journey/user-reviews?dist=negative.

Valdez, A. and Halley, J. (1996). Gender in the Culture of Mexican American Conjunto Music. *Gender and Society, 10*(2), 148–67.

Valdivia, A.N. (2011). This Tween Bridge over my Latina Girl Back: The US Mainstream Negotiates Ethnicity. In C. Kearney (Ed.), *Mediated Girl Back: New Explorations of Girls' Media Culture* (pp. 93–110). New York: Peter Lang.

Valkenburg, P. M. and Peter, J. (2009). Social Consequences of the Internet for Adolescents: A Decade of Research. *Current Directions in Psychological Science, 18*(1), 1–5.

Van Bauwel, S., Dhaenens, F. and Biltereyst, D. (2013). Queer Gazing and the Popular: A Study on the Representational Strategies of Queer Representations in Popular Television Fiction. In A.N. Valdivia and S.R. Mazzarella (Eds.), *The International Encyclopedia of Media Studies, Volume III: Content and Representation* (pp. 225–39). Malden/London: Blackwell.

Van Dijck, J. (2009). Users like you? Theorizing Agency in User-Generated Content. *Media, Culture and Society, 31*(1), 41–58.

Van Doorn, N. (2011). Digital Spaces, Material Traces: How Matter Comes to Matter in Online Performances of Gender, Sexuality and Embodiment. *Media, Culture and Society, 33*(4), 531–47.

Van Eijck, K. and Lievens, J. (2008). Cultural Omnivorousness as a Combination of Highbrow, Pop, and Folk Elements: The Relation Between Taste Patterns and Attitudes Concerning Social Integration. *Poetics, 36*(2/3), 217–42.

Van Hintum, M. (2013, 16 January 2013). 'Vrouwen krijgen banen juist níet omdat ze vrouw zijn'. *Volkskrant*. Retrieved from http://www.volkskrant.nl/vk/nl/6177/Malou-van-Hintum/article/detail/3378015/2013/01/16/Vrouwen-krijgen-banen-juist-n-iacute-et-omdat-ze-vrouw-zijn.dhtml?utm_source=dailynewsletter&utm_medium=email&utm_campaign=20130116&utm_content = .

Van Zoonen, L. (1988). Rethinking Women and the News. *European Journal of Communication 3*(1): 35–53.

——(1994). *Feminist Media Studies*. London/Thousand Oaks/New Delhi: Sage.

——(2002). Gender the Internet: Claims, Controversies and Culture. *European Journal of Communication, 17*(1), 5–23.

——(2004). *Media, cultuur & burgerschap: Een inleiding* (3rd edition). Amsterdam: Het Spinhuis.

——(2005). *Entertaining the Citizen. When Politics and Popular Culture Converge.* Lanham: Rowman & Littlefield.

——(2014). *Foucault 2.0. Moral Panics and The Question of Sexual Liberties*. Paper presented at the Opening Event Amsterdam Research Center for Gender and Sexuality, Amsterdam.

Verboord, M. and Brandellero, A. (2013). Globalisering in popmuziekhitlijsten in negen landen, 1960–2010. *Tijdschrift voor Communicatiewetenschap, 41*(4), 364–86.

Vygotsky, L.S. (1978). *Mind in Society: The Development of Higher Psychological Processes*. Cambridge, MA: Harvard University Press.

Wallace, L. (2000). Continuous Sex: The Editing of Homosexuality in Bound and Rope. *Screen 41*(4): 369–87.

Want, S.C. (2009). Meta-analytic Moderators of Experimental Exposure to Media Portrayals of Women on Female Appearance Satisfaction: Social Comparisons as Automatic Processes. *Body Image, 6*(4), 257–69.

Weber, B.R. and Steffens, K. (2010). Genre Transvestites: Testosterone Tales and Feminine Textual Bodies on Fox's *24* and *The Swan*. *The Journal of Popular Culture, 43*(4), 860–80.

Weedon, C. (1987). *Feminist Practice and Post-structuralist Theory*. Oxford: Basil Blackwell.

Werner, J.F. (2006). How Women Are Using Television to Domesticate Globalization: A Case Study on the Reception and Consumption of Telenovelas in Senegal. *Visual Anthropology, 19*(5), 443–72.

West, C. and Zimmerman, D.H. (1987). Doing Gender. *Gender and Society, 1*(2), 125–51.

WikiHow. (2014a). How To Be a Good Brother. Retrieved 27 June, 2014, from www.wikihow.com/Be-a-Good-Brother.

——(2014b). How To Be a Good Sister. Retrieved 27 June, 2014, from www.wikihow.com/Be-a-Good-Sister.

Willem, C., Araüna, N., Crescenzi, L. and Tortajada, I. (2012). Girls on Fotolog: Reproduction of Gender Stereotypes or Identity Play? *Interactions: Studies in Communication and Culture, 2*(3), 225–42.

Williams, J.E. and Best, D.L. (1990). *Measuring Sex Stereotypes: A Multination Study.* Thousand Oaks/London/New Delhi: Sage.

Williams, N. (2010). Is Lady Gaga a Feminist or Isn't She? *Ms. Magazine Blog* (Vol. 11 March 2010).

Williams, R. (2003). *Television. Technology and Cultural Form* (2nd edition). London/New York: Routledge.

Williams, R. and Edge, D. (1996). The Social Shaping of Technology. *Research Policy, 25*(6), 865–99.

Willis, P. (1998). Notes on Common clture. Towards a Grounded Aesthetics. *European Journal of Cultural Studies, 1*(2), 163–76.

Wittel, A. (2001). Toward a Network Sociality. *Theory, Culture and Society, 18*(6), 51–76.

Wohn, D.Y. (2011). Gender and Race Representation in Casual Games. *Sex Roles, 65* (3/4), 198–207.

Wollin, L.D. (2003). Gender Issues in Advertising –An Oversight Synthesis of Research: 1970–2002. *Journal of Advertising Research, 43*(1), 111–29.

Women's Studies Group (2007 [1978]). *Women Take Issue: Aspects of Women's Subordination.* London/New York: Routledge.

Wood, J. (2011). *Gendered Lives: Communication, Gender and Culture* (9th edition). Boston: Wadsworth.

Wouters, C. (2010). Sexualization: Have Sexualization Processes Changed Direction? *Sexualities, 13*(6), 723–41.

Writers Guild of America, W. (2014). *Turning Missed Opportunities Into Realized Ones: The 2014 Hollywood Writers Report.* Retrieved 8 November, 2014, from www.wga.org/uploadedFiles/who_we_are/HWR14.pdf.

Zhu, J. and Wang, X. (2013). Unveiling the Political Elite: High-Ranking Chinese Officals on Television Talks Shows. *Journal of Chinese Politcial Science, 18,* 117–37.

Ziamou, T. (2000). *Women Make the News: A Crack in the 'Glass Ceiling'.* Paris: UNESCO.

Zillmann, D. (1988). Mood Management Through Communication Choices. *American Behavioral Scientist, 31*(3), 327–40.

Zuiderveld, M. (2011). 'Hitting the Glass Ceiling' – Gender and Media Management in Sub-Saharan Africa. *Journal of African Media Studies, 3*(3), 401–15.

Index